W9-CCR-219

PRIMETIME
POLITICS

Polemics

Stephen Eric Bronner, Series Editor

The books in the Polemics series confront readers with provocative ideas by major figures in the social sciences and humanities on a host of controversial issues and developments. The authors combine a sophisticated argument with a lively and engaging style, making the books interesting to even the most accomplished scholar and appealing to the general reader and student.

PRIMETIME POLITICS

The Truth about Conservative Lies, Corporate Control, and Television Culture

Philip Green

ROWMAN & LITTLEFIELD PUBLISHERS, INC.

Lanham • Boulder • New York • Toronto • Oxford

ROWMAN & LITTLEFIELD PUBLISHERS, INC.

Published in the United States of America
by Rowman & Littlefield Publishers, Inc.
A wholly owned subsidiary of The Rowman & Littlefield Publishing Group, Inc.
4501 Forbes Boulevard, Suite 200, Lanham, Maryland 20706
www.rowmanlittlefield.com

PO Box 317
Oxford
OX2 9RU, UK

Copyright © 2005 by Rowman & Littlefield Publishers, Inc.

British Library Cataloguing in Publication Information Available

Library of Congress Cataloging-in-Publication Data

Green, Philip, 1932-
   Primetime politics : the truth about conservative lies, corporate control, and
television culture / Philip Green.
      p. cm. — (Polemics)
   Includes bibliographical references and index.
   ISBN 0-7425-2106-0 (cloth : alk. paper) — ISBN 0-7425-2107-9 (pbk. : alk. paper)
   1. Television broadcasting—Social aspects—United States. 2. Television and
politics—United States. 3. Television broadcasting of news—United States. 4.
Television broadcasting—Ownership—United States. I. Title. II. Series.
   PN1992.6.G73 2005
   302.23'45--dc22

                                                            2005006400

Printed in the United States of America

∞™ The paper used in this publication meets the minimum requirements of
American National Standard for Information Sciences—Permanence of Paper for
Printed Library Materials, ANSI/NISO Z39.48-1992.

CONTENTS

❶

THE SYSTEM:
MONOPOLY AND ALIENATION

This book is about three related subjects. Primarily, I attempt to describe the nature of American television's self-presentation and the institutional, ideological, and structural reasons it takes the form it does. However, it is impossible to undertake that task seriously without devoting special consideration to what has become one of the big lies of the twentieth—and now the twenty-first—century. That is the conservative lie about "liberal domination" of the media, and it is of crucial importance, not just because it constitutes a falsehood about an institution so central to all our lives, but because it is deliberately designed to distract our attention away from the third, most important subject of all: the impact of television on cultural and political democracy. We should begin, of course, with the facts of the matter: the real nature of the institution itself.

In the fall of 2002, a Time Warner billboard that appeared around New York City told passersby that "everything you thought about TV has changed forever" and added that "anything is possible." The first statement is certainly true; in some ways the world of cable (e.g., Time Warner), pay-per-view, and satellite television has relegated the past in which network programming was the sum of all television experience to the same era of the talkies or the dominance of radio. Moreover, as we shall see, the world of television continues to change under pressure from new technologies that make it possible not only to receive more types of programming but, more important, to avoid the mainstay of traditional television: commercials.

However, the French adage *plus ça change, plus c'est la même chose* (the more things change, the more they remain the same) still holds. One version of a new genre, imported from abroad, takes hold, and, within a year, every network is inundating the audience with variations of it, playing copycat and catch-up, thus momentarily reviving the same old system of stale imitation posing as fresh innovation. In other words, "anything" is still far from "possible": not because of any technological deficit and not because the creators of television's output remain mired in a vast wasteland of bad taste, but rather because the economic *structure* of television—that is, the structure of who owns and controls it and to what purposes—remains essentially as it always was. Until that changes, much remains impossible: above all, the prospect that television might become an institution compatible with the maintenance and progress of a democratic social order.

This is the context in which I suggest the desirability of abolishing television as we know it. By "television as we know it," I do not mean the technology that delivers distant communications into our private living spaces or even the general possibility of receiving distant communications in those spaces by means of some organized and readily available delivery system. Rather, I refer to the specifically American (and increasingly worldwide) system that delivers the great bulk of televised communications commercially from providers organized as immensely powerful and profitable nationwide networks of (in the United States) locally sited stations. These networked stations are legal monopolies; together they make up a dominant oligopoly.

That is, networked stations have been granted an exclusive license such that no one else can legally use at any time the parts of the bandwidth they are said to own (i.e., have been granted exclusive access to). They are also common carriers—that is, any communication could in principle be sent over that bandwidth, just as any material good can be shipped in a truck. As common carriers, such stations are licensed by public authority to use public space—the airwaves over which broadcasting takes place or the ground over which cables are laid—for private profit and private purposes in return for providing vaguely specified public services. However, they never in fact provide, have no intention of providing, and are not compelled to provide, any such services; every service they provide, with only the partial exception of news coverage during moments of national crisis, is part of a profit-making structure. In this respect, the licensing system for television stations —and thus for monopolistic networks, as few stations are independent, that is, totally outside the control of one or another network—constitutes a simple and straightforward giveaway of unimaginably valuable public space to private persons. Moreover, this system of public communications for private profit not only fails to provide public goods and services (i.e., goods and services determined by democratically legitimate authority to be in the public interest); for the most part, it does not even provide commercial goods or services for user fees or consumer payments (as do the sellers of other cultural commodities); thus there is no aggregation of individual pursuits of private profit into an alleged public good, à la "the invisible hand" described by Adam Smith. Instead, the television monopolies, as has often been said, make their profit by delivering consumers to advertisers who, rather than the consumers themselves, in turn foot the television bill and thus largely determine its content.

The distinction is more fundamental than it might appear at first glance. This is a unique arrangement in the history of popular entertainment in that content is determined not by the propensity of audiences to consume that content, but by their (imagined) propensity to consume the goods sold by its sponsors. To take the most obvious example of disparity between these two propensities, the fastest growing population segment in the United States is senior citizens, but a television program that achieved its greatest popularity with that group would melt from our screens like a snowfall in July. It is as though the market success of *Chicago* were measured not by box office receipts but by the sale of fishnet stockings; or the success of Steven King's horror stories were measured not by book sales but by the sale of fright masks.

In sum, the American television system is a system of (1) publicly licensed private monopolies (2) controlling a public good in what is supposed to be a democratically constituted polity, for (3) their own purposes and the purposes of corporate advertisers. This is the system I propose ought to be abolished.

There are several reasons why anyone interested in sustaining the broad outlines of a democratic political system ought to support such a proposal, and these are elaborated in the rest of this chapter. Essentially, however, the television system's owners monopolize a space that is vital for democratic life: the space of collectively undertaken social discourse. Among themselves, moreover, belonging all to the same social class, they do not have opposed or—to use John Kenneth Galbraith's term—countervailing interests. It is possible (though only by an act of infinite imagination) to imagine a benevolent monopolist, or collection of monopolists, who would altruistically reserve that space for types of discourse dedicated to citizen enlightenment, the stimulation of appetites for creative works of the imagination, and so forth. This does not happen. Instead, the monopolists maximize their control of public space, which is the heart of their system, by substituting one-way communications for citizen involvement and subjecting all communications, whether their purported purpose is to inform, entertain, or uplift, to a uniform test of commercial profitability (to the networks and their advertising partners).

Most crucially, as has been pointed out by many commentators, the system is organized so as to make the consumption of its products habit forming (just like the system for distributing addictive substances or pornography). If watching television replaced all other avenues of social absorption or self-expression, the sellers and buyers of television time (i.e., producers and advertisers) would consider this a financial blessing rather than a blow to collective or individual human improvement. No other contemporary social institution can be described in this way. The goal of the system's guardians is always to increase time spent by consumers with the TV set on and, preferably, actively viewing it. Thus, the number of hours devoted daily to this way of passing time by hundreds of millions of Americans, if devoted to almost any other private, nonoccupational enterprise (e.g., watching movies, shopping for fashionable clothing, sitting in bars, reading newspapers, playing video games, surfing the net), would be considered an obsession, a sign of depression, or a failure of complete adult socialization. Most other leisure-time activities, moreover, have the comparative virtue that they entail at most a temporary withdrawal from public space rather than immersion in someone else's version of it.

Why do I use the phrase "habit forming"? Imagine that the so-called war on drugs took place in a world where drugs were legal and free: anyone could walk into the nearest chain drugstore, pick up his or her daily shot of heroin or sniff of cocaine, and walk out still an upstanding and law-abiding citizen. Or imagine that the multibillion dollar pornography industry, currently the most successful sector of mass entertainment in the United States, gave away its products for free to all comers, its costs and profits being met instead by advertisers who bought space on video cassette covers or in hard-core magazines (or anywhere, for that matter). Imagine also that most of the production and distribution of drugs or pornography was controlled by four or five major international corporations, their behavior virtually unregulated (except perhaps for the distribution of their goods to preteen children). Among them, with very little interference from any government, they would decide the content of the product, how to cut or edit it, to whom to distribute it, and how to advertise it. And finally imagine that, because these products had such successful mass distribution, candidates for political office, and celebrities from all other walks of life, spent millions of dollars to promote themselves on drug packs and porn videos.

What I have just described is not some fanciful world of either drugs or pornography (thankfully), but rather the very real world of American network television. There is no point in trying to make a moral distinction among these distribution systems as each is immensely popular and profitable and, apparently, fulfills a widespread if not universal need. (Pornography is geared primarily toward male consumers—but probably less so than professional football or the world of ESPN generally.) In a universe of desires and fulfillment that, according to economists, offers "no such thing as a free lunch," the most ubiquitous and ostensibly one of the most habituating substances is distributed almost completely free of charge. To be sure, we consumers must pay a price of entry—the cost of a television set—that can be amortized at no more than a few dollars a month over its lifetime. In addition, nowadays most of us also pay a monthly rental of either cable capacity or satellite access that costs a minimum of twenty to fifty dollars. However, given the logic of habituation developed over the past half century, the wherewithal for paying this rental cost is simply transferred, usually without any thought whatsoever, from some other sector of our current consumption (or, more likely for those who have the least resources, added onto our existing consumer debt). If anyone reading these words has ever had a friend or acquaintance who said, "We used to watch TV when it was free, but now that they're charging for cable we've gotten rid of our TV set," it would be an astonishing event. Such a person would have dropped out more thoroughly than did the inhabitants of, say, the 1960s Vermont commune known as Total Loss Farm. To surrender the set is to surrender, effectively, one's citizenship. It is as though our free drugstore started charging a thirty dollar monthly fee for access to its product; it would be making more profit than it used to, but the world of addiction would not have changed. Compared to all other goods, the cocaine lunch would still be virtually free, as is television now.

To put it another and perhaps more precise way, once a person agrees to pay the price of entry to the television system, any particular good within that system—pay-per-view and premium subscription services aside—is absolutely free, and the consumer need not discriminate among them in order to conserve scarce resources; not even time, in that the capability to watch one program while recording another renders the television universe virtually free of time constraints as well. A repetitive pleasure that costs, or seems to cost, nothing: that is the very essence of addiction.

Seen in this light, much of the usual discourse about television is largely beside the point. "Consensus" and "domination" are the antithetical terms most regularly used, by apologists for or critics of television respectively, to describe the relationship between the producers of mass communications and their mass audience, but the thesis of this book is that neither descriptor is adequate to the task. Rather, American commercial television is a *total system* within which consumer choice of a kind seems to rule but which itself is not merely an option among other options. In discussing Milton Friedman's notion of the free market, the political theorist C. B. Macpherson once said that while we are "free" to purchase any one consumer product rather than another, we are not "free" to make the much more fundamental choice of not entering into market relationships at all; there are many other ways of exchanging or distributing material goods and services, but they are not generally available in a capitalist society.[1] By the same token, we are free to watch *E.R.* rather than *60 Minutes*, or vice versa. However, we are not free to seek out visual news and entertainment sources for home consumption that are not created, owned, and distributed by a handful of people belonging to the same social class and sharing the same profit-making purposes; there is no alternative system for distributing independently created cultural products to a mass audience. Almost all of the so-called cable channels, those which we receive as part of the regular but not basic cable package, are actually creations of the major networks: for example, Lifetime, USA, ESPN, Disney Channel, Court TV, etc. Even so-called public television is simply a set of channels funded mostly by the same corporations that fund programs on network television for distributing programs that do not fit into the networks' program mix. That public television belongs to the same system is evidenced by the fact that it is not allowed to produce or show competitive types of programming. Its role is defined by the private networks: it can only be what they are not; it is part, though on balance a slightly more independent part, of the commercial system.

Thus, the most useful account of the relationship between the television system and its audience is that, as consumers of mass media, we alienate certain of our capabilities and powers to its producers but have no option to do otherwise, given that the producers have been granted a monopoly over the only public space in which those particular capabilities and powers could be exercised. This is most evident in the sphere of democratic politics (or what might be democratic politics), in which the avenues of political action theoretically available to all of us are blocked to a fantastic extent by the necessity of spending immense sums of money to buy time on television for the reduction of political speech to every conceivable lowest common denominator. This giveaway of public space to private persons with nothing but their superior financial resources to justify their takeover is so obvious and so crude that it requires no explanation but, rather, action that never seems to be forthcoming. However, the action required to reclaim public political space becomes clearer once we explicate the deeper, more systemic sense in which alienation, conjoined with monopoly, is the most appropriate description of the sphere of public communication. (I write about the United States but, in all wealthy parts of the world, the tendency of television systems is toward convergence on the American model as the traditional European system of state regulation and quality control dwindles away under the pressure of cable and satellite distribution networks that cross national borders with the same ease as electronic transfers of dollars.)

Although I shall describe it in more detail later, the nature of the commercial monopoly of television is almost self-evident; volumes have been written describing it both in broad outline and in detail.[2] Here, therefore, I want rather to describe the nature of the alienation to which we are subjected. All human beings have the capacity to create images of the world in their minds and to communicate those images to others. The most amateurish, untrained home photographer or video camera operator does this regularly and often with surprising effectiveness. In the world of mass communications, however, we give over that capacity, in the guise of communications policy. Using the monopoly power "we" have given them by way of such policy, a small group of persons create, or supervise the creation of, their images of the world and then return them to us as though they were our own. These images are produced as though they are what we generally call commodities, and we become willy-nilly their consumers. When we begin to regard these so-called commodities as representations of the world's reality rather than of their producers' powers and interests, then we participate in what Marx called (in Volume I of *Capital*) "the fetishism of commodities," in which "a definite social relation between men . . . assumes, in their eyes, the fantastic form of a relation between things."

But these "commodities" are not just any commodities. In the first place, as I have said, they are mostly *free*, like the air we breathe, so that we their consumers are subject to a double illusion: not only do they seem to be "ours" ("this is what I like to see"; "this is the program I've been waiting for"; "he is my favorite newscaster"), but they seem to come to us without cost despite the fact that, one way or another, "we" are spending billions of dollars for them and our national economy is built on their base. In other words, they seem not to be commodities at all in the traditional sense of the word; to fetishize them is to mistake not only how they have been produced (i.e., by the same kind of labor that produces everything else) but also how they are distributed.

Second, again unlike the commodities Marx spoke of, these products come to us not as a small part of the material world, like shoes or automobiles or canned tuna fish, but as a *simulacrum* of that world. (This distinguishes television from the internet, which rivals it as an object of obsession but carries with it no pretense of being anything but what it is.) The television universe seamlessly fits together episodic, fictional narratives; commercials, many geared specifically to sexual titillation; news broadcasts of all events, especially wars and other forms of violence; "infomercials"; soap operas; promotions for products from other media owned by the same corporation ("synergy"); "docudramas"; relays from, or imitations of, other media (especially film); political campaigns; game shows; pseudoreal competitions; police force and military proselytizing; propagandistic talk shows; genuine and fake courtroom trials; celebrity promotion and gossip about people who are at the same time appearing elsewhere in the system; public psychological confessionals and physical confrontations; athletic games and contests either created by the television system or molded to its specifications (and, as with almost all the other genres I have mentioned, adapted to its own channels); self-referential hype; and many other genres too numerous to go on listing, not to mention repeats of all these when the creative imagination of TV's producers has flagged. With the occupation of public space twenty-four hours a day, seven days a week, and replication in all sorts of print mediums for those who still have time left over to read, this endlessly repeated world is in fact not so much a simulacrum of reality as a replacement for it—a more vivid world than the workaday one we live in, and often more demanding of our attention if we are to remain in touch with our surroundings. Famously, more people voted on the question, "Who shot J. R.?," than in the presidential election of 1980; the small-town Texas sheriff who resigned his office some years ago to be a guest on an afternoon talk show knew what he was doing. The fetishism of commodities, as Marx explains it, reflected a misconception about reality afflicting mostly economists and whoever took them seriously. The fetishism of television afflicts everybody, including people who write sentences such as "the fetishism of television afflicts everybody" but go right on enwrapping themselves in it.[3] Science-fiction movies about protagonists who are trapped inside their television sets aren't so much science fiction as an ironic commentary on whoever is watching them. Television is often analogized to film in that millions of people view the latter very seriously as part of their world, closely follow its celebrity culture, take social cues from it (e.g., how to kiss or manage a first date). But few people think that the financial, political, judicial, or medical worlds have any similarity to what they see in movies as movies make very few direct statements about those worlds; it's generally considered economic death to do so. Television programs, however, every day make thousands of direct statements about the world, effortlessly interweaving them with its supposedly distinctive fictions, most of which are themselves made up to look as though they were real lives on which we just happened to be eavesdropping. They are an abstraction from reality posing as the reality they are an abstraction from.

A third aspect of the audience's alienation is that the distinction between delivering programs to audiences and delivering audiences to advertisers is more fundamental than might appear at first glance. "Delivering programs to audiences" suggests a kind of democratic pleasure principle. It is the principle that informs the justifications that television executives always give for what they do: they are just giving us what we want. "Delivering audiences to advertisers" is aimed, quite differently, at giving *advertisers* what they want. But these two versions of "want" are not the same. Advertisers want television to deliver not pleasure but what I've called habituation, a condition in which the set is never turned off, in which one viewing experience always leads to another. "Pleasure" suggests the possibility of a variety of aesthetic experiences. "Habituation" suggests a narrowing of aesthetic experiences only to those that do not provoke thought, passion, excitement, engagement, or any state of being that might preclude watching more television or, specifically, watching commercials. This was put nicely by the chief executive officer of Turner Broadcasting: "Your contract with the network when you get the show is you're going to watch the spots. Otherwise you couldn't get the show on an ad-supported basis. Any time you skip a commercial or press the button you're actually stealing the programming."[4]

Here, the distinction is clear for all to see, as a social contract between viewers and advertisers (mediated by programmers) replaces an aesthetic transaction between viewers and programmers. But this is a peculiar contract in that viewers will be provided only with programs that the advertisers want. Whether and to what extent the viewers want them too is incidental as we can see by imagining a system in which the publication of books or the production of movies was ad-supported. The list of movies and books that would never have seen the light of day would include a good number of each that people actually enjoyed. More to the point than the issue of censorship, though, is the revelation of how consumer alienation is institutionalized and systematized. The constitutive purpose of the television system is to *prevent* people from realizing their own aesthetic purposes in watching it. It is not that we can really imagine an alternative system in which people directly produce and realize their own aesthetic desires through the medium of long-distance telecasting; that would be a utopian project in the same sense as was Marx's project for abolishing alienated labor (in *The German Ideology*): the "communist society where nobody has one exclusive sphere of activity but each can become accomplished in any branch he wishes, society regulates the general production and thus makes it possible for me to do one thing today and another tomorrow, to hunt in the morning, fish in the afternoon, rear cattle in the evening, criticise after dinner, just as I have a mind, without ever becoming hunter, fisherman, shepherd, or critic." Rather, we should try to imagine a system in which alienation is not the consuming purpose—a system that might deliver a plurality of experiences, among which individuals might find those resembling their own purposes in the world, and none of which would have the deliberate intention of numbing their critical and creative faculties.

A comparison to a superficially similar, yet actually quite different, medium can clarify this point. There are people (other than professional reviewers) who watch so many movies—sometimes even more than an average of one a day—that everyone who knows them recognizes their relationship to film as an obsession; an abnormal psychic state; yet such people may well spend less time watching movies than the modal TV viewer spends watching television. Why then do we not call such TV viewers "obsessed"? We don't, and no one would think we should, for in a sense they are perfectly normal (and not just because they are modal). They are normal because it doesn't take any particular expenditure of psychic energy to do what they do nor any sublimation of ordinary life—watching TV is just what they do when they're at home—whereas their counterparts in the movie theaters seem to have given up most of their private lives to their obsession. And yet, in fact, television has subtracted more of their lives from the world of common action than film has ever done to anyone; and it does this by substituting for the world of common action a common world of inaction. This is the peculiar nature of alienation in this sphere. It deprives viewers of a whole range of experiences, both aesthetic and social, and replaces them with a nonexperience, the contours of which are entirely determined by someone else. This form of alienation has particularly grave consequences for what we like to think of as democratic self-governance. Political emancipation, that is, democracy, begins to lose its meaning when thinking our own thoughts—the real foundation of such symbolic institutions as voting and religious freedom gives way to distraction from thought when the political value of those institutions is replaced by their entertainment value.

In sum, television, specifically American commercial television, is the field of cultural consumption in which the process of alienation in production has been taken to the furthest extent, for it is a field in which no social or artistic tradition or formal or informal regulation operates as a brake or limit on the enterprise. The whole point of the commercial television system is to create abstract audiences for products conceived abstractly, and the first thing that happens to a project when it comes to the attention of the actual producers is that they explore how to adapt it to their conception of its market. The second thing that happens is that they instruct the original creator, if there is one, how to accomplish that. This is as true of so-called informational programming as it is of narrative fictions. This is why certain kinds of independently conceived programming simply can't appear within the system and are relegated to the second division of pay services such as HBO. Commodification is not just an aspect of productive labor or even of the distribution system. Rather, it defines the way the commercial system works root and branch; nothing within that system is allowed to escape its grasp. How then does a product that appears to its audience to cost nothing get to be the ultimate commodity?

The answer to that question was famously given by Marshall McLuhan: the medium is the message. The message was encapsulated best by Jean-Luc Godard: "When I see a movie, I see it in a cinema with hundreds of other people, and yet I see it absolutely alone. When I see a television program, I see it alone in my living room and yet I see it with millions of other people." What he meant—and we should remember he was talking about nothing more artistically complex than the Westerns of Samuel Fuller—was that movies, because of their appeal to the inner world of fantasy, speak directly to the members of their audience as individuals; just as novels, because of their appeal to the inner world of reflection and intellection, speak directly to their readers as individuals. The commercial television system—as it has developed—not only fails to speak to its audience as individuals but, also, forbids any attempt to do so. For example, as we shall discuss later, there are network censors whose purpose is to prevent any individual program episode from taking a stand on any social or political issue deemed "controversial" at the moment, so that, if, say, the protagonist of *Judging Amy* were to state opposition to capital punishment, someone else would have to speak for it. Thus television speaks only to our outer world, as citizens of a polity—media land—in which neither reflection nor intellection nor fantasizing are encouraged and in which, therefore, no escape from its world is to be allowed. That is what makes it the ultimate commodity.

Why should this matter, though? It isn't, after all, as though I myself don't enjoy spending a weekly hour with *Judging Amy*. And I could cheerfully have watched *Xena: Warrior Princess* every week for the next ten years if it had not, typically, been networked out of existence in a dispute that had nothing to do with its capacity for pleasing audiences. There is surely nothing wrong with passing the time pleasantly, or even unpleasantly (while enjoying fantasies of set destruction, say), with one television program or another for a few hours a week. Moreover, it is not possible to argue that the minds of people who don't watch *Six Feet Under*, or didn't see *Mulholland Drive*, are somehow deprived of a basic human good. So what exactly is the problem?

The problem is that these pleasure-giving moments are isolated instances of a system, whereas the system as a whole has characteristics that transcend in impact any moments of pleasure within it. Something crucial happens with the virtually free distribution of creative communications that television represents. We might put it like this: From the liturgical works of Bach to the raps of KRS-1, from the novels of Flaubert to the novels of Steven King, from the ritual theater of Athens to the overblown musicals of Broadway, from the paintings of Rembrandt to the paintings of Rockwell, creative works of the imagination sometimes enlarge our experience, sometimes leave it pretty much as it was, but even at worst never *narrow* it. But that is precisely what the system for delivering commercially televised communications does. And it does not just narrow our experience if we watch it, though it can certainly do that. With its total lack of accountability and truthfulness, the news and other misinformational television might as well be presented by a cultural commissar; and the rigidly ideological communication of most fictional TV, though its effects on consciousness are probably somewhat less than we imagine in our worst fantasies, surely is intended to put a damper on the social imagination of anyone watching it. That is especially true in that the system (at least its American version) lives and can only live by delivering pseudoexperience to us in the form of stereotypes, as the format and time constraints of the broadband monopoly allow for no other artistic possibility. But much more crucial, in the end, is that TV narrows our range of experience even if we *don't* watch it, perhaps even especially if we don't watch it. Watch it or not, it draws people farther away from the realities of each other's lives rather than bringing them closer to an at least partially trustworthy knowledge and understanding of each other, as cultural works were traditionally supposed to do.

The television system, put simply, colonizes public space and discourse. There is little room left over for other discourses in that space for the reason that television, as an imperial system, tends to subsume them all. Public discourse becomes unreal unless it can be reproduced on TV, but when it is reproduced on TV, it becomes, precisely, unreal, so that you, a person, cannot participate in that discourse without paying tribute to the most common, that is, most falsified, version of it. In addition, the television system colonizes time, for it is constructed and delivered not just as an alternative way of spending leisure time (that was the old BBC model, for example) but as the *primary* way of spending leisure time. Possibly the most frequently uttered sentence in post-dinnertime America is, "Is there anything on the tube tonight?" Try to imagine asking, "Is there anything in the house to read tonight?" and the meaning of that question becomes clear. Even movies are, in that sense, only weekend entertainment for most people; only dedicated cinephiles, sitting around after dinner on a Tuesday night, would think to ask "what's at the movies tonight?"

Nor should we allow the burgeoning of cable television, with its allegedly myriad alternatives, to confuse us about the nature of this colonization for at least two reasons. First, even on the occasions when cable, in its sometime role as a common carrier, provides moments of creative imagination on one or two of its four hundred channels, these merely take their place among the mass of indiscriminate product, the sole function of which is to keep us in our living room, and away from the social world as part of an abstract, disconnected audience. Second, on all but the handful of pay or subscription channels, what we receive are not in fact cultural commodities, not even bad ones, but rather carefully crafted advertisements, designed to place us within the system of material consumption as a whole, interspersed with the simulacra of narratives or information that are only the system's subsidiary content.

For all these reasons, my approach to the world of television is different from that of some other critical theorists in that I treat both "entertainment" television and "information" television together. Usually these are seen to pose different problems. As the titles of their books often indicate, writers about "information" television tend to discuss questions of content, structure, and alleged political effects: "the sound-bite society," "no sense of place," "the politics of illusion," "inventing reality," and "manufacturing consent." This is the discussion that produces most of the best writings about the relationship between television and democracy: who controls the flow of information rather than who provides the flow of entertainment. Conversely, most criticism of entertainment television is explicitly or implicitly about matters of taste ("the vast wasteland" or "gratuitous sex and violence"); alternatively, most often in the form of feminist or neo-Marxian cultural criticism, it projects supposed ideological or moral effects on the psyches of audiences (although the two faces of critique, aesthetic and sociological, are often barely distinguishable).

By and large, this distinction is certainly correct, and therefore I have reproduced it within the text that follows: chapter 2 focuses on the presentation of television news and chapter 4 on entertainment television. But the distinction contains only a partial truth. For the crucial thing to understand about commercial television, at least in the United States, is that it is a total system with a comparative hegemony over public space. To maintain that hegemony it must constantly reproduce its own social conditions.[5] The chief of these is what we might think of as an interface between its own structure and that of society as a whole: the more they come to look *like each other*, the stronger the system's position and thus the potential for profit and power of its leaders. Seen in this light, the system's inner dynamic (perhaps consciously internalized by some of its producers, but surely not by most) is to make sure that what's shown as "news" looks like what's shown as "entertainment" and that what's shown as "entertainment" looks like what's shown as "news." To the extent that this aim is realized, real public activities—politics, the legal process, other modes of entertainment, and class conflicts—are no longer able to compete for our attention, or even our belief, with their televised representations; and, conversely, the private realm as an arena for the communication of potential resistance and dissidence disappears. What is most revolutionary and frightening about TV, and explains the moral panic that surrounds its ubiquitous presence (see the discussions of "the culture wars" in subsequent chapters), is the ease with which we bring its images into our homes—homes that gradually become separated instances of a privatized culture. That the public sphere is privatized, and the private sphere made public, are the operative conditions of TV's hegemony, the root structure of the alienation process in which we are all embedded.

Not all elements of television's productions contribute equally to maintaining its social interface. Several are especially crucial: above all, the treatment of "crime" (which is highlighted in chapter 4). Both as a news structure (in Gaye Tuchman's phrase) and as the bedrock narrative of fictional (noncomedic) TV, crime is the glue that holds society together by defining outsiders in a way that includes almost all viewers while at the same time emphasizing television's visual dominance of the public sphere. "Crime" is what television sees it to be, in whatever genre; any potential dissonance between fact and fiction is erased by Court TV or programs such as *Cops*. What is seen as crime is also nothing else, so that drug use is always a crim-

inal activity; political protests (unless in an ad for "free fries" at McDonald's)
are seen only as problems in crowd control for legitimate police forces;
"crime waves" are represented in remarks by real or fictional cops about the
urban jungle, irrespective of whether the incidence of crime is rising or (as
recently) declining. In a similar manner, the news frames labor as an "interest group," a vector of conflict; and, on entertainment television, labor
simply disappears, to be replaced by cops and waitresses—the only working-class people that the system regularly shows us, and both only in a helpfully non-unionized frame.[6] Social policy issues, similarly, are reduced to
stereotypes that stand for social conditions, for example, as single mothers
stand for "welfare." As the news is given to us solely by middle-class men
and women who can counterfeit authoritativeness, as less-educated non-
professionals cannot, almost all "serious" television (i.e., excluding sitcoms,
soap operas, etc.), whether informative or entertaining, consists of pictures
of middle-class people talking to us or to each other and saying things we
are meant to believe. In fact, the expected hierarchy of authoritativeness is
inverted: Mariska Hargitay and Chris Merloni have as much to tell us, or
more, about life in New York City as do the actual district attorney or police chief of the city.

In general, it is becoming increasingly difficult to separate dominant cinema or television from the marginal world of cable TV, fact from fiction, and
narrative from documentary. To take one obvious example, the adventure-
suspense genre has been so greatly transformed that its most popular representations are now fake reality programming such as *Survivor* or *Temptation Island*. Such programs are to real life what televised wrestling is to
real sports but make no lesser a claim to the "truth" of their content than
can any segment of, say, the Fox cable news channel. Again, this is especially true for the realm of criminal justice in which *Homicide* or *Law and
Order* (and all its clones) are part of the same world as *America's Most
Wanted* or *Cops*. Police forces in cities such as Houston, New Orleans, and
Los Angeles even have their own television shows; cameras peer into juve-
nile courts in which delinquents judge each other; "deadbeat dads," most
wanteds, and other public enemies are hunted down by viewers. Whether
reality television is truly "more real" (whatever that might mean) than the
networks' fictional version is a moot question, for the whole is part of one
unified metatext. Though individual lawyers or judges may occasionally be
satirized, as on *L.A. Law*, dominant television in the end always treats the
institutions of the law with the reverence that courtroom protocol requires
of the law's supplicants except on occasion, to criticize them (in the *Dirty
Harry* tradition) for not being authoritarian enough. Rarely does it show us

the endemic corruption of local courts, the sadism of judges, and the help-
lessness of individuals confronted by the resources of wealth or the powers
of the state. The same thing is true of hospital shows, those bastions of pa-
ternalism. On *E.R.*, for example, the audience is usually forced to take sides
between rigid hospital rules and the judgment of doctors; it is never given
to think that perhaps the American system for delivering medical care is a
major part of the problems that arise within it. So if and when we do encounter defects in these systems, once again their fictional representations
benefit from any comparison we might be tempted to make. This substitution of the fictional for the real turns us away from the possibility of social
insight, for what would that be insight into? In the watchword of the era,
"Whatever."

Even more fundamentally, both subsystems, whether or not conceptually
separable, work together to produce, or try to produce, the habit of watching; neither functioning by itself could succeed in doing that because the
limitations of each would become too obvious as well as boring (endlessly
conventional narrative stereotypes on the one hand and unrelieved know-
it-all bluster on the other). The habit-forming system, in other words, is
seamlessly integrated. The clearest example of that integration is that the
formally identifiable subsystems are allotted their own time slots, neither of
which is allowed to invade the other. But the obvious disparity here (dinner
time for news and prime time for entertainment) suggests a final reason not
to distinguish "information" and "entertainment" too sharply. The two
worlds are not at all equal; one dominates the other totally; that is, information culture, as I have said, is in every respect subjected to the standards
of commerce and advertising. The commercial, its placement, and its potential drawing power is the *only* criterion for the entire system of network
television. Once or twice a year, an exception to this rule—a wholly or partially ad-free program—is announced with such hoopla that it only calls
more attention to the normal way of doing things: the exception that proves
the rule. Moreover, every advertising segment on contemporary television
has at least one commercial, possibly more, which is told as a narrative in
the same way as, though often with more flashy technique on display than,
the fictional narratives or newscasts in which it is embedded. In short, at the
deepest level, the system reproduces the world it attempts to dominate and
its domination of that world.

Because network information belongs at least partially to the world of
propaganda and because it may be untrue to reality in specific ways that
cannot be alleged of even ideologically slanted fictions (which except for
the hybrid genre of docudramas proclaim their status as fictions), I do con-

sider it in a separate chapter. But for all the reasons just given, the distinctive features that chapter highlights are ultimately of less importance than the broad nature of the system as a whole, in which the information subsystem participates as an unequal but contributing partner in the assault by communications monopolies on culture and, thus, on democracy.

At the same time, as I have indicated, it is not enough merely to describe the fictional and nonfictional worlds of television before grappling with the complex and fateful relationship between television and democracy. Chapters 3 and 5 therefore surround the empirical and theoretical analysis of television with a dissection of the conservative critique of "liberal domination." Although that critique is mostly undertaken by the same people regardless of whether the subject matter is information or entertainment, and the assumptions and biases that undergird the critique are the same in either case, the materials of the critique are different enough that I have separated the two versions of the conservative critique just as I have separated the consideration of information and entertainment television themselves.

I have also found it impossible, in considering especially entertainment television and its conservative critics, to avoid the delicate question of taste and the content of programming. The most important distinction I make, in opposition to much liberal and radical media criticism, is that it is not the business of serious democratic critics of the mass media to promote or attack particular subcultural tastes or programming that attempts to satisfy those tastes; this argument is the gist of chapter 6. Even if it were possible on some philosophical ground or other to defend Herbert Marcuse's notorious argument (from his essay on "Repressive Tolerance") that regressive ideas or behaviors should be censored, it is not possible to defend the proposition that censorship will be limited to such ideas or behaviors. Censorship, whether formally or informally achieved, always proceeds by defining an "other" who is effectively to be excluded from the democratic polity; those who are regularly in the business of defining alien others are without exception antidemocratic. Instead, it is the business of democrats to seek democratization of the means of cultural production and distribution so that no person or no group is able to monopolize the cultural arena and so that the mass audience is able to escape from the habituation and fetishization that disfigure that arena and turn what ought to be a democratic communications system into a one-way street.

In sum, for those who pay a great deal of attention to the television system —and there are serious payoffs, at least in American society, for paying attention to it and serious disincentives for not paying attention to it—at its most dominant, it leaves little time left over to think about what you might want to think and how you might want to think it, if left to your own devices or in cooperation with other people. In fact, a lot of the thinking that many intelligent people do with their leftover time is thinking about the nature of television. Thus culture in the larger anthropological sense, the field of symbolic meanings that give structure to people's common lives, willy-nilly becomes "culture" in this narrower and distorted sense. The most profound problem confronting us with this version of cultural alienation is that it translates directly into political alienation, in that who controls its images controls the symbolic life of a society. Thus the absence of a genuinely free market for televised communications is not a politically negligible matter, as might be, for example, the absence of a free market for the production of steel or aluminum or cholesterol-lowering medicines. The former case might have a negative effect on our material standard of living or the nation's balance of payments; the latter case might generate deleterious effects on public health or individual incomes. In either case, though, the polity is not less democratic than it otherwise would be. Communications are different, however. They are the lifeblood not of the corporeal body but of the metaphorical, yet very real, body politic. And television is the most problematic area of cultural production and distribution: omnipresent, intrusive, addictive, and irresistible. Above all—and this is the one finding consistent across all empirical studies of television watching—it is demobilizing; it accelerates and strengthens any other tendencies toward a retreat from civic consciousness that may already exist. So my ultimate purpose is to define the approach that democrats ought to take toward this now uncontrolled and uncontrollable institution.

The creation and preservation of a democratic polity depends ultimately on the creation of a democratic, rather than alienated and fetishized, culture: that is, on our jointly and equally reclaiming the capacity to communicate images of the world to each other. This does not, and cannot, mean that every individual is able to participate equally in doing so; that was the myth of participatory democracy, and it is not a myth worth clinging to. What this does mean is that the control of public space—and the abstract space of the broadband is today the most public of all public spaces—ought to be representative in a particular way. What I mean by "representative" here is not that we elect scriptwriters or producers or network executives but, rather, that no set of persons monopolizes, or controls entry to, those positions. An actual, classical, free market, rather than the parallel series of monopolized, corrupted, and dominated markets that go by that honorific title in the contemporary world, is probably the best we can do. My intention in the final chapter of this book is to provide at least a sketch of what a *free* market for televised communications, as opposed to a *dominated* market for free communications, might look like.

NOTES

1. C. B. Macpherson, *Democratic Theory: Essays in Retrieval* (Oxford: Oxford University Press, 1963), 145.

2. For a recent overview by the best American historian and critic of the American television system, see Robert W. McChesney, *Rich Media, Poor Democracy: Communication Politics in Dubious Times* (New York: New Press, 2000).

3. The most important and informative work on the fetishizing effect of visual culture is Sut Jhally's *The Codes of Advertising: Fetishism and the Political Economy of Meaning in Consumer Society* (New York: St. Martin's, 1987).

4. Jamie Kellner's remarks appeared in *Inside*, April 29, 2002; they are quoted in *Extra!*, June 2002, 2. He is quite correct; critics such as myself are greatly cheered by the existence of commercial-skipping "buttons" and hope for more and better such technologies. See my proposals for ending network monopoly in chapter 7.

5. See Gaye Tuchman, "Consciousness Industries and the Production of Culture," *Journal of Communication* (Summer 1983), 330–41. The discussion in this paragraph owes much to Tuchman's seminal article, "Consciousness Industries and the Production of Culture," from which I've also taken the quotation about reproducing "its own social conditions."

6. See also Michael Kimmelman's remarks in *New York Times*, November 5, 2000. On this point, see Stanley Aronowitz, "Working Class Culture in the Electronic Age," in *Cultural Politics in Contemporary America*, ed. Ian Angus and Sut Jhally, 135–50 (New York: Routledge, 1989).

2

IDEOLOGY AND PROPAGANDA

I began this book with a theme about the nature of American commercial television in my mind. However, during the course of the book's preparation, the media was overtaken by events, that is, by America's invasion of Iraq in March 2003 and its pursuit of the novel and morally shocking doctrine of preemptive warfare and by an American unilateralism that, on many fronts, repudiated the foundations of the last half century of international politics. These events, following shortly after the collapse of the Soviet Bloc, transformed international relations from an arena of balance-of-power politics amid struggling but real institutions of international law and rights to one of naked empire, without law, or rights, or balance. Although at first American commercial media responded to the nascent, post-September 11th imperialism with some hesitancy and balance, that almost entirely disappeared after the March invasion, when the hyped-up "War on Terrorism" (as the news channels uncritically style their politically inspired "alerts") became interchangeable with the badly misreported war in Iraq.

However, the change in media behavior went much deeper than merely the uncritical supernationalism of most American newspapers and television outlets (ABC-TV being at times an honorable exception). The disgust that non-American journalists evinced at American television's war coverage and the "embedding" of American journalists would have been more persuasive if they could attest to a more objective stance of their own national media outlets during their own nations' foreign or civil wars. Whereas it is reasonable to explore ways of freeing media from the perversions of corporate control, it is naive to expect any national mass media, no matter how structured, to preserve journalistic integrity when the population imagines itself to be at war.[1] In this respect, indictments of media nationalism have the air of Claude Rains chiding Humphrey Bogart in *Casablanca*: "I'm shocked, Rick, shocked, to find that gambling is going on here." Thus, although we must criticize media one-sidedness, we have to realize that it is, after all, subsidiary to the one-sidedness of the nation-state itself. Moreover, the television system has been no worse than the daily print media in the way that George W. Bush has been given a free ride for questionable behaviors both past and present (which even in the *New York Times* are fodder only for page fourteen or the columns of Paul Krugman).

To be sure, a little more than that must also be said. It is simply the case that nowhere in what might loosely be called the democratic world, and even very few places in the rest of it, could one find out less about events in Iraq than one could from American television; that is still so even as I write in mid-2004. With the occasional exception of a few newspapers, the collapse of American mass media, their complicity with power, is complete. A comment by Michael Moore about the filming of *Fahrenheit 9/11* is applicable. Asked by an interviewer how it was that the U.S. Marine Corps let him follow its recruiters around the streets of Flint, he replied, "When we called the Marine Corps headquarters for permission, they didn't even ask what the point of view or the purpose of the film was. They automatically assumed that if the media was calling it would be good."[2]

Still, there being nothing new about the ideology of nationalism or subservience to authority, the truly subversive, revolutionary impact that the invasion had on American commercial television lies elsewhere. Even as compared to the first Gulf War, in which the new tendency first surfaced, or the invasion of Afghanistan, the invasion of Iraq made evident a *formal* rather than merely ideological transformation of media. This was a transformation uniquely grasped, at least at first, by a few daily or weekly media critics (e.g., Allesandra Stanley, Frank Rich, Michiko Kakutani, and Jon Pareles of the *New York Times*; and Nancy Franklin of the *New Yorker*), who are used to watching television as television rather than as politics carried on by other means. What they observed, and reported in the immediate aftermath of the invasion, was the representation of "war" no longer as an awesome, terrifying moral event, but now "sanitized" and "airbrushed" (in Frank Rich's words) as a reality show above all reality shows, although its ratings would never equal those of the latest version of *Survivor* were the politicians and generals not allowed to commandeer the broadband. All genres are

broached by the presentation of "news" as entertainment: soap opera, family drama, adventure, and cops and robbers. "The Year of the Fake," one
commentator called it, in which "the real Jessica Lynch—who told Diane
Sawyer that 'no one beat me, no one slapped me, no one, nothing'—has
proven no match for her media-military-created doppelganger, shown being
slapped around by her cruel captors in NBC's movie, *Saving Jessica Lynch*."[3]
But above all, this was killing as superspectacle, as video game, as a real-
world "Mission Impossible," watchable as such by the mass audience only
because the "mission" had no real suspense at all but more the air of a box-
ing match between a brass-knuckled Mike Tyson and a hundred-pound
teenager with one arm tied behind her back. Awe was indeed one product
of the spectacle, but it was the awe of the beauty of the Baghdad night sky
seen through night-vision scopes from miles away: the beauty of the bombs
falling, rather than the horror of the corpses on the streets (seen regularly on
their own television channels by the rest of the world's nations, but only
rarely in the United States). Instead of "seeing" the event, and interposing
at least some minimal distance between ourselves and the seen, we were
placed safely in the middle of events, able not to interpret but only to enjoy;
we were spectators of a virtual though deadly game. Moreover, as opinions
about the event were formed almost entirely by watching its representation
—often that was true of the invaders themselves, safe in the rear echelon
watching the flow of images as though they too were "audience"—the mode
of representation itself became one of the chief determinants of the invasion's "outcome;" that is, the way it could be perceived by contemporary history. As one observer asked, "Are the television cameras the witnesses to war,
or are they part of the weaponry? Or both?"[4]

So, when television gave the president a photo opportunity to declare as
"won" a war that had hardly begun, it was months before any mainstream
commentator on television bothered to notice the evident falsity of his dec-
laration. This development marked the end of any notion that television
journalism might be an at least partially independent institution within the
belly of the media beast. And, as I have noted, there was more at work than
merely predictable nationalism which, after all, can take diverse forms.
Shortly after the invasion of Iraq, an internal network study at NBC found
that Phil Donahue was "a tired, left-wing liberal out of touch with the current marketplace" who would be "a difficult public face for NBC in a time
of war," and could be "a home for the liberal anti-war agenda at the same
time that our competitors are waving the flag at every opportunity." Donahue, moreover, had resisted the request that he "had to have more conservative or right-wing guests than liberals on the same hour show."[5] NBC then

hired, to replace Donahue on its cable outlet, MSNBC, the openly racist, anti-Semitic, homophobic, and misogynistic hate-talker Michael Savage (who would later go too far even for wartime and be fired by his new supporters). This move had to do only with "the current marketplace," not with any value in what a talk show host might be talking about. In other words, far from being thought of as a loss leader that networks have to produce in order to fulfill their "public" responsibilities, as different from and lesser than "entertainment television," news and opinion had now beaten entertainment at its own game—had (if only momentarily) replaced entertainment *as* entertainment. If we could have endless wars—precisely the doctrine of the second Bush administration—then television, following along in their wake, might finally achieve the longed-for goal of all advertisers everywhere: that the set *never* be turned off. Not only that, but the entire presentation itself is a series of advertisements: for the networks, the military services, the administration, the technologies and their producers, and the "might of America." Mere commerce seems harmless by comparison. Even the fake footage of Palestinians allegedly celebrating in the streets after the fall of the Twin Towers belongs to the quaint era of old-fashioned chicanery.

The comments below that I had written earlier, about the uneasy relationship between "news" and "entertainment" and the total dominance of the latter on network television, should be read with this transformation in mind. I have left them for the most part as originally written only because they represent the consensus of critical thinking about television news as it was *before* the events of March 2003.

I begin by distinguishing the institutions that collectively make up the world of network news and documentaries, national journalism, and the like, and are best thought of as the institutions of information culture. Centered in Washington, D.C. and New York rather than Hollywood, they are anatomized beyond compare by Edward Herman and Noam Chomsky in their monumental (even if somewhat dated) *Manufacturing Consent*.[6] As I have noted, the presentation of news and other forms of "information," even when the subject matter is war (e.g., the Gulf War) or political campaigns and elections, is slanted as much toward entertainment values and is often as much imbued with fiction as are the so-called fictional products of "entertainment television." Moreover, news presentation is as saturated with ideology as the average feature film or television series, if not much more so. However, except on those rare occasions when a "news" event is so dramatic in its own right that it is already being packaged as a feature film before it has concluded (for example, the rescue of the nine miners of Creed in the summer of 2002), news events usually lack narrativity and thus emotional distance. Their presentation is therefore probably better viewed through the optic of what Chomsky and Herman call "the propaganda model." A propaganda model "traces the routes by which money and power are able to filter out the news fit to print, marginalize dissent, and allow the government and dominant private interests to get their message across to the public." "Filter," "marginalize," and "dominant" are the key words in this partial definition, emphasizing both qualitative and quantitative gaps in the ability of different social groups to gain access not merely to the news-room but, also, to what finally goes on the air. Ideology in the realm of in-formation culture is too intertwined with propaganda, that is, the conscious, deliberate attempt to mold minds and distort information for a political purpose, to be easily assimilated to the less purposively argumentative world of narrative fiction.[7] There are no artists intervening between infor-mation and audience in the strictly didactic world of propaganda (though its didacticism is disguised on most of the news channels by the suave, bland authoritativeness of the newscasters).

Also, unlike ideology, propaganda is always abstracted from its objects, whom it often defines as internal or external enemies. It cannot afford to al-low them to confront us with their actual humanity, which we might then contrast with the reduction to which propaganda has subjected them. For visual media, the "fanatical" or "militant" "Arab" or "Muslim" is a "terrorist" until proven otherwise (as has so often been the case since 9/11), and we are not treated to sob stories about his hard work, his sick mother, etc. A prominent example from a different arena entirely makes the contrast even more clearly. In his influential Reagan-era book, *Losing Ground,* the writer Charles Murray propagandized ceaselessly about "welfare mothers" but never once introduced us to a real "welfare mother," her history, her needs, and her actual "incentives" or "disincentives." Were he to have done that, his work would have been revealed as the tissue of fictions it was. Instead, he actually invented a couple on welfare and had them "respond" to incen-tives and disincentives of his own devising; a few years later the American Medical Association did exactly the same thing in its television advertising campaign against President Bill Clinton's medical insurance proposals. This is the dehumanization that accompanies propaganda.[8]

To elaborate, propaganda is always noticeably present, but its objects are always absent. In contrast, ideology, whether of the nation or the commu-nity, minimizes the scope and significance of internal dissent, which can be seen, in virtually any network series episode where it occurs, to eventuate in some kind of reconciliation. Ideology therefore always attempts to human-ize the subjects of its discourse because "we" are going to be reconciled with them by the end. In this respect, entertainment television is preeminently, almost totally, ideological. A textbook example of ideology at work, for instance, was visible in a 2002 episode of the series *Crossing Jordan*, in which a Boston office building was blown up and over one hundred persons killed. The first suspect was, as we might expect, an Arabic man, but he was eventually cleared by one of the show's male leads, a local policeman who resists the ignorant fanaticism of the FBI. (In the ideology of American cultural production, the local is always morally preferable to the national, which only recovers its prestige when external enemies are being confronted.) The real "terrorist" turns out to be a "normal" American man trying to make a statement about the law firm that had settled a case against a corporation whose products killed his wife and child, and who believes that the building would be unoccupied when his bomb was set to go off. We begin by thinking him an innocent victim trapped in the ruins; then we find out the truth and, throughout the whole episode, Jordan, the titular female protagonist, holds his hand while he dies, full of remorse. No human being—the faceless corporation being the exception that proves the rule—is really excluded from the social contract. TV's ideology, in other words, is almost always an ideology of inclusion, into a concept of the nation, community, or family broader than we started out with. Outsiders exist not to be scapegoated but to be absorbed into the whole. In Hollywood cinema, for example, this has been the central motif of almost every war movie from World War II to the Vietnam War (occasional epics such as *The Battle of Midway* aside) and typically figures as the integration, or reintegration, of the skeptic: Rick Blaine in *Casablanca* and Ripley in *Aliens* (a standard war movie set in outer space). On television the same theme prevails, although on a smaller scale: Carroll O'Connor's Archie Bunker, the almost-good-hearted bigot of *All in the Family*; Blair Underwood as the token black man of *L.A. Law*; and Richard Belzer, the cynical nihilist of *Law and Order: Special Victims Unit* (by way of *Homicide*), whose immersion in cases involving the mistreatment of children keeps drawing him back into the conventional social order. In the same way, it would only be a slight exaggeration to say that, in Hollywood, Jews (or, one might say, "out" Jews) have existed primarily to point out the evils of anti-Semitism and blacks to highlight the existence of white racism. As we have seen, the end result of this ideological framing is to affirm, despite temporary obstacles, the underlying unity of the nation, the small town, the big city, the work world, and the family.

In performing these unifying operations, ideology is always apparently absent—no one stands in a corner of the screen saying "let me tell you what this episode is about, and what a wonderful place the United States would be if we could all get together"—but its subjects are apparently present. We are encouraged to identify as one or more of them without being lectured about it. If television were, for example, to produce a film about "welfare" (generally, in fact, too grim a subject for television to want to address), it would be about the recovery of a lost soul by her family or by some community institution of the kind typified by "Boys Town" (i.e., not supported by tax dollars). The female viewer would be encouraged to identify with that woman, who would be carefully distinguished from her irrecoverable sisters (e.g., the hopeless drug addict or sociopath). The male viewer, in most cases, would be led to see himself as an authority figure who distinguishes the salvageable from the unsalvageable and oversees the righting of a social wrong. No one would be identified as the author of a supposedly truthful, analytical text. Even more crucially, the creative artist, by the very act of creating the distance between ourselves and the page, or the canvas, or the celluloid, that generates works of the imagination (as opposed to direct statements of beliefs), demonstrates a consciousness of what he or she is doing that is incompatible with any attempt at creating the *systematically* deluded state of mind that propaganda aims to produce in us. We know we're watching a story. If there were the smallest doubt that it is only a story, if it were meant to be taken as a literal revelation of the state of the world, then it would not have been made as a fictional narrative but as a newscast or documentary: an illustrated lecture.

On the face of it, therefore, it would seem that the subsystems of information culture and entertainment culture are sharply distinguishable. In fact, though, this is not the case. The network divisions that produce information and news are actually subsectors of the whole; and the whole is not just predominantly, but entirely, about entertainment. It is meant to deliver audiences to the network and thus, ultimately to advertisers or, metaphorically, addicts to pushers. The takeover of information by entertainment is most prominent in the central arenas of war, as we have already seen, and politics, as the substance of political argument is replaced by the analyses of newscasters and commentators, who are much more intent on finding points of immediate audience interest—the "horse race" aspect of campaigns or legislative conflicts—than they are in illuminating the issues. But, everywhere, the differentiations between the various subsystems are, although real, only marginal. For example, what is the difference between the recent craze, reality television, and, say, a human interest story on *60 Minutes*? Both are allegedly about "real" things happening to "real people." Presumably, the "reality" of reality television is a fake reality, its conditions having been preestablished by the producers of the show. But this is also true of most of the stories we encounter on the television news magazines, which stories are chosen from among the many possibilities because their protagonists come across as sympathetic and articulate, and their point is either noncontroversial or can be slanted in such a way as to fit in with what the networks see as mainstream ideology. By the same token, much of what comes to us as "news" is primarily an account of what variously anointed public figures in government agencies, the White House, the military, various police forces, and so on, have said, and is thus only notionally real. That is, it is "real" in the sense that it is a true report of what someone has actually said—like the Bush administration's claim that the infamous "sixteen words" were not "false," even though they were false, in that the British, to whom they were correctly attributed, had actually said them. However, whether what is said has any correspondence with what an independent observer might find to be the case is another question entirely. Russell Baker's famous words, "only a fool expects the authorities to tell him what the news is," merely highlight the fraudulence of the celebrity newscasters' pretensions to be taken seriously. Like the public relations and promotional spots that come to television from the corporate world in the guise of business news, official pronouncements are prepackaged to get their message across, and the people who put them out are on familiar terms with the people who read them and comment on them. This "news" is not exactly false; but it is, as W. Lance Bennett has called it, an illusion; a particular version of "what is" masquerading as the actuality and entirety of "what is."[9] Indeed, as the second Bush administration has shown, the bigger and more frequent the lies that official sources present to the world, the easier it is to get away with them, as the newscasters will not challenge an official spokesperson until long after the fact.[10]

In the same way, cop shows, which represent an early version of reality television, are merely action-packed and extended versions of the perp walks and prosecutorial news conferences that pass for the coverage of crime on local news programs. All of this, with very little exception, is about entertaining the audience. News clips about people and institutions only enter the system if they are slick and easy to read or can be interpreted by alleged experts who have been carefully chosen to be noninflammatory. In this respect, the coverage of breaking events is professional, but only in the same way (and using the same techniques) as is the production of fictional television. Above all, the people who bring us our "information" are celebrities, paid on the same celebrity scale and for the same virtues as Jennifer Anniston or Jerry Seinfeld. No one reading these words could run into Diane Sawyer or Barbara Walters or Tom Brokaw or Ted Koppel or Dan

Rather or Chris Matthews on the street and not recognize them instantly; no one reading these words has the faintest idea what *New York Times* reporters David Sanger or Floyd Norris look like (unless their good friends happen to have picked up this book), though the latter are trained journalists and intelligent news analysts.

This interweaving of "information" and "entertainment" exists not only in news magazines and the nightly news but, even more so, in the local news that imitates the latter's format at eleven every night. This is most obviously true in its constant highlighting of the ideology of the nation, not only during actual wartime but also during confrontations of any kind with other nations (two categories that cover almost all of recent U.S. history). But ideologizing also takes place on the small as well as the large scale in, for example, those feel-good anecdotes that end almost every edition of the nightly news on every network and that are invariably about how decent ordinary Americans are. These anecdotes, in the world of television, are the glue that holds together the uneasy American amalgam of muscular nationalism, rugged individualism, and communal conformity. They are the individualist antidote to the endless reification of the whole that we otherwise encounter on TV, such as those images and slogans of the nation at war after 9/11 that showed the martial spirit everywhere across the continent but sedulously avoided New York City's Union Square, only two miles from ground zero, with its acre of signs asking us to "give peace a chance." In television's reified world, the government always speaks for "us," politics consists of Democrats and Republicans, cities are in trouble or trying to get out from under it, and "the economy" is weakening or strengthening. The class, ethnic, and regional conflicts that underlie this strength and prosperity rarely escape into the light of day or do so for a moment, only to be dragged back (like Rick Blaine or Ripley) into some concluding picture of harmony.

However, the amalgamation of ideology with propaganda does mark an important difference between the two sectors. Ideological narrative, as we've seen, is marked by the *absence* of visible presenters who stand for, and try to persuade us of, an argument that is clearly being made. Instead, it substitutes a narrative line that presents several arguments but winds up foregrounding and, through the actions of protagonists already identified as "us," endorsing just one of them. In this respect, ideological narrative still differs in obvious ways from newscasting in that the presentation of news is most of the time descriptive rather than narrative and, thus, the presenters are very much there. Here, though, the newscasters divide into those who try very hard to mute the propagandistic aspect of their work, to not be seen as making arguments or attacking persons who might have different political standpoints (e.g., most network newscasters), and those broadcasters and soi-disant pundits who make no effort to avoid that appearance (e.g., Brit Hume).

As to the first group, who might be called pseudoprofessionals, their main effort is to seem politically neutral—the system's dominant ideological mode. Their presentation—in essence their potential rating power—is primarily one of style, looks, and even dress, rather than content; their appeal is to the general ideology of the popular consumer "democracy" that in the United States, at least, undergirds most notions of communal or national harmony. This pseudoprofessional outlook of the network news operations, conjoined with the relatively subdued ideological grounding of TV's narrative fictions, also carries over, in a slightly different manner, to the human interest stories and exposés that are the bread and butter both of the newsmagazines and of so-called docudramas that mix fact with a presumably acceptable degree of entertaining fiction. On straight news shows, the kinds of coverage different events or persons get is very often dependent on the distinction between what Herman and Chomsky call "worthy" and "unworthy" victims. For example, strikers who are also the victims of apparent racial discrimination are more easily positioned as worthy victims deserving of human interest coverage, whereas strikers who are depriving the populace at large of some needed good or service (or a product that owns a network or sponsors some of its shows) are more likely to be treated with suspicion or criticism; unruly demonstrations on behalf of firemen are more likely to gain sympathetic treatment than more peaceful antiwar demonstrators. On the magazine shows and in docudramas, this distinction is also crucial, but so too are the programming decisions that have to do with the kind of action the producers want "the public" to take or the attitude they want it to adopt. These two types of discrimination are woven together; that is, it is easier to gain support for policy initiatives on behalf of worthy or "innocent" victims, easier to drum up anger against the unworthy or undeserving. Such decisions cannot be treated as simple exercises in journalistic dishonesty, for their direction is overdetermined; the attitudes of the immediate producers, above all their desire to seem professional, are balanced by the perceived attitudes of the conventional viewing audience, the demands of sponsors, and the overriding need to be entertaining and thus popular, rather than gloomy and off-putting.

Two examples from almost two decades apart illustrate how television pulls off this balancing act in the face of normative uncertainty. Prior to the revolutionary decision of *Roe v. Wade*, network television produced four documentaries on the abortion struggle. As one critic describes them, their central thrust was the same regardless of what stance one had on the issue before watching them, in their "effacement of the women's movement and ultimate framing of the 'pro' side within the discourses of population control." In doing this, television "distorted the terms in which abortion was discussed, maintaining social hegemony and constraining the medium's more emancipatory possibilities," as "particular spokespeople in the abortion debate were invested with authority and approbation and others—specifically women and feminists (both white and women of color) were not." In the end, in other words, "TV participate(d) in defining abortion as a government- and medically controlled practice, and a moral, ethical, and medical quandary, rather than an unequivocal and socially based right of women"[11] In effect, for the pro-abortion argument, medical and demographic "experts" were worthy spokespersons; women who actually needed abortions were not. If they were victims at all, they were unworthy victims. To understand how the search for conventionality and balance stifles real debate, we need only envision how different the landscape of visual culture would have been if the real issues of principle, right, and justice had been put forward to the nationwide audience, face to face, by the persons who stood for them most dramatically—women in need, advocates from the women's movement, and representatives of antiabortion religious groups. But such persons were shut out of television's world because real drama, and uncompromising people, are the last thing the system wants.

In more recent times, perhaps the most glaring example of this balancing act was the difference between television's kid-gloves treatment of the AIDS crisis in the late 1980s and the confrontational tactics and images of radical activist groups such as Act-Up. As one retrospective account puts it, after years of a hands-off approach that barely concealed a deep repugnance, commercial television began the process of "'putting a human face' (a handsome, white, and not-too-gay human face) on the disease for middle America. In turn, the human face evoked a change in social attitudes that enhanced the success that activists and artists were having on other fronts. And did so, in my judgment, with acceptable losses to art and history."[12] Speaking of the made-for-TV films *An Early Frost* and the more-or-less docudrama *The Ryan White Story*, the author goes on to say, "If it was perplexing to be moved by these movies while acknowledging their contextual dishonesty, *that dishonesty was how they managed to function at all.* (It's also how the nation's first major AIDS legislation got passed: the Ryan White Comprehensive AIDS Resources Emergency Act of 1990). You might as well call metaphors dishonest. In any case, the divorce of AIDS from homosexuality in these early narratives was universally understood to be a ploy." The key phrase here is the one I have italicized; the information-dissemination aspect of television is unimaginable, if divorced from the sentimental approach to subjects and their images that makes television the medium of popular *entertainment*, no matter what the collateral costs.

However, there is more to television information than its immersion in the conventional ideologies of the day (which might be summed up by saying, "Bad things should happen to bad people, and good things should happen to good people, and never the twain should meet"; see chapter 4). News programs, totally unlike straightforward entertainment television, can also be, and especially on cable news channels often are, founts of propaganda, which is often confused with, but is yet wholly different from, ideology. Rather than the appearance of harmony, they can deliberately present the angry partisanship of the populist or, in wartime, the aggressive nationalist. Populist and nationalist propaganda, unlike the subdued and neutral ideology of the intelligent consumer, is spoken by visible spokespersons whose words we are meant to believe exclusive of any possible contradiction and who proceed not only by omitting, but often by slandering, all contrary positions. Their propaganda relies on an appeal to "real people," that is, those who are like-minded, and on the exclusion and scapegoating of all others. On talk shows, this is done very openly, though the pretense that we are merely listening to opinions is maintained. That is, the word "opinion" is used to suggest that what we are hearing just happens to be the thought of the individual persons who are talking instead of being, as is most often the case, one element in an already existing, dogmatic, and externally organized political position for which the speaker is propagandizing. Propaganda, moreover, does not just exist on the cable news channels but in the major network news magazines, as well. Presented as in-depth explorations of a particular topic, they are, in addition to being invariably superficial, not always but very often advocacy pieces for the particular reporter's viewpoint on a topic that might have one or more quite contrary interpretations. These are sometimes presented as counterweights, but the standard mode of presentation is for the weight of the program, especially the visual and anecdotal evidence, to be massed on the favored side, while dissent, carefully marked as such, is relegated to brief statements by a spokesperson for "the other side"—often a person of lower status, such as a woman, responding to a case made by white men.[13] In any event, like all propaganda, these programs make their arguments mostly by selective anecdote or one-sided interpretations of statistical data; the kind of back-and-forth discussion and presentation of evidence that one might find on a panel of social scientists is nowhere to be found on commercial television.

Moreover, the pull of audience appeal is such that the most common type of magazine report is the exposé, which gives viewers the excitement of being on the inside of some hidden story. The exposé is a hardy American journalistic tradition, but to see the genuine thing, one has to look at noncommercial television, such as the documentary investigations *The War Behind Closed Doors* (February 2003), *A Family's Fortune, A Legacy of Blood and Tears* (January 2003), or *Failure to Protect: The Taking of Logan Marr* (July 2002) on PBS's *Frontline*, or at HBO, which has produced such major cinematic documentaries as *The Farm*. Despite their highly dramatic contents (an inside look at policymaking on Iraq, unregulated and toxic industrial pollution in Birmingham, Alabama, the failures of one state's child protection system, and a terrifying depiction of a Louisiana prison farm, respectively), these programs do not fit into commercial television's mode of having used-car salespersons (such as ABC's John Stossel; see chapter 3) throw anecdotal arguments at a mass audience within an overall news-as-entertainment format. In other words, they induce reflective thought about profound systemic imbalances and the immense difficulties to be encountered in any effort to right them. Conversely, even when most sober, the commercial magazines on the whole give added weight to the strange antigovernment propaganda of the right wing in American politics, which propaganda is strange in that it accompanies an insistence on authoritarian respect for government as long as it is not engaging in welfare-oriented activities. Rarely do they feature accounts of federal or state programs, such as Head Start, that do what they are supposed to do or explain how entrenched deformations of government budgets or tax structures disable attempts at reform. The one-sidedness of commercial news magazines is not so much that of overt propaganda, but more often of simple failure to explore in-depth simplistic, and thus propagandistic, accounts of public policy. They are neither genuinely political nor genuinely professional but, rather, riders of the curve.

This concentration of the news divisions on either pseudoprofessional or propagandistic reporting styles puts a different light on the conventional wisdom of the business pages, as well as of Michael Powell, chairman of the Federal Communications Commission (FCC) during the second Bush administration, that oligopoly actually increases "diversity." This bit of corporate propaganda was presented by reporter Jim Rutenberg in the *New York Times* on December 2, 2002, as though it were simple fact, under the headline, "Fewer Media Owners, More Media Choices"; as Powell was quoted,

"When I look at the trends in television over the last 20 to 50 years, I see a constant and increasing explosion in variety." What followed in the rest of the story, however, was not a single word about variety of content but, instead, many words about multiplicity of sources—an entirely different issue—as though BBC-America's truncated newscasts, which are often not even available on the basic cable service, play on a level playing field with CNN. As the FCC under Powell, despite belated congressional opposition, attempted to relax historical prohibitions on cross-ownership (of newspapers and television channels, or cable companies and television channels, in the same city), apologists argued for accepting local or regional monopoly as a way of accommodating the traditional demand for diversity of viewpoint, rather than in spite of it. They argued that the proliferation of network and cable channels, each with its own separate news operation, has brought forth a plethora of independent news sources never known before and supported by the strength of centralized ownerships. ABC, NBC, CBS, Fox, CNN—what more could one ask for?

The power-seeking Rupert Murdoch, in actuality, could ask for much more, as shortly thereafter the administration (now with the acquiescence of a supine Congress) was about to allow his News Corporation to control the nation's largest satellite service, DirecTV, and thus greatly expand Murdoch's reach and power. At the very same moment, former presidential candidate Al Gore was "begging, literally, Vivendi/Universal to sell him a single, poorly distributed news channel."[14] This contrast casts a different light on the centerpiece of the argument in Rutenberg's story, that allowing Murdoch, owner of New York's Channel 5 (among many other media outlets in various places), to buy the *New York Post* in 1993 "saved a local voice in New York that would have been lost." This is simply false, as Rutenberg must have known, because barely a month later he was reporting on the almost total domination of broadcast media, especially Murdoch's empire, by conservative and Republican Party partisans. Aside from its "Letters to the Editor" section, and a commitment to leaving no bloodshed or cleavage uncovered, the *Post* is no more a "local voice" than any other of Murdoch's worldwide monopoly holdings. Its voice is that of right-wing partisanship anywhere in the United States, and it covers no local news that cannot also be found in the *New York Daily News* or, much better, in such community weeklies as the *Villager*. On the contrary, it was the management of AOL-Time Warner's local access Channel 1 in New York City that really did add a distinctive "local voice" to the city's television offering. Channel 1's all-day format, via its interviews as well as its various discussion programs, gives a discussion forum to a wide range of New Yorkers who would almost never be heard from on the half hour or one hour news segments provided by the network channels—including, on rare occasions, even labor leaders, paraprofessionals, minority voices, social service workers, etc. No network has created any such enterprise. Far from adding local voices, in fact, Murdoch's overarching goal is to subtract them and leave only his in their place; for some time, the *Post* has been engaged in a circulation war with the *Daily News* in an overt attempt to destroy the latter's circulation base.

In any event, even the technicalities of cross-ownership, as devastating as they are to pluralism in the world of communications, are not the real issue. The "more one could ask for" is, precisely, diverse and equally funded news channels (not to mention radio stations) that counterbalance each other to the extent that information in easily digestible forms inevitably tends toward the propagandistic; that are able to encourage a sense of professional responsibility independent of someone else's conception of what will motivate the audience economically or politically; and that are independent also of a giant economic monopoly that forbids criticism of (or even news about) itself in particular, the commercial system that sustains it generally, and the insider politics that acquiesces in its demands. Perhaps the condition of oligopolistic domination would not matter if "news" were just what the name is intended to imply—a representative sampling of facts (i.e., roughly accurate statements) about some corner of the world of interest to a representative sampling of citizens. But it is far from that. Or, rather, that kind of information is one small, usually very small, portion of what comes to us during the half hours or hours that are carefully set off from all other programming as "news." This is true even on the twenty-four-hour news channels; their coverage of what the network news programs consider "national" or "international" news is only marginally more extensive than what the networks provide; they, instead, earn their reputation for more complete coverage through constant repetition of the same stories. In any event, and whatever the network, most of what we receive is communiqués (more often, summaries of them crafted to conceal the truth of what is actually happening or being proposed) from the official organs of power. These are interpreted, if at all, from some conventionally centrist standpoint by celebrity newscasters or their chosen guests, an A-list of spokespersons carefully selected so as not to be likely to say that everything we've been listening to is simply a lie; and supposedly exemplary anecdotes are chosen to leaven the fundamental dryness of one-minute, official news bites.

Three aspects of this oligopolistic system, in particular, lead to a degradation of the idea of "news" or "information." First, as I have already emphasized, the news divisions of the major networks are a minor, but integral,

part of the total *entertainment* structure. As with sports, there is adminis-
trative separation but no separate standard: the basic principle of operation
is to win the ratings war within the news sector and, thus, to sell advertising
time at the highest possible rate. Achieving this position does entail maintaining a certain status with the viewers, commentators, and public figures
who confer prestige within the world of public information (as opposed to
the academic world, which has much stricter standards). But the fight for
status is strictly instrumental, and, if ratings and thus advertising revenues
fall, it will be sacrificed to whatever bottom line is being enforced on the
news divisions. In any event, however prestige is pursued, it is pursued
within the boundaries of what is construed as "entertainment"; it is not to
be pursued at the expense of audience appeal. The commercial television
audience may be segmented—into whites and blacks, men and women,
adults and children, informed viewers and casual viewers—but every segment must fit into the overall structure, a structure that is heavily skewed
to entertaining audiences rather than informing them and to appealing to
likely consumers between the ages of eighteen and forty-nine. It is as
though a publisher might occasionally—to great fanfare—publish *The
Lovely Bones* or *Midnight in the Garden of Evil*, but not poetry, or *Ulysses*,
or a probing history of abstract expressionism.

The most important aspect of news-as-entertainment, though, is the way
the commercialization of news affects its very meaning. Taken individually,
the various means by which news is coded in the television system might be
merely irritating or intellectually questionable. Taken together, they add up
to more than that: to a whole that is *predominantly* rather than incidentally
entertaining. To begin with, the news is presented as "sound bites"; that is,
as a series of capsule descriptions that don't so much *summarize* the news
content but, rather, as demonstrated in Jeffrey Scheuer's compelling analysis, *replace* it. In addition, the presentation of news, especially on the cable
channels (but now the networks as well), is punctuated by an accompany-
ing commentary, spoken or written, that Neil Postman years ago called
"Now . . . this."[15] The slightly portentous "Now . . . this" also takes the more
excited form of "This just in," and nowadays the inescapable headline,
"Breaking News," as well as the "crawl" at the bottom of the screen, pioneered by CNN but now to be found everywhere. The effect of this constant invocation of heightened expectation and subsequent surprise is to
present "news" not as an ongoing report on the social (or world) state of affairs, but as a continuing drama, a play with a cast of stars and supporting
actors who are leading us to the amazing (but really completely foreseen)
revelation that always comes at the end of Act II in any well-made Ameri-

can play. "America Strikes Back" was the ultimate version of the way in which the drama itself thus *becomes* the "news." Any failure of the administration to actually strike back would have been worse than a political failure; it would have been a failure to play its assigned role in the drama, as though Cherry Jones or Swoosie Kurtz, appearing in some Broadway play, were to say "Excuse me, I don't like this speech," and walk off the stage.

To return to the theme I expounded at the opening of this essay, the propagandistic aspect of national television has thus taken a long step beyond the erstwhile power of the press, as exemplified by the drumbeat of war talk in the Hearst papers that led, after the sinking of the battleship Maine, to the Spanish-American War of 1898. Television news does not *incite* to war but reports it as though it is already happening, and it is now simply a matter of leaders catching up to events, many of which are simply invented or transmuted from trivia into history. As *TV Guide* noted during the run-up to the invasion of Iraq, "every time we drop by CNN or Fox News Channel or MSNBC, we see some sort of 'breaking news' alert—only to find a simple live report from some minor event."[16] By February's worldwide antiwar demonstrations, CNN's website was reporting that "antiwar rallies delight Iraq," and every mention of the Mideast on CBS was accompanied by the logo, "Showdown with Saddam," surrounding an American flag. Anyone else in the world, one could presume, could hardly wait for the play, that is the war, to begin.

The appearance of news as drama (or, most usually, melodrama) is also determined by two other factors: the encapsulation of news by commercials and the entwining of the important with the trivial. As with straightforward entertainment television, it's never quite certain which is the tail and which is the dog; the more so in the case of news, in that commercials, when they are not conceived as clever dramatic or comic narratives, often take on the form of information themselves, thus not only distracting from the "news" but actually competing with it. Moreover, commercials are often longer than the news bites that interrupt them. With commercials in the form of those late night or early morning "infomercials" that clog the non-network channels, letting dubious doctors and the like peddle their questionable products for hours at a time, the boundary is finally breached beyond any repair; anyone who has seen enough of them would have to be forgiven for wondering exactly what *is* the difference between Tom Brokaw and the latest well-muscled enthusiast of NordicTrack. In this total structure, even the best intentions of would-be professionalism are suborned.

In much the same way, the boundary between the significant and the trivial is constantly being breached. One of the most striking—but hardly unique—examples of this phenomenon occurred on NBC on February 5, 2003. That morning, as always on weekdays, NBC began with the *Today* show from seven to ten a.m. The supposed climax of the show, its advertised highlight, was the appearance of Adrian Nicole LeBlanc, author of the recently published *Random Family*, a book that reported on her experience of living for ten years with a poverty-stricken and crime-prone Puerto Rican family in the Bronx. In the few minutes of interview time that could be spared for her, she gave a subtle critique of the "culture of poverty" approach to the behavior of the poor, focusing instead on what she called the internal logic of their lives and suggesting that such traditional approaches to poverty as higher wages, better housing, and more support for public education would do much to improve those lives. The interviewer did not pursue this line of thought but thanked her and then informed viewers that, after the commercials, the show would return with a discussion of another new book on "men who avoid commitment." The interview with LeBlanc had also included, at its beginning, an interview with one of her subjects, a reformed addict and felon who spoke feelingly of the depth of his commitment to his family, even from behind bars; only a dedicated seeker of irony would have noticed the juxtaposition. As if that were not enough, the entire LeBlanc segment (all twelve minutes of it) had been preceded, not too many segments before, by an interview with ex-madam Heidi Fleiss, who was pushing *her* recently published book, *Pandering*. What is *Today*, the most watched morning show in America, telling us its audience?

The best answer to that question would be—nothing—absolutely nothing, except that there is no meaning. But there was more to come. At ten a.m., NBC (and all other networks) broke away from regularly scheduled programming for a "Special Report": Secretary of State Colin Powell's speech to the United Nations (UN) in which he justified war against Iraq. This speech was presented in its entirety free of commercial interruptions: an approach that seems to testify to the seriousness of the networks but, in fact, only underscores their relegation of most news to the second division. The call to war was then followed, at noon, by a series of commentaries on the speech, most of them by carefully selected centrist Democrats who endorsed the Secretary's words with few reservations. No one was consulted who might have asked embarrassing questions, such as why the United States had never put its intelligence capability at the service of the UN inspection team but, instead, had apparently deliberately withheld it in order to make a case for war. No time was given for reflection or for a potentially wide-ranging exchange of informed analyses that might turn up unconventional ideas. But how could there be time for that, as at one p.m. NBC's nation, now having been prepared for an event that might well result in thousands of deaths and tumult in the Mideast for years to come, was allowed to return to its more serious business: the extended commercials for cosmetics and cleansers known as daytime soap operas. This is "the news" as we have become accustomed to it. With only minor variations—mostly on the cable news channels, especially Fox—it was repeated on every outlet. As for those twenty-four-hour news channels, by prattling on forever (interrupted only by the undeniable commercials), they merely underscore the system's primary purpose of delivering viewers to advertisers: their message is "don't turn us off" for "you might miss something [the same something we were telling you half an hour ago]."

None of this should be any surprise, because the second important aspect of the information system is that the condition of oligopoly in any sector is always to preclude innovative change and to promote only pseudoinnovations that intensify existing methods of production. Oligopoly fosters convergence of product: there is little to be gained by innovations that deviate substantially from the norm, as one's competitors can copy the innovation in short order (one season, in television). If it is a success, then the innovator has gained nothing but a short-term advantage; if it is a failure, the innovator is the sole loser. The potential returns are not worth the gamble, so the gamble is rarely taken. Competition among network news operations, therefore, consists in such nonevents as, for example, being the first to hire a woman in a major role, stealing celebrities from another network (e.g., Paula Zahn), leading with a different story from among the six leading stories that everyone is going to carry that night, carrying a different kind of logo or crawl, and so forth. This is sales competition rather than product competition. The only innovation in American newscasting since its origins was the introduction of 24/7 cable television. This is a perfect example of oligopoly at work, in that, on one hand, the round-the-clock news format was soon copied by every major network (though CBS's attempt failed) and, on the other hand, this is an innovation without innovation. Nothing has changed in the fundamental relationship of news to audience or audience to advertising. With cable news, the audience is now talked at around the clock by photogenic pseudoexperts instead of only for an hour a day. But official institutional and other approved sources still dominate the news arena; complex situations and interpretations are still reduced to commercially manageable sound bites; and the overall system degenerates as the propaganda content of "information" escalates, reaching its peak with the conscious decision of Murdoch's Fox News, under the direction of a leading GOP campaign strategist, to become an arm of the Republican Party.

Moreover, in times of real or so-called crisis—the Gulf War, the O. J. Simpson chase, the 2000 election fiasco, the attack on the World Trade Center, the invasion of Iraq, and the death of *Columbia*—even minor differences among the networks disappear, as the safest way to compete is to do what everyone else is doing. As a perfect illustration of this point, we can recall that, from the moment on the morning of September 11, 2001, when CNN first posted its "America strikes back" logo, it was only a few hours before every other network had adopted that slogan as its own. Indeed CNN, the leader then, is now (as of this writing in 2004) the follower, as it hastens to adopt the newscaster-as-celebrity mode of presentation that it had originally eschewed, but now pursues under pressure from Fox and the major networks.

Third, virtually none of this news and information is factual in the sense of being as close as we can get to an objective account of what is going on— what the philosopher Thomas Nagel calls "a view from nowhere," a consciously disinterested, professionally dictated attempt to describe a situation as fully as possible, as though the person describing it had no stake in its outcome.[17] The body of what is chosen to pass as fact (without being so) is not in the slightest a reasonably representative sample of what might have been chosen; and the audience whose putative interests are elevated to that of the whole is not to the faintest extent representative of the whole but is, instead, representative of the persons doing the reporting. These are not all the same persons, for different representations of the audience compete with each other. Without exception, the celebrity network presenters adopt the standpoint of the pseudoprofessional, which by and large entails good-looking, white, male, upper-middle-class persons delivering dramatic but inoffensive summaries of what the news producers have determined to be "news," for a middlebrow audience of intelligent consumers. In what way these men are supposed to be professional is never clear, given that their only activities, for the most part, are to read the summaries that other people have written for them or to provide platforms for superficially important persons by asking them noninflammatory questions. Meanwhile, the on-site reporters, most of whom are not celebrities (though females and males both are invariably attractive in some standard sense and, over time, may become celebrities), pretend to be journalists, as though the sound bites they deliver were actual stories that had been covered instead of, as they really are, reports of what yet other people have said, or written as communiqués, and invariably repeating almost exactly, but with more verbiage, what the newscasters have said in introducing them. Together, the different role-players maintain a patina of professionalism. At the local level, this pattern is repeated without the movie-star aspect, although over time the local news-casters also may become minor regional celebrities in their own right. In ei-ther case, nothing that might be unpopular, that is, potentially depress rat-ings, is permitted; nor is anything permitted that might reveal the hidden agendas of the various multinational, national, and regional business inter-ests that maintain the commercial television economy. Once again, "infor-mation" turns, almost outside our line of vision, into propaganda. Under the second Bush administration, indeed, propaganda has taken over without a hint of resistance from a supine TV system, which accepts and reproduces fake "news" from fake "journalists" without a whimper.[18]

If we cannot find a path to the "view from nowhere," then the most ob-vious way to achieve at least a simulacrum of it is to multiply types of sources, to find countervailing powers. This is what "diversity" ought to mean, but it does not. Labor leaders are hardly ever interviewed to talk about business and the economy; nurses, social workers, and general prac-titioners are not interviewed to talk about the disasters of the for-profit health system; women on welfare are not asked to analyze welfare reform (i.e., its abolition); and professionally commissioned reports on the im-mense racial discrimination inherent in the legal system rarely receive air-time (how many readers of this page know that convicted black persons re-ceive, on average, sentences that are five times as long as the sentences that convicted white persons receive for the same crimes?). Political commen-tators outside the closed framework of Washington's one-and-a-half party politics need not apply unless to fill this year's role of the token outsider; in-dependent filmmakers aren't asked for comments on the state of Holly-wood; and so on.

None of these absences is repaired by cable's adoption of the populist ap-proach, which instead only makes the propaganda model even more hor-rendously applicable. It is true that, with commentators such as Chris Matthews or Sean Hannity or Bill O'Reilly or Rush Limbaugh, the pretense of professionalism disappears, along with the Hollywood-style manner and along with, on occasion, even the faintest effort at truth-telling (although if these men presented themselves as stand-up comics offering an entertaining alternative, à la Jackie Mason, to the pompous self-satisfaction of the pro-fessionals, their preference for bon mots over truth-telling might be a little less repellent).[19] In their place, though, we find not an attempt to probe be-neath obvious social surfaces but instead a macho-inflected, barely con-cealed anger on behalf of a populist construct—yet another reification—known as "the ordinary guy." Beneath that superficial difference, the only thing that really changes with the populist news style is the ratio of open propaganda to concealed ideology, as unspoken ideological assumptions of middle-class unity are replaced by the overt and partisan scapegoating of enemies. Thus, whereas the pseudoprofessional style freezes out what are considered the extremes, the populist style freezes out all political opponents: in the case of right-wing populism (virtually the only populism to be found on television), all who are not Republican partisans. The last time anyone counted, about 80 percent of cable channel talk show guests whose political affiliations could be identified were Republicans; and, although the cable talk shows have even less traffic with genuine information than do the cable newscasts, together they form a unified whole, as little effort is made to separate them as different kinds of informational sources. If we were to believe the allegation that, at one time, there was a larger proportion of Democrats than Republicans on news shows (a pre-cable phenomenon, if it really existed at all), then one partisan imbalance has been replaced by another, but the predisposition of the news system toward inside-politics, out-of-control partisanship has worsened considerably.

In any event, the similarities between cable and network are as significant as the differences. The most important similarity often goes unnoticed: authoritative information is resolutely male and white. Women, hired to emit a kind of middle-range glamour, are traded among the networks and cable news channels like a utility infielder; the acme of their accomplishment is to become famous for interviewing people more interesting than themselves. Nonwhite men, despite the onetime exception of Bernard Shaw, usually need not apply. Substantively, on most important issues, the two styles converge on a common content. As Gaye Tuchman has written, "The content [of news] is implicit in the process of its production. . . . Given possible multiple readings of mass media, the power of the news lies in its ability to ensure that readers or other active users are presented with the same or similar bureaucratically created and ideologically embedded accounts."[20] To take just one example, from PBS to CBS to Fox, all news groups within the system have at least a daily summary of the stock market and of what they call business news. Yet a small proportion of Americans have personal stock market portfolios of any consequence compared to the many, many millions who have immensely consequential (for themselves) holdings in pension funds. However, no information about pension funds leaks out of either pseudoprofessional or populist news coverage: nothing about which companies are scaling back their pension funds, how they are being invested, what their mutual fund holdings are doing, what is happening to the expectations of those who thought they had secure future pensions but in truth do not, etc. In the same way, news about "the economy" or "business" contains no information about the immensely profitable business of union-busting, though millions of Americans belong to unions and breaking those unions is the primary task of certain major law firms, "security" agencies, and the like. The soi-disant people's representatives never talk about the ways in which corporate profit drives and distorts the health-care system or how the tax system favors the wealthy. So too, industrial accidents and workplace toxicity, which kill more Americans annually than homicide, never appear in television's version of the economy. And the all-encompassing social system of American apartheid, with its separate schedules of jail time, mortgage loan rates, rental housing openings, etc., for blacks and whites, goes virtually unmentioned: right-wing populism is for whites (mostly white males) only.[21]

One can find out about these matters from time to time (but not very often) in the serious press; but there is no serious television. Neither the pseudoprofessional nor the populist newscasters, in other words, care about the actual lives of the audiences they are trying either to sell lifestyles to, or, in the case of the populists, to "represent" politically. But then, they know nothing about those lives. Bill O'Reilly and Chris Matthews, those multimillionaire tribunes of the ordinary guy, get their seven-figure paychecks not for having a socially productive skill (unless we agree to call the presentation of falsehoods with a dogmatic air of certitude "productive"), but for being good at what Heidi Fleiss's prosecutors would call pandering. On this basis, they presume to lecture other celebrities (e.g., Susan Sarandon) for having opinions based on just about the same amount of information (to be charitable to the news hawks) as they themselves have. As representatives, wherever they originally came from, they now live on the same block, with just about as much "street cred" as "Jenny from the block." Rather, Brokaw, and Jennings live there too. At least, though, it can be said of J-Lo that what she gives to the world is exactly what she purports it to be: the pleasure of talent and the embodiment of dreams. She does not try to sell us ignorance and bias posing as facts.

The results of this insulation from social reality are profound. Within the news subsystem, just as much as in its strictly fictional counterpart, consumer television pretends that there are no fundamental class differences in the way people live—after all, "everyone" drinks Bud. To be sure, populist television (properly called "authoritarian populist"; see chapter 3) insists on the existence of class differences but pretends that they are all a matter of political ideology. Liberals are upper-class twits, and conservatives are the real people; one could never guess to which class George Will, not to mention Matthews or O'Reilly (or George W. Bush), belongs. The Clinton impeachment imbroglio was temporarily disastrous for the populist style, as it exposed an immense gap between the way most "ordinary Americans" actually felt about the attempt to impeach the president and the way the case was being presented by the would-be populists. However, the 2000 election crisis, which the system delivered to the GOP and its cable propagandists before anything had truly been settled, recouped much of this lost ground (the high-handed and bullying contempt with which Chris Matthews, for instance, treated Democrats and other protestors against the electoral coup de main has to have been seen to be appreciated; there is no way it can be described retrospectively). And the terror, outrage, and inflamed nationalism consequent on 9/11 recovered much of the mass audience for the populist style and even delivered some of pseudoprofessional television into its hands. But, in either case, as far as television information is concerned, the economic power structures that delimit the way most of us are able to live might as well not exist.

Some years ago, a critic of the system presented an imaginary nightly newscast that featured movements in the prices of basic necessities, rising or falling incomes in different segments of the society, an occupational health and safety report, a consumer product safety report, and a "plant shutdown monitor" report. It concluded, "And that's the way it was, Tuesday, November 1st, 1983."[22] That is *never* the way it is or has been on any American television newscast, whether pseudoprofessional or populist.

NOTES

1. The BBC's honest coverage of the invasion was made more tenable by the fact that British public opinion was overwhelmingly against the invasion and Prime Minister Tony Blair's support of it.

2. Quoted from an interview with Gavin Smith in *Film Comment*, July/August 2004, 26.

3. Naomi Klein, *Nation*, January 26, 2004, 10.

4. Sara Boxer, *New York Times*, Arts section, April 3, 2003.

5. As reported in Jim Navreckas, "MSNBC's Racism Is OK, Peace Activism is Not," *Extra! Update*, April 2003.

6. Herman and Chomsky, *Manufacturing Consent: The Political Economy of the Mass Media* (New York: Pantheon, 1988). See also Elayne Rapping, *The Looking-Glass World of Non-Fiction TV* (Boston: South End Press, 1987); and Michael Parenti, *Inventing Reality* (New York: St. Martin's, 1986). I exclude documentaries, as most of these are overt efforts to persuade and therefore belong also to the informational culture world.

7. By "ideology," I mean "the ensemble of beliefs and practices that support a (partially) fictitious sense of community among the members of an organized human group." See Philip Green, *Cracks in the Pedestal: Ideology and Gender in Hollywood* (Amherst: University of Massachusetts Press, 1998), 15. Chapters 1 and 3 of that book take up the specific topic of ideology in visual culture at greater length than I can give it here. For a more detailed discussion of the concept of "ideology," see my "I Have a Philosophy, You Have an Ideology: Is Social Criticism Possible?" in *Massachusetts Review* 32, no. 2 (Summer 1991), 199–217.

8. See Murray, *Losing Ground: American Social Policy, 1950–1980* (New York: Basic, 1984).

9. W. Lance Bennett, *News: The Politics of Illusion,* 2nd ed. (New York: Longman, 1988).

10. See chapter 3, note 25.

11. See Julie D'Acci, "Leading up to *Roe v. Wade*: Television Documentaries in the Abortion Debate," in *Feminist Television Criticism: A Reader*, ed. Charlotte Brunsdon et al, 273–89 (quotations at 274–75) (Oxford: Clarendon Press, 1997).

12. Jesse Green, "When Political Art Mattered," *New York Times Magazine*, December 7, 2003, 72. The "human face" quote is from the playwright Larry Kramer.

13. A December 1, 2002, *20-20* "report" on Title IX, the federal legislation that has mandated equal participation by women and men in intercollegiate sports, was a classic case in point, as sympathetic interviews with male wrestlers and coaches whose teams had been dropped by some universities in order to meet the requirements of Title IX were counterposed to brief rebuttals by a woman who was carefully positioned as an ideologue and a representative of feminism rather than as the deprived individuals that we saw in the males. The woman came across as a "tough woman"; they came across as helpless persons whose side was clearly the side of the angels, as far as the reporter was concerned. Decades of sometimes vicious and even coercive discrimination against female athletes, and the special role of football teams in creating an imbalance among scholarship athletes, were glossed over. The wrestlers were never asked, for example, if they thought it would be reasonable to drop, say, ten men from the inflated football rosters (in Division I competition, twice the size of what the National Football League finds satisfactory), in order to make room for themselves.

14. See Jeff Chester, "A Present for Murdoch," *Nation*, December 22, 2003, 22.

15. See Jeffrey Scheuer's *The Sound Bite Society: Television and the American Mind* (New York: Four Walls Eight Windows, 1999); Postman's *Amusing Ourselves to Death: Public Discourse in the Age of Show Business* (New York: Penguin, 1985); and Bennett's *News: The Politics of Illusion.*

16. Consider for example this Fox "news alert" from mid-January 2003: "The American military campaign to reach Iraqi generals and people in leadership positions by e-mail, appears to be working." What exactly was working, and how we knew it was working, remained a mystery. See *TV Guide*, February 1, 2003, 10.

17. See Thomas Nagel, *The View From Nowhere* (New York: Oxford, 1986).

18. See David Barstow and Robin Stein, "Under Bush, a New Age of Prepackaged News," *New York Times*, March 13, 2005.

19. On the lies of Bill O'Reilly and Sean Hannity, see Al Franken's *Lies (and the Lying Liars Who Tell Them)* (New York: Dutton, 2003); also, see chapter 3. Rush Limbaugh has been anatomized most famously in Franken's earlier *Rush Limbaugh Is a Big Fat Idiot and Other Observations* (New York: Delacorte Press, 1996). But since the publication of Franken's book, Limbaugh has outdone himself with his notorious remark on Monday Night Football in September of 2003, that Donovan McNabb was an inferior quarterback but the media had puffed him up because he was black. The characterization of the media was a simple lie. In fact, as a sportswriter in the *New York Times* pointed out, the Philadelphia media have been vicious to McNabb at times during his career. More to the point, perhaps, Limbaugh's statement about McNabb was ignorant, leaving his mouth at just about the moment when McNabb recovered from earlier injuries and began to lead the Eagles toward the playoffs, as arguably the best quarterback in the NFC. Limbaugh has never apologized for either the lie or the ignorance; the faux populists are never wrong as long as there are enough resentful white men out there to cheer them on.

20. Gaye Tuchman, "Consciousness Industries and the Production of Culture," *Journal of Communication* (Summer 1983): 333.

21. The definitive account of entrenched racial discrimination in the United States is Douglas S. Massey and Nancy A. Denton's *American Apartheid: Segregation and the Making of the Underclass* (Cambridge, Mass.: Harvard University Press, 1993).

22. See Peter Dreier's "The Corporate Complaint Against the Media," in *American Media and Mass Culture: Left Perspectives*, ed, Donald Lazere, 78–79 (Berkeley: University of California Press, 1987).

3

DISTRACTIONS:
THE LIE ABOUT LIBERALS

In this chapter I must necessarily grapple with the obvious fact that the description of the TV system I have just written is, on its face, incompatible with the most common contemporary account of mass media, that they suffer from "liberal control." The nature of this account as it relates to the television system is a simple matter of record: the subservience of news departments to the business interests that "own" them; the conservative domination of news and opinion shows (including those on PBS, that special target of the smear campaign) and the prevalence of Republican Party and other right wing spokespersons who deliver a daily, mostly one-sided, mostly unchallenged, barrage of contempt for liberals and liberalism; the exclusion of women-as-feminists from visual media (whereas men speak as masculinists all the time); the relegation of minority spokespersons to the sidelines, unless they deliver conservative propaganda; and the fawning reliance of media on government sources during the Reagan and both Bush administrations contrasted with their skeptical and often sneering treatment of Clinton and his administration. The record has been established by Eric Alterman in his definitive account, *What Liberal Media? The Truth about Bias and the News*.[1] As we shall see below, it can also be found regularly in *Extra!*, a bimonthly publication of the New York-based media watchdog group, Fairness and Accuracy in Media (FAIR). Rather than simply repeat what they have demonstrated, I think it would be useful here to address two questions that still leave a sense of puzzlement after one has plunged into the literature on TV "bias." The first is this: how can the right-wing critics of "liberal" television possibly even be attempting to make a case that is so evidently counterfactual? And the second question is why, in a period of long-term conservative triumph, both institutional and ideological, do they have such a burning desire, such a rage, to make a case that denies their own power? How can the ubiquitous Ann Coulter see Susan Sarandon or Sean Penn, demonized as they are, as important threats to the polity? The first is a question of methodology and is more easily and clearly answered than the second, which is a question about the ambiguities of psyche and identity, to which answers can only be speculative.

Most accounts of alleged bias on television consist of the piling up of instances, and this poses three problems. The first problem is the tendency of these accounts to ignore the context in which "instances" and "mentions," to use two of the critics' favorite words, occur. The second is reliance on what I call anecdotalism, the telling of random stories that are neither representative of the whole universe from which they are isolated nor relevant to a theory or generalization that they strengthen and that, in turn, testifies to their relevance. The third is the regular substitution of the storyteller's judgment about content for that of the newscaster, with respect to a particular story that allegedly is biased; that is, deviation from your beliefs does not show bias on my part, as an equally plausible explanation of my deviation is that your beliefs about reality are wrong.

The first tendency is especially important, for the counting of mentions is the main, often the only, support for the conservative propaganda machine's claim to be doing genuine empirical analysis. Mostly this consists of showing how various newscasters have made an excessive number of negative comments about the policies of Republican administrations. L. Brent Bozell and the Center for Media and Public Affairs are especially prone to take this tack, but, in order to make their point, they must pretend not to be aware that the entire normative context, and the agenda for public discussion, have already been set by the political leaders whose communiqués and pronouncements (see chapter 2) come to the public with much more substantial authority than any single reporter can possibly muster. The so-called news is so dominated by officialdom that newscasters, far from being "biased," are remiss if they do not take pains to counteract official claims. In the case of George W. Bush especially, the entire tenor of his administration has been to tell outright lies about the intended effects of policies. For example, a tax cut intended to benefit the wealthy is heralded as benefiting the poor; legislation intended to maintain drug company profits is said to be designed to lower the cost of drugs to the elderly; above all, the decades-old campaign of the Right to undo the concept of social security by turning it into a privatized, risk-based system is offered, with conscious falsity, as an attempt to "save" the system from a fiscal collapse with which it is not in fact threatened. In such cases, simply reporting what the president has said is already distorting the realm of policy discussion.

As for anecdotalism, the problem here is that an anecdote is not an argument; even a thousand anecdotes do not add up to an argument. For example, piling up quotations from Edward Kennedy and Barbara Boxer and Tom Daschle could make the U.S. Senate sound "liberal," but it isn't; it's just that all the contrary evidence has been omitted. The worst example of this kind of incompetent methodology in action is Bernard Goldberg's recent addition to "liberal-elite" bashing, *Arrogance: Rescuing America from the Media Elite*.[2] From a field of thousands, perhaps millions, of available quotations about policy, politics, culture, and power from "media elites," Goldberg has managed to find a few dozen that are satisfactorily "liberal" in order to make his case. Some of these are actually defensible arguments or simple statements of fact (see, e.g., the quotations from Maria Liasson and Carole Simpson)[3]; some are recycled from his previous book *Bias*, as though the well of liberal duplicity and "arrogance" has actually run dry; and some are not relevant to anything at all. (At one point, Goldberg asks us to match "offensive quotations" with the presumably liberal celebrities who uttered them, under the heading "That's Entertainment!" What does this have to do with anything? Why shouldn't there be liberal celebrities?) Anyone—Eric Alterman, for example—can with ease find an equal or (more likely) far greater number of quotations or behaviors to support the contrary case for conservative bias and arrogance. This is simply not the way to make an argument. Where the data set is infinite, and classifications are arbitrary and tendentious ("liberal," "conservative," etc.), we need a way to test our characterization of the whole that goes beyond one-sided countings of the uncountable. In this context, anecdotes or examples only become a genuine argument when they can be fitted into the confines of a theory, that is, a hypothesis which accounts for the given examples by showing how the theory they support explains what is happening in all its profusion and variety.

In the case of media "bias," there are indeed two competing theories, though only one of them is usually made explicit. Theory one may be described as follows: a small number of corporations, and the persons who control those corporations, own and oversee the activities, the institutions, and the organizations of American mass media. Particular media outlets, therefore (and especially visual media outlets because of their greater concentration of ownership), behave in such a way as to forward the agenda of those corporations and persons. That agenda includes, first, making a profit comparable to that made by other similar corporations (and by all corporations generally, as they all compete for funds in the same investment markets); second, ensuring that the profit-making activities—in the case of visual media, audience-pleasing cultural commodities—do not impair the reputation or economic viability of the parent companies or of important capitalist entities and operations, most importantly the operations of "private enterprise" and "the free market" in general; third, supporting and reproducing the conditions of economic monopoly that define the visual media field; and fourth and quite definitely last, producing and distributing the kinds of audience-pleasing commodities that the immediate producers (though not the laborers, who Marx would have considered the "immediate producers") are comfortable producing. We might call this the class/structural model of media control.[4] Herman and Chomsky's "propaganda model" is the most worked-out contemporary version of the class/structural model; what distinguishes it from many other critiques of the role of intellectual workers is its focus on ownership and control of the media, not on the political or moral beliefs of journalists, teachers, etc. (i.e., "intellectuals"). They show how both political leaders and capitalists exercise power and authority to ensure that newspaper and television journalists will not, in the end, subvert the interests of their masters: the dominant class. Some sociologists of the media who are not conservative critics, such as Herbert Gans and Gaye Tuchman, have offered a view of journalistic behavior which might seem to undercut the propaganda model, as they emphasize the extent to which journalists learn to follow "professional" rules of conduct in determining what is "news" and when.[5] However, "professionalism" itself, as they show, is defined within the confines of the dominant ideology; one has only to look at how news sources *become* sources, become quoteworthy, to see this process in action. (Chomsky himself, for example, is never quoteworthy on the subject of Israel in the United States, though he is so everywhere else in the world.) Moreover, in the information culture, viewers are often devoid of any means for checking the reality of the propaganda to which they are subjected, especially if it is about faraway events. News can be manipulated or suppressed, as by the Department of Energy after Three Mile Island and the U.S. military during the Gulf War or the Iraq invasion; or it can fail to become news, as in the case of American complicity in the East Timor massacres or strikes that are only reported locally. It is also true, as conservative critics point out, that some owners may personally be politically liberal (Ted Turner, e.g.), but that is of little relevance in this account. Few are, and, in any event, there is no evidence that any of them will ever contravene long-established rules of corporate behavior.

The second theory, because the whole of it is rarely made explicit, must be teased out of what is available. According to this theory, control of the production of cultural commodities rests in the hands not of newspaper chain proprietors, television network owners, and so forth but, instead, in the hands of the immediate producers, including studio executives, visual media professionals, journalists, creative artists, and the mid-level overseers of production and distribution; it is not economic oligarchs but communications and educational specialists exercising intellectual hegemony. In this account, intellectual hegemony has mysteriously become detached from the actual economic and political hegemons; it rules with a life of its own. Moreover, the elite that incarnates it has the strangely conceived agenda of pursuing its own political and ideological purposes, according to which audience pleasing as an economic goal is subordinated to the ideological goal of subverting and degrading traditional American values. This approach is a particular version of the explanatory schema best known as the theory of "elite domination"; it is also an outré, even bizarre version of that theory.

Elite-oriented theories of decision making come in several forms, but the most well-known, stemming from the work of the modern Machiavellians Robert Michels, Max Weber, and Gaetano Mosca, expounds the persuasive (if arguable) thesis that all complex organizations, including governments and even democratic governments, are necessarily dominated by small groups of activists. These may consist of apparatchiks (Michels), experts and bureaucrats (Weber), or exceptionally ambitious and politically talented men (Mosca and Machiavelli). In any case, it is perfectly clear how they got where they are, and why (if you accept the theory) they have to be there. From the standpoint of classical elite theory, it is possible to criticize the society that requires such a form of organization (though all the elite theorists would regard such criticisms as utopian). It is neither required nor relevant, though, to impute nefarious motives or behavior to the elites themselves, who are just doing a necessary job. "Who says organization," in the words of Michels, "says oligarchy." In the most developed of these theories, that of Weber, it is also important to note that "the capitalistic entrepreneur is, in our society, the only type who has been able to maintain at least relative immunity from subjection to the control of rational bureaucratic knowledge."[6] This remarkable caveat is omitted from most reductions of Weber's work, including the one we are now discussing.

Clearly, the kind of contemporary reasoning that sees opposition and subversion as the work of educated and even well-off persons is not the same kind of analysis as Marx's notion of class warfare; but it is far from the reasoning of the classic elite theorists as well. Instead, this neoconservative critique imputes nefarious motives and behaviors. As Stanley Rothman puts it, "The Hollywood elites . . . seek to propagate an ideology that they believe should be held by all decent people."[7] The most straightforward version of this approach is the one that has been made familiar by some African-American nationalists and an English conservative: visual culture has been and is dominated by a cabal of Jews. Many of the conservative cultural critics are themselves Jews, but, unembarrassed, they adopt this version of elite theory wholesale and simply substitute "liberals" for "Jews" as its core category.[8] The ideology revealed by this move, rather than being that of true elite theory, is the twentieth-century European variant of populism, the nationalist ideology which proceeds by dividing society into two camps, the virtuous *people* and the malignant *elite*. This right-wing populist ideology—what Stuart Hall has called "authoritarian populism"— has always argued for the inherent harmony of self-evidently inharmonious communities by attributing all dissidence and division to a subversive enemy within.[9] Because the enemy, according to this version of ideology, is always a deviant subculture (Jews, liberals, feminists, homosexuals, Communists, pornographers, Satanists, the criminal underclass, etc.), we need only expel it from the body politic to produce communal reintegration: conveniently without having to challenge patterns of *economic* and *social* elitism, of corporate capitalist power and patriarchalism, in the slightest. The point about these competing theories of the media system is not to proclaim which we prefer but, rather, to ask how they help us to understand what actually goes on.

For here, suffice it to say that one of them is debatable but plausible. The other—that is, the contemporary, neoconservative version—is totally implausible, especially in its depiction of a system in which underlings exercise power outside the control of the owners who employ them, in which it is better to be Diane English or Steve Bochco than Rupert Murdoch, if one wants to amass ideological power. When the more than 300 radio stations belonging to the Clear Channel Network boycotted The Dixie Chicks, or when the Sinclair Media Group instructed its sixty-two "independent" local television stations to run an anti-Kerry film just days before the 2004 presidential election, anyone not living in a right-wing fantasy world could discover who has the real power in the world of monopolized media. (And when no conservative of any kind criticized either of these corporate fiats, the same observer could discover the politically inflected limits of the right-wing media criticism discussed below.) What is of more moment, however, is the starkly different ways in which these theories amass and use evidence to support their main outlines.

Here, to begin, are some examples of media bias taken from the publication *Extra!* during the past decade. A great many of them pertain to *ABC News* reporter John Stossel who, as *Extra!* puts it, "enjoys a special position in broadcast network news: Though not usually identified as a commentator, Stossel is routinely allowed to use his one-hour primetime specials and his regular 'Give Me a Break' features on *20/20* to explicitly promote his personal ideological agenda—from singing the virtues of corporate greed to attacking child labor laws—a perspective that is distinctly different from the generally muted centrism that pervades broadcast TV news." Following that agenda, Stossel has made verifiably false claims about the record of the Occupational Safety and Health Administration; about SAT scores and public school graduation rates; comparative death rates from Parkinson's and AIDS; factory workers' compensation compared to executive compensation; government spending on the poor; and a host of other policies and scientific warnings that don't fit into the right-wing view of the world.

Unlike Stossel, PBS's *National Desk*, being a "public" entity, is supposed to give voice to all sides of issues and purports to do so. But this too is a fiction. On a series on "the gender wars," for example, the three hosts were all well-known conservatives and allowed virtually no persons of any other viewpoint to respond to their opinions, which were offered as though they were facts. The various segments were underwritten by four explicitly right-wing foundations, and the show's promotional material claimed to afford "a look at how the Social Engineers use Government to manipulate behavior—even to the point of fooling with Mother Nature!" A segment entitled "The War on Boys" included such false claims as that female athletes were given athletic scholarships at the expense of minority boys, and the "experts" who supported the false claims were actually not experts but publicists funded by the very same foundations that were underwriting the program. The same violation of ordinary journalistic ethics marked a program on public education, à la John Stossel, which offered thirty-eight conservative "experts" from (again) the underwriting foundations as well as for-profit and religious school employees. In defense of public education were four guests, two of whom were National Education Association officials and denigrated as such. None of the thirty-eight offered any credible data supporting the claim that private and for-profit schools offer, as they put it, "a better education." They did not report on the major current study of vouchers in Milwaukee, Wisconsin, a mixed verdict, or on another study showing that reduction in class size, unlike school voucher programs, has produced notable test-score gains for African-Americans; and they allowed one prolific litigator on behalf of conservative causes to assert without rebuttal that public education has been in serious decline for several decades, without offering the faintest evidence (much of which, to be sure, contradicts the assertion).[10]

More tellingly, in the winter of 2002, all major network news programs supported the Bush administration "fire reduction" plan: a plan based on arguable if not false claims about that fall being the "worst season" ever, as well as false claims about the tendency of fires to destroy soil forever, that quoted a Forest Service report but not the repudiation of such report by the General Accounting Office of Congress on the grounds that it was based on incomplete and misleading statistics. At the same time, ABC's Peter Jennings (another supposed liberal) gave a special report on the proposed reintroduction of wolves into Idaho; his report suppressed interviews with supporters of the program, who included ranchers as well as environmentalists, and falsely claimed that most Idahoans were against the program. Only in his reply to critics did Jennings acknowledge that, by "most," he had meant "the body politic of the state, responding to the wishes of the livestock industry"—that is, the wealthiest and most powerful industry (and lobby) in the state.

During the invasion of Iraq, *Extra!* also documented the extent to which media coverage was completely subservient to the military, accepting Pentagon communiqués about hostilities and the existence of, and search for, weapons of mass destruction (WMDs) without question, and putting down anyone who managed to express an on-camera dissent. The *Extra!* reports focused especially on Fox, the most extremely one-sided of all the networks, hosting Bill O'Reilly's unembarrassed self-contradictions on the administration's supposed knowledge about WMDs and his outright lie that Hans Blix had accused Saddam Hussein of not letting UN inspectors interview Iraqi scientists (rather, Blix had said that the list given to the inspectors was incomplete), as well as reporters who called dissent "treasonous," or "unpatriotic," and boasted of being "slanted and biased" and who spread the ugly lie that foreign journalists who'd been killed in a shelling of the Palestine Hotel had been used as "human shields" by the Iraqis. Meanwhile, the network itself, supposedly a source of news, posted scathingly critical signs about antiwar protesters on its New York news building. In this same period, the periodical also documented O'Reilly's racist slurs (a recording group might be out "stealing hubcaps," "wetbacks" were infiltrating across our borders, the "most unattractive women in the world" are Muslim, and black athletes "can't speak English"). Fox was not alone in its priorities, though, as demonstrated by NBC's treatment of Phil Donahue and his replacement by Michael Savage, documented by *Extra!* (see chapter 1). *Extra!*'s approach to Savage and his murderous expressions of homophobia, incidentally, was not to suggest that he should be fired, but to ask why he'd been hired in the first place, when there were plentiful coherent, decent, civil voices (like the "liberal" Donahue) who are never asked to appear on cable TV.

In addition, *Extra!* also documented egregious conflicts of interest and instances of advertiser control over content, such as CBS in New York running a newscast that promoted a medical procedure it had advertised on its website; Barbara Walters turning eight shows into paid infomercials for Campbell's Soup; a Washington state channel presenting an infomercial by the Washington Forest Protection Association, a timber industry group, as though it were a documentary on how the timber industry is "Saving the Salmon"; General Electric's NBC bashing Oregon's universal health-care initiative with false assertions and propaganda out of the medical industry's playbook; and other examples from ABC's *The View* and NBC's *Today* show. Worst of all, it reported on a Fox affiliate in Tampa that fired two reporters *for refusing to report false information* about growth hormones in milk; the station did not dispute the facts but simply asserted (with the agreement of a federal appeals court) that it had a right to discipline its employees for violating orders. *Extra!* also noted various instances of cross-promotion by so-called news programs, such as *CBS News* promoting the network's *Survivor* as if it were a news topic and NBC doing the same with its Olympic coverage. All these are just a few among the many instances of conflict of interest it has noted since its founding in 1988.[11]

Two comments about this record (actually, just a tiny portion of it) are critical. First, we should note that none of the examples I have cited involve questions of judgment, that is, differences of opinion about ideas or policies or appropriate amounts and types of coverage. They are all verifiably about distortions of fact or unethical behaviors, and, in this respect, *Extra!*'s coverage differs sharply from that of the Right in its allegations of liberal bias.

Ann Coulter's hysterics aside, the most well-known "documentations" of that supposed bias are the two books by Goldberg (*Arrogance* and his earlier *Bias*) and two by L. Brent Bozell III (the first with Brent Baker): *And That's the Way It Isn't*, published in 1990 at the height of the "liberal media" scare, and the more recent *Weapons of Mass Distortion*. These are often taken to be some kind of conservative counterweight to the Left critiques of Alterman, or *Extra!*, or the contemporary collection *Through the Media Looking Glass*.[12] However, instead these books demonstrate the fallacy of relying on anecdotes and partisan substitutions of judgment.

Bozell and Baker especially make no effort to pursue facts or document their critical accounts of news broadcasts. Rather, they begin with an irrelevant review of the alleged political leanings of "journalists"; irrelevant because, despite the Right's presumption that every thinking person is an ideologue and

every statement dependent on a concealed ideology, most journalists are neither politicians nor ideologues nor academics, and their political postures,
comparatively "liberal" as in some cases they may be, are changeable and
evanescent. Moreover, the presupposition that beliefs lead directly to behavior is utter nonsense. In the case of the would-be professionals of network
newscasting, quite the opposite is equally likely, as they often make conscious
efforts to bend over backwards and not follow their own immediate inclina-
tions. (Anyone who watched the "liberal" Judy Woodruff's badgering of Democratic spokespersons during the 2004 campaign, or the generally skeptical approach of mainstream newscasters toward John Kerry, will recognize the
phenomenon immediately.) Bozell and Baker, and later Bozell by himself,
then proceed by criticizing news judgments and interpretations that they (and
the Right generally) disagree with, as though finding them bore out the implications of the "political leanings" study—a methodology also followed by
Goldberg. Instead, these "findings" simply tell us what would have been "the
news" had Bozell and Baker been reading it instead of Tom Brokaw (a favorite
whipping boy), but it is impossible to tell why Brokaw's reading constitutes a
particular bias. Bozell and Baker were incensed, for example, because network
news in the 1980s gave more coverage to human rights abuses in South Africa
and Chile than in the Soviet Union and treated Mikhail Gorbachev as a re-
former rather than just another Stalinist tyrant; just as Goldberg is later incensed because television news gives more prominence to the injuries of
American women than to those of American men. In fact, there are all sorts of
good reasons for the former disproportion, if it really existed, and, on Gorbachev, the "reference guide" is simply wrong. As to the travails of men in
schools or divorce courts, Goldberg does not attempt to account for the fact
that almost all the people making these decisions about coverage are themselves (white) men, though the most obvious distinction here is that the men
whose injuries Goldberg wants covered are mostly lower-class men, and, as
compared to its focus on the middle and upper classes, male or female, the system has never been comfortable with, or much interested in, such "victims."
Nor is he, apparently, given that, when he discusses homelessness and AIDS
in *Bias*, his approach is to castigate the media for overestimating the extent of
those conditions and for "prettifying" the victims when they ought to be blam-
ing them—that is, for showing homeless people as attractive persons instead
of drug-ridden down-and-outs or AIDS victims as white victims of blood trans-
fusions (e.g., Ryan White) instead of black, homosexual drug users. But again,
this is simply disingenuous. "Prettifying" is what television always does, and, as
a long-time TV reporter, Goldberg knows this. He simply refuses to notice
prettifying when it doesn't make his point, as in the prettifying of giant corpo-

rations, advertised products, President Bush, cops, college athletics, professional football, male and female news anchors, or the devastation of Iraq—but one could go on and on. It is sufficient to add here that, as AIDS has become a worldwide heterosexual epidemic, television's avoidance of this topic is ignored by Goldberg. American TV's isolationism, much more central to its mode of operation than any liberalism, is of no interest to its ideologically invested critics.

Goldberg at least occasionally takes the media to task for what might be actual falsehoods, though his lack of research and almost total reliance on one-sided, ideological sources is not very encouraging. Bozell is all about being "right" or "wrong" (or "left"), which are matters of emphasis and judgment, rather than about "true" or "false," which are not. To take another example, network coverage during the 1980s allegedly featured more anti-SDI (Strategic Defense Initiative, or "Star Wars") than pro-SDI coverage. The former, in a particularly slanderous bit of slanting, was called by Bozell and Baker "the Soviet side," despite the fact that many thoughtful Americans shared Gorbachev's belief that Star Wars deployment would unbalance the arms race and despite the consensus of the expert scientific community that a workable missile shield was a pipe dream. Perhaps the networks were too much slanted *toward* President Reagan's initiative in giving it any credence at all; there's no way of even considering the matter intelligently simply by conducting an arcane count of "mentions" and "instances."

Bozell, in 2004, offers more of this kind of faux analysis. To see the method in action, one can compare his treatment of the 2000 presidential election with Alterman's.[13] Bozell merely repeats wholesale the Republican Party's version of the campaign and of the Florida fiasco and indicts the networks for the few deviations from the Republican script he can find. One has to read Alterman to find out that Gore's so-called "lies" about his past were mostly invented by the GOP or by journalists themselves; that Katherine Harris orchestrated a campaign of intimidation and voter-purging against black voters; that a Republican Supreme Court majority departed from its own oft-affirmed principles in halting the recount; and so on. Nor would we know from reading Bozell that, as anyone who watched knows, television newscasters and commentators, led by the supposedly liberal Dan Rather, declared and welcomed Bush's election night "victory" with cheerleader enthusiasm and, thereafter, made a constant mockery of Gore and the Democrat's case and welcomed the halting of the recount as a victory for stability and good sense. The media's treatment of President Clinton draws the same evasive treatment from him, as Alterman's parallel account makes clear; it is especially noteworthy that Bozell simply accepts the

Starr Report wholesale and considers any deviation from its partisanship to be evidence of "liberal bias." In the same way, Goldberg plays the game of searching for ideological rectitude and acceptable news judgment as an index for the existence of his liberal unicorn, turning a handful of statements by particular reporters into "the media" and (mis)reading the evidence to suit his own bias. To take a particularly salient example, Goldberg (in *Bias*) argues at various points—it is his central, even crucial, argument—that television news departments bend over backwards to be uncritical of black people. It is undoubtedly true that millions of American white people—not just "liberals"—quite properly feel so much guilt about the history of American racism that they do not trust their own responses to events that could be perceived as negative revelations of African-American culture. But as Eric Alterman points out in his critique of *Bias*, Goldberg, apparently without realizing what he is doing, quotes supposedly telling remarks from network moguls that actually make the opposite point. In fact, what they say (according to Goldberg himself) is that they look for stories that they think will sell and downgrade stories that they think won't sell; and that is the sum of their thinking—most of which is in practice not at all beneficial to African-Americans, whose interests and ideas and problems are on the whole perceived as not saleable.[14] As these examples taken together show, front-running and conventional opinion are the main desiderata of newscasters' ideology.

To be sure, the thought process that produces decisions about what constitutes an interesting story is undoubtedly influenced by years of both exposure to racial stereotypes and attempts to rise above stereotypical behavior. That conflict is real in most Americans, and its result can go either way depending on circumstances and the particular person's various predispositions. But, in the media world, all of those efforts are ultimately trumped by the desire to do what will be acceptable to the largest possible audience: a black man killing a white woman is news; a black man killing another black man isn't, unless the other black man is a police officer. If a wealthy suburban student attending an elite university is killed in Manhattan, or kills someone himself, this is news no matter who did the killing, or who was killed. All such decisions faithfully track rules of choice, alluded to above, that have been built up over centuries of journalism: man bites dog is more interesting than dog bites man; lower is better than upper but wealth is more interesting than poverty; sympathetic victims take precedence over unsympathetic victims; and so on. These occupational prejudices intersect with race, obviously, in that people do not come into the world with "sympathetic" or "unsympathetic" marked on their foreheads; where and how they fit into their particular social milieu determines that identification. In this respect, we can truthfully say that, by their own account, most news producers in the TV system make little or no attempt to submit the "popular" determination of what is interesting to their own independent moral interrogation; they give in to it without asking how "the popular" came to be "popular." From the standpoint of the people making them, then, none of these business-like choices and non-choices are either liberal or conservative. Those are after-the-fact characterizations; they substitute the critic's version of what the decision maker must have meant for the decision maker's own understanding, however limited, of what he or she was trying to do. Thus, we could never understand from the ideologue's perspective why affirmative action programs (another instance of liberal elite favoritism according to Goldberg) have been more entrenched in the corporate world than anywhere else. It could hardly be because personnel administrators and CEOs are "more liberal"—than whom? No, they simply want to score points with a potentially critical community, avoid lawsuits and government regulation, and thus protect long-run profit potentials—all without engaging any of the nagging philosophical questions they would have to confront if they were, say, academics at a liberal arts college.

On the other hand, where no controversy beckons, because any possible oppositional constituency is too weak (either in spending power or in legislative halls) to make itself heard, we can see the system in its true colors; there is not any variation of red. There is, for example, a recent university press book that relates negative views about welfare (of the kind that led to its abolition under President Clinton) to the way television has portrayed both welfare costs and welfare recipients; another scholarly work similarly indicts the media's standard portrayal of labor strikes and protests.[15] But the conservative media critics don't recognize the existence of actual research; their only interest is in each other's polemics, as though multiplying criticisms makes them more likely to be true.

In other words, the methodology of this search for "liberalism" is worthless; whatever the case might actually be, it can't be found by substituting interpretations for data, and it can't be found by giving multiple examples taken only from the body of evidence that can be tweaked to support the case. One collection of pieces from *Extra!*, in comparison, offers a list of news items that television could have covered, but did not: how agribusiness firms used donations to key congressmen to prevent nutritional labeling on products; how certain congressmen parlay fealty to powerful lobbies into personal riches; how Philip Morris bankrolled a misnamed California initiative for "Statewide Smoking Restrictions"; how industry groups similarly misname themselves in order to present themselves as friends of environmental reforms they actually oppose; how "General Electric lobbyists . . . helped draft the corporate tax law that reduced the company's taxes to below zero"; and how representatives of "public interest groups" propose legislation that would solve the problem of corruption by big money.[16] There is *no* TV coverage of these issues. Moreover, the authors of *this* guide report evidence of liberal as well as conservative malfeasance (the list I've just adumbrated notes large contributions from the chairman of Archer Daniels Midland to the campaigns of both George Bush and Bill Clinton). That is because they are looking for bias in the *news reporting rather than in the reporters*. The hated "liberal" Peter Jennings is a wonderful example of the payoff in looking at *all* the evidence, rather than just the ideologically acceptable. But then Bozell and Baker did not find it worth mentioning that another "liberal," Ted Koppel with his nightly "America held hostage" report during the Iranian hostage crisis, possibly had more to do with discrediting Jimmy Carter and delivering the 1980 presidential election to Ronald Reagan than any other individual. Was this a triumph for liberalism, or more importantly a way for ABC-TV to compete with *The Tonight Show* at last?

None of this is to say that journalists as a group are not in some ways (but certainly not all ways) more liberal politically than the American electorate. It could hardly be otherwise. What I have called the ephemeral views of journalists are ephemeral because they are the views of the established consensus, and the established consensus changes very slowly. In the 1980s, it was still the consensus of a very watered-down New Deal Keynesian welfare state in domestic policy and of détente in foreign policy. The first of these had been confirmed, and the second initiated, by the last elected Republican president, Richard Nixon. Ronald Reagan, even in his second term, despite his sweeping electoral triumph of 1984, was still a counterrevolutionary; he had lowered expectations but not reversed them (even some of his approaches to the Soviet Union, such as his universal nuclear disarmament speech in 1985, were in the earlier spirit). That the politics of the 1980s Right looks prescient now should not blind us to the fact that, then, it was still more of a hope than an accomplishment; it was a later Democratic president after all, not a Republican one, who ended "welfare as we know it" and, with it, the last remnant, Social Security and unemployment insurance aside, of the New Deal welfare state. Having implemented the Republican agenda, Bill Clinton received much more contemptuous treatment from the so-called liberal media than Ronald Reagan ever had. And, as to that, conservatives were making up their story about the liberal media just at the moment when, whatever the "reference guide's" documentation of negative attitudes toward Reagan might suggest, its posture toward him had become visibly "on bended knee," and the whole terrain of political discussion on television and in newspapers had shifted drastically rightwards.[17]

Thus, the methodological contrast with what *Extra!* does is complete. The latter, as I've said, is published by the media watch group FAIR, and the notion of "fairness" and "accuracy" that motivates it is that of *fidelity to the material.* If you see an orange and they tell you to call it a lemon, you must call it an orange; that is the definition of journalistic integrity. The right-wing critique has no interest in fidelity to the material which, though often hard to describe and difficult to interpret, is there. Instead, the Right prescribes fidelity to an ideology, that is, a collection of abstractions that exists only in the minds of various observers. An egregious example from *Arrogance* is Goldberg's description of the volubly antifeminist, and much quoted, Christina Hoff Sommers as a "feminist" who "wouldn't toe the party line" and was sent "to the gulag," which appears to have set up one of its surprisingly cushy camps at the American Enterprise Institute. (This kind of fraudulent invocation of "victim" status is standard in right-wing media criticism; see chapter 6.) Goldberg manages to find a few instances of silly media mistreatment of Sommers but none of the many instances of the fawning treatment received by this antifeminist; and he makes no effort either to track down the existing critiques of her work that demonstrate not its ideological deviation, but its own shortcomings.[18] Looking at her work in toto, we find, as might be expected, ambiguity: some of what she says is just, some unjust, and some still needs to be clarified a decade later. But Goldberg can only assume ideological correctness: his enemy's enemy must be his uncriticizable friend. This whole approach, in sum, makes journalistic integrity impossible, for the material that ought to be the source of the observations that follow it now becomes merely fodder to realize one's own desires and fantasies. There is no such thing as liberal news or conservative news, liberal facts or conservative facts; there is only what has happened, of which there is so much that it is impossible to reduce it to a name, let alone get it all "right."

Even given that impossibility, however, if we subject these contrasting approaches to the test of how well they function in support of their respective hypotheses, there is something to be found out about television news. The Left hypothesis fares fairly well, if not decisively so. The priorities it predicts—maximizing corporate profits, reproducing the conditions of monopoly, producing audience satisfaction, and last and least producing personal satisfaction—on the whole seem to be as predicted; though, like all

Marx-influenced class theory, it arbitrarily assigns popular nationalism to ruling class influence without considering whether the causal arrow might not at times be the other way around. The blatherings of Fox's pundits may give personal satisfaction, but they are also very popular with a particular audience (mostly resentful white males), and they comport wholly with the views of the owner, Rupert Murdoch. As to the owner himself, *Extra!* (and others such as *The Nation*) points out that, despite his ferocious anticommunism, he too surrendered his own presumed personal satisfaction to market imperatives by deleting the prestigious and much-watched BBC World Service from his Sky network and ordering his book publisher HarperCollins not to publish a book critical of the Chinese regime, in order to satisfy the demands of his putative Chinese hosts and their prospective billion-person audience. Nor does the class/structural hypothesis have any difficulty accounting for the evidence on the other side, such as it is. Thus, at the end of one of his books on media, Michael Parenti, an unabashed socialist and perhaps the most outspokenly left-wing voice among American social scientists, writes that "the ruling class rules but not quite in the way that it wants. Its socializing agencies do not work with perfect effect, free of contradictions—or else this book could not have been written or published or understood."[19] There is no reason why some, or at times many, journalists employed by monopoly capitalists should not be liberals. They rarely bring any harm to their employers; their dedication to any liberal agenda is negligible compared to the dedication of their right-wing counterparts (as Alterman shows over and over, the "liberals" typically bend over backwards to show "the other side"); and, in their partial professionalism, they provide the best possible facade for the claim that the mass media are not under their owners' thumbs. There are capitalist nations that have been governed by people well to the left of Dan Rather and Tom Brokaw for decades at a time, yet remain capitalist. None are, or have been, threatened by the fuzzy, nonmobilizing, and nonthreatening ideological stances of professional media spokespersons. What is impermissible in the privatized media in any of those nations, however, is that such persons should tell the truth about the interests and activities of their employers; and this, at least in the United States, does not happen. A comparison of BBC News, even on domestic British matters, with any American television news operation is simply embarrassing.

The "elite domination" hypothesis is another story. The factual statement that many news persons are politically liberal can account for some of the instances of one-sidedness highlighted by Bozell and Goldberg—only some, because it is quite possible that the nature of the actual facts dictates the others. But the attempt to turn these instances into the generality of "elite domination" fails miserably. Unlike the class/structural analysis, this analysis brooks no quarter; it is impossible to imagine any right-wing equivalent of Parenti writing such a sentence, or perhaps even thinking it. Conservative ressentiment seems to preclude taking any notice of how politically and culturally successful one actually is. Yet nothing in its story about liberal elites can account for the documentation to be found in *Extra!*, not to mention Herman and Chomsky's *Manufacturing Consent*, the articles in the special issues of *The Nation* referred to in note 4, or the work of Robert McChesney, the premier Left media commentator. The hypothesis cannot explain why or how station or network executives kill stories unpalatable to themselves or their bosses or advertisers and twist the "news" to promote or whitewash associated products; it cannot explain the censorship to which Michael Moore's satirical show *TV Nation* was subjected during its brief run in the summers of 1994 and 1995, nor the refusal by CBS to air an anti-Bush ad during Super Bowl halftime in 2004.[20] It cannot explain why there has never been a visibly liberal opinion show on either commercial or public television, though many conservative ones on both.[21] It cannot explain the vindictive assault on a more-or-less liberal president, and the salacious prurience on which that assault was based, during the Monica Lewinsky scandal.[22] It cannot explain, inter alia, why television analysts gave George W. Bush a free ride about his defects of character, behavior, and intelligence while mocking Al Gore during the 2000 election. It cannot explain the medium's uncritical acceptance of the ideology and hype (and lies) of the most war-like administration in American history (though to be fair, as I've suggested in discussing the force of popular nationalism earlier, this is an observation that also gives class/structural analysis difficulty); nor its supine acceptance and repetition of one after another palpably false statement by the Bush administration about its intentions and accomplishments, while spreading contempt for the 2004 candidacy of Howard Dean and his wife Dr. Judith Steinberg (so much for TV's "feminism"); nor the total domination of post-Inauguration coverage in February 2005 by representatives of the Republican Party.[23] Above all, the elite domination hypothesis cannot refute the contrary hypothesis—what an analyst might call the "null hypothesis"—that, within structural and institutional limits (as developed by the class/structural theory), the behavior of the "liberal" media commentators can often be explained by their appropriate, even if occupationally narrow, pursuit of what they conceive to be the truth. To refute this counterhypothesis, Lichter and Rothman (the "empirical" source for most popular right-wing media critics) can, as we have seen, offer only the argument—what they seem to think is a critique—that journalists have "more liberal" views than the population at large.

This charge is echoed by both Bozell and Baker, and Goldberg, as in the latter's comment that "the elites remain in denial . . . despite the surveys that show that large numbers of Americans consider the elite media too liberal."[24] There are two serious problems with this accusation, though. The first is its confusion of a word, "liberal," with a condition, alienation. Of course, "large numbers of Americans" are *alienated* from the media; as I have argued in chapter 1, they ought to be, because alienation is the condition that monopoly domination of mass media creates (or, rather, "alienation" is the best description of that condition). That many among that number attribute the nature of the media monopoly to "liberals" tells us nothing except whose propaganda is more successful in "the marketplace of ideas." The second problem with this reasoning shows up if we ask, does Goldberg really believe that everything "large numbers of Americans" believe is true? In making this move, he and his fellow critics insist, as a justification of their own reasoning, on precisely the shallow intellectual pandering that they have already sternly rejected as an explanation of the media's behavior: "my audience, may it always be in the right, but my audience right or wrong." This defense of media by its controllers is certainly not offered in good faith (think of the comment quoted earlier about audience violation of the social contract through fast-forwarding of commercials); but then neither is the populist attack on liberalism, as it would have to be happy with, even to demand, media endorsement of whatever liberal views the majority happens to share—and there are many, according to Lichter and Rothman's own data (see note 17). Is the media's distaste for single-payor health care an example of liberal conspiracy at work? But intellectual consistency is not the goal of the attack on liberal elites.

The elite domination hypothesis, in sum, is a hypothesis that fails every test except the ultimate test of being politically acceptable to the men who pay the pipers and call the tune. That such a tendentious, partisan, palpably false, and intellectually superficial argument about the alleged power of liberals should have become the conventional wisdom is the most telling possible refutation of its own claims to truth.

To ask why the right-wing propagandists assert a thesis with such obvious limitations is to waste time; people will say anything that helps them attain power. The more interesting question is why they should *believe* what they say so passionately, as they obviously do. Given the burial service for liberal politics that has been going on ever since 1968 (at the latest), the frantic concern over a few television commentators seems paranoid. But even paranoids, as the saying goes, have enemies, or at least what appear to be enemies. We therefore want to ask, what is it about the commercial TV system that makes it seem inimical to the conservative, despite all the reasons for dissatisfaction with the system that are evident to persons such as Chomsky, or Robert McChesney, or myself. Some of the answer to that question has to do with the peculiar nature of fiction television, and I shall deal with that later (see chapter 4). The most crucial point, however, is this: the right-wing critique, unlike Chomsky's, is in fact not a complaint about the *manufacturing of consent*, but is rather a complaint about the manufacturing of *dissent*.

This is a significant difference. The argument of Chomsky, McChesney, and others is that if public space is monopolized by certain kinds of communications with which people are regularly bombarded, then some of those people may be led to believe falsehoods, such as the asserted connection between Al Qaeda and Saddam Hussein, that they wouldn't otherwise believe in the presence of truly free, unmonopolized communications. The right-wing critique is, instead, that people may be led to disbelieve what they *ought to believe* and really do believe in the absence of concentrated dissent. But this is totally implausible. In the first place, it is counterfactual. Consent possibly can be "manufactured," though the experience of the Soviet Union shows how difficult this is. But dissent can never be manufactured; it can only be generated. To manufacture it, one would have to control the entire structure and process of communications, and, even then, success would not be guaranteed. (And why would the people who purportedly control the core of a social order want to encourage dissent from it?) But what is wrong with generating dissent? The right-wing argument is that the people's true values—patriotism, religion, etc.—are in danger of being subverted; the flak machine, as Chomsky and Herman call the Right's cultural interventionism, exists to prevent this subversion. But, at the same time, the Right denies that people really change their beliefs; at worst they're confused by liberal lies. And yet the right-wing critics are always quoting so-called public opinion to show that the people are really on their side.

What then is the problem? How can people be led to dissent from a truthful account of their material world if the conservative account is really truthful? The answer, and the reason for the discrepancy between the two types of argument, is that the Right's world is one of ideas and symbols rather than material welfare or ill-fare; the material world hardly counts as such, because our perceptions of it are infinitely malleable. In the twenty-first century, right-wing politics has consisted to a great extent of outright lies (all of which are taken as self-evident truths by Bozell) about the material realm—the effects of tax cuts, the causes of war, the nature of environmental problems, and so on.[25] This being the Right's own view of life, conservatives project this as the real world. "Culture" then stands above the economy and politics; it is all-powerful because only it is really real.

A comparison with *Manufacturing Consent* is instructive here. *Manufacturing Consent* is largely a description of structures and processes, called by Herman and Chomsky "the propaganda model":

> A propaganda model suggests that the "societal purpose" of the media is to inculcate and defend the economic, social, and political agenda of privileged groups that dominate the domestic society and the state. The media serve this purpose in many ways: through selection of topics, distribution of concerns, framing of issues, filtering of information, emphasis and tone, and by keeping debate within the bounds of acceptable premises. We have sought to show that the expectations of this model are realized, and often considerably surpassed, in the actual practice of the media in a range of crucial cases.

Speaking of Watergate and the Iran-Contra affair, Herman and Chomsky go on to add,

> Contrary to the usual image of an "adversary press" boldly attacking a pitiful executive giant, the media's lack of interest, investigative zeal, and basic news reporting on the accumulating illegalities of the executive branch have regularly permitted and even *encouraged* ever larger violations of law, whose ultimate exposure when elite interests were threatened is offered as a demonstration of media service "on behalf of the polity." These observations reinforce the conclusions that we have documented throughout.

And they conclude that "as we have stressed throughout this book, the U.S. media do not function in the manner of the propaganda system of a totalitarian state. Rather, they permit—even encourage—spirited debate, criticism, and dissent, as long as these remain faithfully within the system of presuppositions and principles that constitute an elite consensus, a system so powerful as to be internalized largely without awareness."[26] Despite their book's ominous title, and aside from the initial and concluding generalizations in the above passage (with the language of "inculcate" and "internalized"), Herman and Chomsky actually have little to say about the state of people's beliefs, what they do believe, what they might believe, and, especially, what they ought to believe. Their complaint is that the media frame issues in such a way as to diminish the possibilities for achieving fuller and more accurate knowledge about them. The structure is pluralistic, and it provides a variety of viewpoints within bounds (the "filters"). Therefore, its communications do not falsify most people's immediate experience, and its main effect is to circumscribe possible interpretations of situations, not to keep them from view (though it sometimes does do that); in this respect also, the Left hypothesis does not deny the existence of pluralism and need not deny it as long as that pluralism does not encompass system-threatening activities. As is shown by big media's consistently hostile treatment of the 1999 anti–World Trade Organization demonstrations in Seattle, or the protests against the Republican National Convention in 2004, these boundaries can be policed as firmly as if a commissar of information were commanding the media instead of a collection of private enterprises. The strength of the propaganda model is that, both in theory and in practice, it doesn't require a commissar to explain how this policing takes place.

In a sense, then, the propaganda model is related to the model of alienation and habituation I offered earlier, in that each describes a situation of what might be called cultural imperialism, in which possibilities of authentic knowledge and experience are removed from people's grasp by the very structure of the situation. But manipulation and deceit are not inevitable (nor are alienation and habituation). They are not built into the existence of modes of mass communication (as Michels, for example, claimed they were) but only into its existing social relations—its institutions. Therefore, to the limited extent that full knowledge of a state of affairs is possible (it is not clear that Herman and Chomsky realize how unlikely or even inconceivable this is), we can all come closer to realizing it; but, first, it is necessary to smash through the limiting frame, to make the structure truly instead of only notionally pluralistic, and that is what they try to do (and enable others to do). Although they are strong critics of contemporary liberals, in fact, their model is the classic liberal position, as best articulated by John Stuart Mill in *On Liberty*. More discussion, more debate, and especially more dissent are always healthier than less. People can increase their understanding; we can overcome our own prejudice and bias; and we can (at least) try to achieve Nagel's "view from nowhere." There can never be "too much dissent," and dissent can never be dangerous or bad for anyone's intellectual health: "If all mankind minus one were of one opinion, and only one person were of the contrary opinion, mankind would be no more justified in silencing that one person, than he, if he had the power, would be justified in silencing mankind."[27]

"Liberal" and "conservative," therefore, are not, as is sometimes said, mirror images of each other, or extremes between which a wiser middle position can be located. The Millian position *is* the middle position (if we must have a middle), between authoritarianisms of Right and Left (say, Castro or the Chinese regime) that would squelch one or another kind of dissent. The authoritarians do not believe that more discussion is always healthier or that arguments in dissent—the questioning of established beliefs, whether patriotic or religious—are preferable, as Mill argues, to conformity. Thus, whereas the Left critique is that there is not enough dissent, not enough voices questioning the monopoly over words and images in public space, the Right critique, contrarily, is that there is too much. Even the feeble questionings of a Brokaw or Rather or Jennings, almost never stated with such force as to threaten the seats of authority, are more than can be tolerated. To see what is really at stake here, we need only compare the hate-suffused, career-destroying campaign of the right-wing "blogosphere" against Easson Jordan for speculating (as does the whole world outside the United States) that American forces had targeted foreign journalists in Iraq, with the same Right's tolerance of the activities of pundit Robert Novak, who literally gave aid and comfort to the enemy by outing an undercover agent whose specialty is the mid-East! The celerity with which CNN allowed Jordan to throw himself overboard suggests a death knell for independent television journalism.

But how can this be? What is the counterargument against dissent? It is hard to tell, as it is rarely made explicit. But there seem to be three justifications for the attack against dissent. The first is that it is not really dissent—that established beliefs are not sufficiently available in visual culture. This is manifestly false. The entire media machine, plus the primary and secondary school establishment everywhere, the publishers of textbooks, the great majority of churches, and so forth, are dedicated to providing almost nothing but established beliefs. With very few exceptions, having mostly to do with the history of slavery and the conquest of Native Americans (and not even that in large parts of the Union), young people rarely hear anything at all like what Howard Zinn calls "a people's history of the United States."[28] As for the visual media, because TV relies mostly on government sources, and secondarily on sources from private business, for its news items, it would simply be impossible to make the case that the established view of affairs is slighted. For example, the instances, as recounted by Bozell, in which network newscasters are skeptical about, say, the 2002 tax cut legislation, merely represent a feeble attempt to establish some kind of counterbalance to the overwhelming effect of authoritatively positive statements (and outright lies) by the president and congressional leaders.

But that is not really the argument either, for the Right doesn't want just the established view, it wants *its own view* put forward: sectarian or even theocratic religiosity; "antigovernment" positions as a matter of abstract ideology but total fealty to "government" when its own personnel are in power; and punitive, authoritarian nationalism in place of a vaguely tolerant and nonspecific patriotism. And this view, its spokespersons clearly think, is underrepresented in visual media. However, this argument is also manifestly false either on the facts or else in its portrayal of the power of the media. For otherwise, the clichés of "liberal media" and "political correctness" would not be mouthed by millions of Americans as though they represented some kind of reality; Americans would have stopped belonging to fundamentalist churches instead of joining them in great numbers; and the various wars the polity has engaged in over the past two decades would have been sabotaged by the populace instead of endorsed by apparently enthusiastic majorities (or substantial minorities). There is no danger of the Right view of the world going unheard; it shouts itself from every radio talk show, every cable TV channel, and most op-ed pages; and it dominates the national government (it has won three of the last six presidential elections, and stolen a fourth). If, as Mill again argues (and would the haters of liberalism endorse any of his arguments?), the "minority opinion" is always the one that most needs to be heard, then with reference to what is available on television, as between the opinions of Bozell, Lichter and Rothman, Tom DeLay, and Sen. Rick Santorum on the one hand, and Noam Chomsky and Robert McChesney or the *Nation* magazine on the other, there isn't the faintest doubt which one more "needs to be heard."

But even this is not the gravamen of the right-wing complaint, for, when we attend to it closely, we discover that the Right really does believe that criticism of its vision of the American way of life is bad because its promulgation in any degree leads to disrespect for authority, anti-Americanism, weakening of faith, and the general degradation of society. This is an extraordinary testimony to the power of pundits who are never seen nor heard on the visual media, and are in magazines that are lucky if their circulation figures reach six figures or, in most cases, five. As Alterman notes, in this perspective, the *New York Times* and *Washington Post*, which (especially the *Post*) carry many conservative and neoliberal voices on their op-ed pages and magazine sections (and book review sections), as well as even sometimes in their editorials, become organs of liberal propaganda, whereas the far-right *Washington Times*, which carries absolutely no dissenting voices at all, is a respectable and even valuable newspaper. The truth is, in other words, that the Right wants the visual media to be *more of a propaganda machine* than it is. What's wrong with Chomsky, in other words, is not (as many conventionally liberal academics would argue) his description of the propaganda model, but his *criticism* of it. "Manufacturing consent," it turns out, is exactly what the Right is after, and the failure to engage wholeheartedly in the struggle is a sign not of good, pluralist intentions, but of insufficient patriotism and free-market dogmatism. Cultural imperialism is a social good; we just don't have enough of it. The standpoint of these conservatives, very simply, is that, if they are not allowed to *dominate* the media, then they are being *excluded* from it. Anything short of their total control amounts to "liberal bias" or even subversion of the polity. As theory, in other words, the elite domination paradigm itself belongs to the realm of propaganda rather than ideology; it is politically useful rather than intellectually serious. As a political practice within the realm of propaganda, it undoubtedly expresses the fondest hopes of ruling groups everywhere: that ideology should be coterminous with propaganda; that all ambiguity or hints of opposition should be leached out of it; and that doing this is the responsibility of those communications specialists who are in their employ. Given the huge outpouring of funds with which right-wing foundations underwrite publications such as *The American Spectator*, *The National Interest*, *The Public Interest*, *National Review*, and the *New Criterion*, a whole host of right-wing campus newspapers, and institutions such as the Center for Media and Public Affairs, it is clear that the elite domination paradigm is better understood as the elite manipulation paradigm; and that, if nothing else, it is an accurate account not of what television or movies accomplish ideologically, but of what right-wing funders are paying their own communications specialists to do.[29]

In this light, there is much more at stake than a debate over control of the media or the power of liberalism. The real issue, rather, is the very meaning of the American constitutional settlement itself. The reason that occasional dissent, skepticism, or even bland neutrality can be read as "liberal domination" is that the contemporary version of conservatism is essentially a fundamentalist religion—a secular authoritarianism that attaches itself to real religiosity in order to validate itself, as the right-wing media critics angrily attack the supposed denial of religion in the media without ever uttering a word of religious belief themselves. It is a weapon for them, rather, a weapon with which to beat their secular enemy (rarely do they admit, or confront the implications of, the official opposition of the Roman Catholic Church to much of what they believe). The religious fundamentalist, and his counterpart the secular dogmatist, views all deviation in belief as Error, and the incompleteness of the domination by Truth (as must always be the case) is taken as the domination by Error. Thus, the authoritarian fundamentalist is always unappeasable. Free expression of opinion is the weapon of the enemy, who seeks to establish the "tyranny" of secular pluralism. This is not so much because the political program of this right wing is totalitarian (though some of it surely is, in its ambition to wipe out all traces of oppositional power), but because its notion of liberty is totalitarian—or, to be more circumspect, authoritarian, as in "authoritarian populism." In contrast to the liberal democrat Mill, who argues that only the doing of actual harm to others justifies impositions on speech and writing, the authoritarian populist holds that *your* liberty to speak and write, if it constrains *my* effort to put my desires into practice, whatever they may be, is a truly harmful constraint on my liberty—in the instant case, on my liberty to monopolize the realm of culture in the name of truth. This rage, never to be thwarted or opposed, can only be understood in the language of the passions. Most of the time, liberals are unable to withstand its thrust, or negotiate its demands, because those are nonnegotiable, and negotiation is, contrarily, the core of liberal doctrine. Perhaps liberals have their own passions, which they have simply learned too well to repress; but in any event, as the attempts of CNN and MSNBC to compete with Fox demonstrate, the unappeasable can never be appeased.

It is for this reason that the conservative flak machine only cites instances of error, that is, of disagreement with its doctrines. It counts up no instances of sycophancy toward Republican authority figures, but only deviations from it. This is why Bernard Goldberg can write about "bias" while offering so surprisingly few instances of it, because he has adopted the stance according to which any deviation from proper behavior is bias; unlike, say Cohen and Solomon, who offer extensive examples of misreporting by supposedly liberal figures, Goldberg does not even mention one instance of the dogmatically promarket, anti-social criticism bias of John Stossel, or of the attacks on environmentalists that his network (CBS) engaged in or of its cozying up to business interests. Neither he nor Bozell and Baker nor Lichter and Rothman produce a structural account of liberal bias—of an institutional weighting against the expression of conventional views—because they couldn't. Conventional views are all around us, night after night, on channel after channel. Goldberg is like the conservative film critic Michael Medved (see chapter 5), who piles up examples of the positive depiction of homosexuality without bothering to notice that almost everything else around us is oriented toward heterosexuality. (Try to think of one TV commercial that "privileges homosexuality," or more than a partial handful of series.)[30] When a writer like Adrienne Rich, conversely, refers to the privileging of heterosexuality, she means by this that almost all institutional supports and expressions in any field of culture are structured in that direction. For the Right that there is any remainder at all is apparently too much. Only the virtual absence of homosexual expression, and only then if marginalized, would be a proper indication of non-bias. For Goldberg, similarly, the sadly thin attempt of big media (at the verbal level only) to face up to the nature of American apartheid and its destructive effects on African-Americans, or to cover up its own exclusion of women from positions of power with occasional gestures toward a genteel version of "feminism," is the only "bias" he can deign to notice.

There can be no understanding of the lie about liberalism without an understanding of this basic asymmetry in political philosophy. Tolerance and intolerance, pluralism and the rejection of otherness, freedom for the speech that we hate and freedom for the speech that we approve of, are not different sides of the same coin, or two visions of democracy. Advocates of liberal pluralism reject authoritarian populism in principle but respect its right to speak for itself. Advocates of authoritarian populism do not reject the right of liberal pluralism to speak. They merely wish to deprive it of the power to do so unless its advocates are safely outnumbered and it is made clear that they are wrong. To these power seekers, the liberal feminist who defends herself against the ravings of Ann Coulter or Michael Savage merely illustrates the French proverb that "*Cet animal est tres mechant/Quand on l'attaque, il se defend.*"[31] Every defense becomes a symptom of aggression; every expressed desire to escape from the dominance of white males over information culture (the monopolists of almost every talk show or round-table discussion, the persona of virtually every news anchor) becomes an example of that helpful evasion, "political correctness." But the lie about liberalism remains just that: a lie.

NOTES

1. Alterman, *What Liberal Media?* (New York: Basic, 2003). On the Reagan years, see Mark Herstgaard, *On Bended Knee: The Press and the Reagan Presidency* (New York: Pantheon, 1989). For an update, see Alterman's "Fantasy Island," *Nation*, February 14, 2005, 10.

2. Goldberg, *Arrogance* (New York: Warner, 2003). One wonders how he managed to get his book published by a subsidiary of AOL Time Warner, one of the worst of the "elites." But lo and behold!, there is no criticism of either AOL or Time Warner to be found anywhere in *Arrogance*.

3. Goldberg, *Arrogance* (New York: Warner, 2003), 125–6.

4. In addition to Herman and Chomsky, *Manufacturing Consent: The Political Economy of the Mass Media* (New York: Pantheon, 1988), see also Robert W. McChesney's *Rich Media, Poor Democracy: Communication Politics in Dubious Times* (New York: New Press, 2000). For detailed, mostly up-to-date accounts of who owns what in the centralized visual and print media, see special issues of *The Na-*

tion for June 8, 1998 ("Who Controls TV?"), November 29, 1999 ("The New Global Media"), and January 7/14, 2002 ("The Big Media," with a pullout section describing media holdings and cross-ownerships).

5. See Herbert Gans, *Deciding What's News* (New York: Vintage, 1979), and Gaye Tuchman, *Making News: A Study in the Construction of Reality* (New York: Free Press, 1978).

6. See Peter Bachrach, *The Theory of Democratic Elitism* (Boston: Little Brown, 1965), for what is still the best critical summary of elite theory. The left-wing version of elite theory, made most famous by C. Wright Mills's *The Power Elite* (New York: Oxford, 1958) and by the many works of his follower G. William Domhoff, is distinctive chiefly for its implication that "democracy" properly reconceived could somehow be free of elite domination. The Michels quotation is from Robert Michels, *Political Parties: A Sociological Study of the Oligarchical Tendencies of Modern Democracy*, trans. Eden and Cedar Paul (New York: Collier Books, 1962), 365. The Weber quotation is from Max Weber, *The Theory of Social and Economic Organization*, ed. Talcott Parsons (New York: Oxford University Press, 1947), 339. This is one significant remark of Weber's of which the leading critic of the "Hollywood elite," Stanley Rothman, who calls himself a Weberian, never takes cognizance.

7. Stanley Rothman, with Stephen Powers and David J. Rothman, *Hollywood's America: Social and Political Themes in Motion Pictures* (Boulder, Colo.: Westview, 1996), 3. "Propagate" is a synonym for "extend" or "spread," as by missionaries—not your average elite. In an earlier formulation, the fictional world of prime time "more often . . . tries to guide middle-American tastes in the direction of intellectual trends emanating from New York and Los Angeles." See S. Robert Lichter, Linda Lichter, and Stanley Rothman, *Watching America: What Television Tells Us About Our Lives* (Englewood Cliffs, N.J.: Prentice Hall, 1991), 4.

8. On Jews in Hollywood, see the article by William Cash in the October 1994 issue of *Spectator*, published in London.

9. See Stuart Hall et. al., *Policing the Crisis: "Mugging," the State and Law and Order* (London: Macmillan, 1978).

10. On PBS, see William Hoynes, "Public TV: More Corporate, Less Public," *Extra!*, Sept./Oct. 1999.

11. The quotes about Donahue are from the *Extra!Update* issue of April 2003, as are comments about Michael Savage, and also in the regular issue of *Extra!* that same month, which also includes the story on John Stossel; Bill O'Reilly is quoted in the issue of June 2003. Many of the items on conflict of interest are in Janine Jackson and Peter Hart, "Fear and Favor: How Power Shapes the News," *Extra!*, May/June 2001. Throughout 2003, *Extra!* also covered mainstream coverage of the Iraq invasion in detail.

12. Bernard Goldberg, *Bias: A CBS Insider Exposes How the Media Distort the News* (Washington, D.C.: Regnery, 2002); L. Brent Bozell III and Brent H. Baker, *And That's the Way It Isn't* (Alexandria, Va.: Media Research Center, 1990); L. Brent Bozell III, *Weapons of Mass Distortion: The Coming Meltdown of the*

Liberal Media (New York: Crown Forum, 2004); Jeff Cohen and Norman Solomon, *Through the Media Looking Glass: Decoding Bias and Blather in the News* (Monroe, Maine: Common Courage Press, 1995).

13. Bozell, *Weapons of Mass Distortion*; Alterman, *What Liberal Media?*

14. Alterman, *What Liberal Media?*, 5–7.

15. See Martin Gilens, *Why Americans Hate Welfare: Race, Media, and the Politics of Anti-Poverty Policy* (Chicago: University of Chicago Press, 1999), and Christopher R. Martin, *Framed: Labor and the Corporate Media* (Ithaca, N.Y.: Cornell University Press, 2003).

16. Cohen and Solomon, *Through the Media Looking Glass*, 16–17.

17. Compare S. Robert Lichter, Stanley Rothman, and Linda Lichter, *The Media Elite* (Bethesda, Md.: Adler and Adler, 1986), Bozell and Baker's most frequently cited source, with Mark Herstgaard, *On Bended Knee: The Press and the Reagan Presidency* (New York: Pantheon, 1989). The Lichter/Rothman work, from the ubiquitous Center for Media and Public Affairs stable (see chapter 6), is a compendium of how to substitute ad hominem appellations for actual analysis of behaviors.

18. See, for instance, Katha Pollit, "Subject to Debate," *Nation*, July 7, 2001; Nina Auerbach's critical review in *The New York Times Book Review* of June 12, 1994; Barbara Ehrenreich's review in *Time* for August 1, 1994; or Megan Rosenfeld's mostly favorable discussion in the *Washington Post* Style section of July 7, 1994, in which Rosenfeld uncovers various questionable accounts of matters of fact by Sommers. In a remarkable "Appendix" to *Arrogance*, Goldberg gives a list of "alternative" sources of information, all of which are right-wing think tanks but gives no reason to believe that their materials are credible; in some cases, there is much reason to doubt that.

19. *Inventing Reality: The Politics of News Media* (New York: St. Martin's, 1993), 228.

20. Moore correctly describes *TV Nation* as "one of the few shows from our side of the political fence that have ever appeared on commercial network television." NBC and, later, Fox censors shot down an interview with an antiabortion terrorist; a follow-up on the Savings & Loan scandal; a story on a school that gave a student extra credit for picketing the funerals of AIDS victims, while holding up a sign that read "GOD HATES FAGS"; a reenactment of the beating of Rodney King; and a segment on condoms. See Michael Moore, "What You Can't Get Away With on TV," *Nation*, November 18, 1996. As for CBS, it has generally refused all "advocacy" ads, but what good is liberal domination if it can't get around a simple rule like that?

21. It is not clear that the class/structural analysis fares any better on this topic. The best explanation here is Jeffrey Scheuer's, in *The Sound Bite Society: Television and the American Mind* (New York: Four Walls Eight Windows, 1999), that liberal policy analyses tend to be too complex and too reliant on ambiguous social science research, compared to those of present-day conservatives; this has certainly been the case since the New Deal era, which cemented a relationship between liberalism and social scientific discourse. I would also add that contemporary liberal opinion is much too frac-

tured to present a clear case on behalf of a united front. In any event, here the "democratic market" apologia of the networks is probably closer to the truth.

22. See the articles by Jeff Cohen and Laura Flanders on "The Media's Obsession With Sex," *Extra!*, March/April 1998. Again, the class/structural hypothesis must be combined with recognition of marketplace effects and audience orientations for a satisfactory account of any phenomenon involving sex.

23. Because one is not supposed to talk this way about presidents in polite society, it has to be reiterated that these are *lies*, and not just "small" lies, and not "honest mistakes," or exaggerations for effect, or playing fast and loose with statistics, but flat-out and often *big lies*. Thus, the president, in the first nationally televised campaign debate with John Kerry, said that the latter had had access to the same information he had had before voting for the invasion. This was a lie, and known to the president as such, as he had received intelligence reports that cast doubt on the rationales for the invasion and were kept from Congress. Earlier, when the vice president told Gloria Borger of CNBC that he had never said of Mohammed Atta's alleged visit to Prague that it was "pretty well confirmed," he lied. She said "OK," and allowed him to continue the lie. As for the Inauguration, as Alterman (see note 1) correctly puts it, "even carefully worded examinations of the speech's most glaring contradictions had no place in America's Pravda-like cable news chat programs."

24. Goldberg, *Arrogance*, 5.

25. See the *New York Times*, August 8, 2003, for a description of a report by Congressman Henry Waxman (D-Calif.) on the ways in which the Bush administration has distorted the findings of scientists about the environment and related issues. That is just one of uncountable such stories. See generally David Corn, *The Lies of George W. Bush: Mastering the Politics of Deception* (New York: Crown, 2003); and Eric Alterman and Mark Green, *The Book on Bush: How George W. (Mis)leads America* (New York: Viking, 2004).

26. Herman and Chomsky, *Manufacturing Consent*, 298–302.

27. See John Stuart Mill, *On Liberty*, ed. David Spitz, Norton Critical Editions (New York: Norton, 1975), 18.

28. See Zinn, *A People's History of the United States* (New York: Harper & Row, 1980).

29. See, for example, the survey undertaken by Beth Schulman and reported by Joel Bleifuss in *In These Times*, November 1, 1993, 13. During the period of their survey, it should be added, "progressive foundations" contributed less than 5 percent as much to a handful of left-wing magazines.

30. Like Bozell (see chapter 5), Goldberg is no slouch at homophobic bigotry. Under the sarcastic heading, "Barbara Walters, Guardian of Standards," the following passage, in its entirety, occupies page 86 of *Arrogance*:

> "News used to be considered a public trust. It was and perhaps still is what gives the networks [their] dignity and integrity. It deserved respect and so, I think, do

we."— *20/20* anchor Barbara Walters, speaking during the furor over ABC's plan to dump *Nightline*, March 2002.

"Up until that point that was . . . the best sex I'd ever had. I felt . . . cared for; loved. . . . on a sensual level . . . that I had not [had] before with a man. I felt . . . sensuous and sensual in a way I hadn't before."—Actress Anne Heche about her relationship with comic Ellen DeGeneres, in a *20/20* interview with Barbara Walters, September 2001.

Somehow, apparently, the mere reference to same-sex love is a betrayal of "standards." It's typical of this repellent literature that one comes away from reading it with much more respect for commercial television's powers-that-be (such as Barbara Walters) than they probably deserve.

31. This animal is very wicked/It bites the foot that tries to kick it."

4

THE REAL WORLD OF TELEVISION

The Right's self-proclaimed culture war is not just about or even primarily about "news." It also depends strongly on a claim about the world of televised entertainment, of narrative fictions: a world which, oddly enough, is supposedly also out of balance with the desires and pleasures of the mass audience that consumes its products. The core of this critique is familiar. Television favorably portrays "too many" single-parent families, sometimes casts big businessmen or government officials as villains, never makes heroes out of "conservatives," ignores religious solutions in favor of "social work" approaches to personal problems, and inundates culture with sexual and graphically violent "trash." All of this is true to a greater or lesser extent; none of it has the faintest relevance to an intelligent understanding of the way mass media work. To see both the occasional plausibility and, much more, the overarching falsity in this accusation, we need to remind ourselves of a few simple truths about media representations.

"The world is a stage, the stage is a world of entertainment," wrote lyricist Howard Deitz for the film *The Bandwagon*. The lyric was intended not as a metaphor but as a summation of the film itself or, more generally, of the closed world of musical comedies in which everything of importance—business rivalries, political scheming, and love affairs—takes place on or around the stage. Show business, the song tells us (recapitulating the plot of the film), gives show people everything they need so that, even though totally insulated from the rest of the world, they don't really need it at all.

The system of commercial television might be said to be the exact opposite: not insulated from, but substituting for, incorporating, and even at times abolishing what we used to call "the real world." No other medium of communication is comparable. Even film, about which it has often been said sentimentally that "we learn how to behave from watching movies," does not come close to achieving this effect and makes no effort to do so.

Overwhelmingly, Hollywood films aim at fantasy, at producing daydreams that seem to emanate from the subconscious of the viewer rather than appearing to eavesdrop, as does television, on the passing social scene as it obtrudes into one's living room. To understand the difference, we need only think of police work. The gritty procedural world of television programs such as *CSI: Crime Scene Investigation, NYPD Blue*, or *Crossing Jordan* can only rarely be found on the silver screen, which instead gives us elaborate jokes on the order of *Beverly Hills Cop* or *Lethal Weapon* and their sequels or, occasionally, wonderfully detailed sequences (a murder investigation or a police station confrontation) at the start of a film that are soon overtaken by melodrama or bizarre flights of fancy. To take other instances, the intense focus on medical procedures that has become a standard television genre is virtually absent from film; the courtroom drama is a more recognizable cinematic genre, but even so there are only one or two such films a year at most, and they get lost in the general pack. No one could possibly think that they give us cues to the actual workings of the judicial system, the way the interweaving of "reality" shows (*Judge Judy*, e.g.), seemingly realistic fictional dramas (*Judging Amy, Law and Order*), and real or fake trials on cable's Court TV channel seems to do on television. Even so-called independent films that take place in observable social milieus almost always focus on the immediate lives and relationships of a small number of protagonists, perhaps with more psychological realism but without the real-people-just-sitting-around-the-living-room-talking ambience that television's family dramas and sitcoms at their most effective achieve.

Thus it is a considerable understatement to say that the commercial television system presents an ideologically consistent worldview to the mass audience and that this is our problem in dealing with television's power. Our problem is much more profound than that. To put it more accurately, despite intense competition among its component parts, and despite the lip service it pays to superficial diversity, commercial television *is* a consistent, inescapable, and omnipresent worldview of its own that, precisely because of its omnipresence, appears to be nonideological. Television in our minds is imperial as was, say, the old British Empire in Africa or South Asia or as is American global capital today. The problem with empire is not that its representatives all behave in exactly the same way and say exactly the same things; they never did that and still don't—think of the opposition to the second Bush administration's Mideast policy among senior American military and foreign policy elites during the run-up to the invasion of Iraq. The problem with empire is simply that it's there—and nothing else is. It has replaced whatever else there might be, and the real complaint about it is not that it's selling any particular ideology but that it displaces (or attempts to displace) all particular ideologies. For them, it attempts to substitute its own apparently universal ideology that seems to comprehend and embrace everything while actually excluding or suppressing entire realms of consciousness and communication.

What then is this universal but less then universal ideology? The major components of commercial television's worldview are national unity, individual competition, the ultimate goodness of the social order, and the sovereignty of commercial television itself—not consumers and not "the people" but the total system—against which and within which all other claims for attention must be measured. The particular themes that the system foregrounds together make up this worldview, which can more usefully be called television's ideological framework, that is, its master illusion that "represents the imaginary relationship," in Louis Althusser's phrase, "of individuals to their real conditions of existence."[1] To begin with, we might expect that ideology, broadly speaking, serves established power structures within the group. However, in a democracy—that is, any group in which formal power is allocated by free elections—the role of ideology is more complicated than that. In the world of televisual culture, the people, via the institution of ratings, have formal but otherwise purely symbolic sovereignty to just about the same extent as they do in the world of democratic politics. Thus, in this realm too, ideological productions work best when they manage to flatter the mass audience at the same time that they confirm its impotence. This circumstance helps foster the illusion, carefully disseminated by the controllers of mass media, that the people only get "what they want." They get, that is, whatever concoction of fictions can be packaged as an apparently seamless byproduct of national—that is, majority—democratic, cultural attitudes.

Thus it should not be thought that ideological framing is just a matter of casual elaboration, or is incidental to television's entertainment function, which includes, to repeat, not just serial narratives and movies and reality shows, but also all presentations of popular culture and gossip about it, as well as narratives such as *Cops* that masquerade as information. Quite the contrary, presenting the appearance of ideological universality is the major task of entertainment television and shows up in, or dominates, virtually every segment of every program, as in, most commonly, the initial wisecrack or epigram or opinionated utterance that is then followed by its equal and opposite riposte, together providing the illusion of balance upon which the more consequential illusion of universality depends. At the same time, this is hard work and difficult to accomplish persuasively. The American nation, after all, is barely a unity, as rife as it is with racial, religious, sexual, class, regional, and sectional divisions. Some of these have lasted hundreds of years. One of them at least resulted in the most destructive war in American history and is, in many ways, still ongoing, as electoral results every two years demonstrate. As for individual competition, its celebration is ultimately self-contradictory and socially destabilizing, for competition is about winning and, because in a competitive social order there cannot be winners without there being losers, every saga of individual triumph is shadowed by a reminder of painful loss—often, were we to investigate, inflicted on many more people than have benefited from the triumph. This is why, for example, businessmen make especially poor protagonists in popular culture, which therefore presents us with very few of them as heroic role models. Belief in the goodness of the social order is also a very hard sell. Real world injustices pile up day after day like autos rear-ending in a California highway fog; and profound moral and religious differences may cut so deep that one person's goodness or fairness is another person's wickedness or sinfulness, as moral positions come to be wielded like lethal weapons. And the hegemony of television itself, the real core of the system, is gradually called into question, for television's insistence on taking no sides looks more and more like the taking of a side as entrenched oppositions harden. The patriotic fervor after September 11 may have temporarily obscured all these divisions, but they are real and cannot be masked for long. It is important, then, to look at the world of entertainment to see both what themes it incorporates, what it excludes, and how, above all, its exclusions are accomplished.

From this perspective, we can only hope to understand what the system tells us by discarding the whole line of criticism that treats television programs as little more than a collection of simple ideological proclamations, fobbing off on a helpless mass audience the hidden messages of a self-styled creative "elite." I set off the last word only in order to replicate the disdain of conservative critics. In fact, the creators of commercial television actually *are* a genuine elite, that is to say, a group of people who are much better at what they do, namely writing narrative fictions, than I am or than almost anyone else reading these words is; anyone who doesn't believe that should try their hand at it. Ideological positioning is certainly an important aspect of entertainment television, and some genres—for example, law and order, family drama, and "reality programming"—would have nothing to say without it. But it is, at the same time, only one moment of any episode of fictional entertainment. For the content of every half-hour or hour-long narrative has several other decisive determinants that have little or even nothing to do with the alleged belief systems of its creators.

What we must remember, above all else, is that the goal of the system is never to be turned off. Preferably one's own channels (if you are a network owner) should be watched constantly, but, as that is not possible, second best is that *something* is always being watched; the system's presence is being maintained. However, the system is subject to the same tendency as any other mass-population phenomenon, namely that its progress (in this case, the extent of its interaction with the mass audience) can be expressed statistically by the standard ("bell") curve. In this case, the system comes into existence after the end of World War II. Demand for its products, and the concomitant supply of television sets, begins slowly, gathers momentum, and then at some point peaks, having saturated its available loci of attention. After that, a steady decline begins, which can only be accelerated by the introduction of competing systems—most notably in this instance, the internet, personal computer games, and video games. The development of more widespread distribution networks—in the case of television, satellite TV and cable—can slow the main drift but can't really reverse it once something approaching audience saturation has been achieved. At this point, the different elements of the television system are competing with each other; the system is consuming itself.

When the television audience actually peaked is unclear, but what is certain is that the peak was reached some time ago. There is absolute agreement on all sides that the number of hours watched by viewers, though immense in an absolute sense, has been and still is declining. The kind of coverage that the system receives in the business pages of, for example, *The New York Times, The Wall Street Journal,* or *The New Yorker,* in which the momentary ups and downs of the competing networks are charted, conceals this overall motion. It is of importance to shareholders but not to anyone interested in the fate of the system as a whole. The real facts of the business are that it can cost over two million dollars to produce a single episode of a prime-time series, and commercial sponsorship typically covers not more than half of these costs. The rest can only be recouped through overseas sales or by going into syndication, or more rarely, DVD distribution, none of which avenues is guaranteed to the networks. As costs escalate, attention dwindles. In this light, it is evident that, from a broad historical standpoint, the enemy of the system's growth, its dark shadow, is inertia: the tendency of momentum once slowed to continue slowing. But inertia in the world of commercial television has a specific content. There it appears as a specific, ever-present threat: *boredom*. Television, like the Red Queen in *Alice*, runs faster and faster merely in order to keep in the same place or, worse, to backslide more slowly. Hour after hour, day after day, week after week, year after year, writers and producers and executives struggle desperately to fill a schedule that, by their own definition of the situation, must never go unfilled for even a minute (hence the existence of the mindless, stupefying, and endlessly unpersuasive advertisements known as infomercials and characterized in on-screen guides as "paid programming"). But given the quite small number of available narrative genres, the only marginally larger number of basic plot outlines, and the thousands of supposedly unique story lines required to fill each genre's time slots, the creative process cannot possibly keep up with the need. Originality gradually disappears, and even franchise programs—*Oprah, Law and Order*—begin to spin their wheels. Is there any variant of criminal activity anywhere that Jerry Orbach and Sam Waterston haven't dealt with three or four times by now? The huge majority of shows are retreads; even the original-seeming *24*, with its click-clack "real time" editing, is essentially a version of the cliffhanger serials of the early twentieth century. Boredom is thus the monster looming over the networks' shoulder. Writers may have ideological messages they hope to get across, but their efforts to do so pale in significance next to the consuming need to *get it watched*—a need that, over time, manifests itself as the inescapable imperative, *be different! be new!* That is why, for example, the explosive, momentarily all-consuming descent of mass entertainment into the nether regions of bad taste known as "reality television" has little to do with the mass audience's declining taste, real or alleged, and much to do with the playing out of the classic genres that film and later television have depended on throughout the twentieth century.

Marx's description of the logic of capital accumulation in a capitalist society comes closest to describing this imperative. Every capitalist must compete with every other capitalist to maintain his hold on the market, and thus a crisis of overproduction must finally ensue. It makes sense for the system to slow down and settle for slow or no growth once a high level of production is achieved, but it doesn't make any sense for any individual capitalist to slow down and so the logic of accumulation drives on and on. The most obvious contemporary instance of this dynamic has been the spectacular rise and implosion of the dot.com industry. Though less spectacularly, the same tendency is at play in the world of visual mass media. The historical imperative has combined with what has so far been striking progress in technological capacity to produce, among other things, the changes in television programming—including reality shows—that the critics of its so-called bad taste are fixated on. For example, violence grows more graphic *of course*, for that development follows the same logic that depicts emergency room surgeries (or, most grossly, the cosmetic surgeries of *Nip/Tuck*) in detail so precise that many viewers find the medical genre unbearably disgusting or watch key scenes with their hands over their eyes. Critics want televised violence to "have consequences," a perfectly reasonable wish, but fail to understand that the chief consequence of producing images of violence, for better or worse, is to make them look more "real," more brutal: surely as appropriate an outcome of violence as its supposed eventuation in lawful retribution. If visual fictions fail to give audiences that thrill of reality, after all, we can always turn to the local news or CNN's latest war or Rock Star or Activision's latest version of mass slaughter.

In the same way, the depiction of human sexuality grows more graphic, and the ways in which it disrupts lives, conventions, and the social order must be displayed more accurately than used to be the case, for audiences will no longer believe sanitized accounts of sexual lives. Once again, if television doesn't give them the real thing, there are too many alternatives in the nearest video store, newsstand, or hotel room that will do it for them. In the early twenty-first century, after all, pornography is the most profitable sector of visual entertainment in the United States (and this account does not even include the returns on soft-core, R-rated movies of the kind that go straight to video shelves or Cinemax). Thus, to take some obvious examples of how this overall logic of visual entertainment plays out, detective stories can no longer be built around illegitimacy as the source of murders; family dramas or soap operas will just be laughable if generations of enmity and vengeance are alleged to ensue because a couple of young people slept together; a sexual villain had better pursue some horrendously unacceptable victims in unbearably horrible ways before we will accept that our police heroes have to dedicate all their resources to tracking him down; and our hero had better see some real flesh on a really attractive heroine (or her body double) before we find their instant mutual lust credible. All this is due simply to the passage of time and the relentless development of a consumer society in which any limits to consumption appear arbitrary, and those which are imposed (e.g., on certain addictive substances) are routinely flouted and go unpunished (unless transgressed by poor or nonwhite people).[2]

There is, in addition, yet another imperative that combines with social and technological change to make television the way it is today. In the world of film, to consider the most obvious comparison, it has become generally acknowledged that directors are the primary creators of what we see on screen. Entertainment television, in contrast, is writer- and producer-driven. It is very unlikely that any readers of these words can identify the director of any episode of any series they regularly watch, but many will instantly recognize the names of writer-producers David Kelley, Steve Bochco, or David Chase. In other words, whereas prestige in the world of cinema accrues to directors, and even the best screenwriters remain largely anonymous, in television land the opposite is true. Moreover, Hollywood directors can gain their fame (perhaps unfortunately) by filming the most original car chase, or blowing up buildings, cities, and planets, but the technology of television is inadequate for this kind of endeavor. Typically, for example, the 2003 episode of *Crossing Jordan* that was built around the terrorist bombing of an office building did not even show the actual explosion. Television's writers thus compete with each other by writing the most prestigious scripts, which usually means being literate, *current*, and *unconventional*. No one will become famous by imitating Booth Tarkington; Mario Puzo is a much better bet. Very quickly, the best writers (in this sense) push the envelope by forcing other aspirants to fame to imitate them, and so the progression continues until some day, without doubt, audiences will watch reruns of *Ally McBeal* and wonder what all the fuss was about.

In sum, the visual and textual content of commercial television is driven by its role as a technologically small-scale medium of mass popular entertainment. Having begun this discussion with a definition of ideology, I clearly do not intend to say that the system is nonideological. However, aside from the delivery of news (especially in its incarnation as propaganda; see chapter 2), television's ideology is peculiar to the system itself. It is neither conservative (though there is some of that) nor liberal (though there is some of that) but insistently, and obsessively, "popular." Within these limits as I've set them out above, then, what is it that entertainment television does, and that its creators think it must do, to survive the test of popularity?

The main point about what television "says" is actually not any particular statement that it makes but, rather, the great lengths that commercial television, in its pursuit of universality, goes to avoid being caught saying anything that is not conventionally acceptable. The unconventionality I have referred to above is not moral or ideological but purely stylistic, a matter of narrative technique and kinetic movement. This is the informal doctrine of balance in the entertainment realm, and it is more stringent than the formal version of "balance" that the FCC used to require for news and opinion programs. It is enforced on every network by an internal official who might as well be called a censor, as censorship is what balance is all about.[3] Balance, of course, has its limits, and these are set by the censors' view of what is so noncontroversial—that is, unlikely to inflame any significant public opinion—as not to require balance or too controversial to permit any mention at all. Thus it is not necessary to balance patriotic sentiments with antipatriotic speeches, nor is it necessary to counter the endless references on law and order shows to judges who "put criminals back on the streets"; by comparison, defenses of due process (e.g., as by Harry Hamlin on *L.A. Law*) are few and far between. On the other hand, abortion, and especially the constitutional right to it, is virtually unmentionable, and there is no balance about that at all, in the sense of as many unhappily pregnant women deciding to have abortions as not to have them (see my comment in chapter 3). Not only does that not happen, but the word itself is hardly ever spoken; friends, counselors, or family members may suggest that "terminating the pregnancy" is a possibility or simply ask in a diffident voice if "you've thought about all the options." Even on the one program that was a major exception to the evasion of abortion (a *Law and Order* episode discussed further in this chapter), of the two women we meet who have actually had abortions, one has become a supporter of Operation Rescue and the other cannot bring herself to use the word. Almost always, the answer to the question is a sharp rejection; the hundreds of thousands of (mostly young) poor women in desperate material circumstances, who have had unwanted intercourse with coercive or careless men, do not exist in television's America. This is because abortion is not debatable among people who are willing to be civil to each other, unlike, say, capital punishment, which is debated on *Law and Order* when one prosecutor supports it and another expresses doubts about it. There are too many people who absolutely *hate* abortion and any support for it, for commercial television to brave their fervor. No one, after all, has ever assassinated a lawyer, or blown up his or her office, for defending an accused murderer. The closest commercial television has ever come to an *un*balanced position on abortion, to my knowledge, is a 2003 episode of *Law and Order: Special Victims Unit* in which an abusive husband tries to prevent his wife from having an abortion as part of a campaign of harassment against her. Her constitutional right is defended in court. But as though to demonstrate everything we need to know about the television system, and nothing at all about the real world of men and women, she then turns around and decides to have the child after all.

The television system's notion of "balance," however, is in other ways quite peculiar. The term is ordinarily used in political discourse or debate, not in the context of narrative fiction. But in visual fictions—that is, in mainstream cinema and even more crucially on commercial television—it functions in a different way, not as the fair representation of both sides to a debate, but as the insertion of, if not emphasis on, conventional viewpoints to counteract suggestions of intellectual dissent or subversion. Balance, then, occurs within each individual narrative rather than as the pluralistic appearance of narratives with different standpoints. On television, ideally, every narrative should in the end have *the same standpoint.*

However, more important than trying to describe that standpoint is describing how it is achieved, for it is that process that is the essence of commercial television. What has to be understood above all is that there is a serious problem to be overcome, and everything in the television system revolves around overcoming it. The problem, as I have written elsewhere, is that ideological justification can rarely be simple or straightforward.[4] The idyllic story of romantic love within the patriarchal family order is given the lie by the experiences of millions of real families. The myth of a classless society is given the lie by the truths of oppressive labor relations familiar to every worker and by the self-evident falsity of the notion that wealth is produced by hard work and poverty by laziness. The picture of community as a coming together of free individuals is given the lie by, to take only one of many examples, the destructions and degradations that the pursuit of industrial profit wreaks on people's lived environments. The self-congratulatory story of democracy is given the lie by racial discrimination, gender exclusion, and a corrupt and often rigged political process, not to mention the imperial resort to force and violence in the relations of the United States to other societies. One could multiply such critiques endlessly, but my point is not to write an exposé of America. It is rather to remind us of all the potential sources of unease and resentment in a society that prides itself on its radical uniqueness as a good society.

To see the significance of this condition, we once again have to look at the difference between ideology and propaganda. Whereas propaganda tells us what to believe, ideology instead appeals to what we are already supposed to believe. When we attend to a particular story, therefore, we derive meanings from the specifics of its narrative and not just from its place in an overall structure. Much of the narrative content of both films and television is supplied by narrative conventions that have become complexly elaborated into various genres, conventions so familiar that they may do their work via the merest glancing reference—visual culture's version of shorthand. (The villain, wearing a black hat, dismounts from a stagecoach and kicks the nearest dog.) However, the various familiar genres require more than merely narrative conventions to be interpretable by us; they also must somehow conjure up for us a familiar moral universe. But that universe is not simple, certainly not as simple as contemporary conservatives make it out to be. Rather, the ambiguities that result from any historical settlement among competing groups and classes—ambiguities which propaganda tries to eliminate—appear as contradictions within ideology and the cultural forms that express it. In the United States, the force of the peculiar and historically unique liberal individualism that defines the difficulty of social reconciliation through cultural integration, thus, defines the limits of visual culture itself. Rebels are criminals, and rebels are heroes; nonconformity is contempt of the community, and nonconformity is a lonely stand for principle.

These underlying counternarratives of the social reality cannot simply be ignored by the creators of visual narrative fiction. If it would be unfair to call the reality they reflect the only reality, it certainly would be even more obtuse to pretend that they don't exist. Moreover, the symbolic resolution of the narrative unease they purvey is always fragile. No matter how much television we watch, no matter how much propaganda we read, we will always find elements of counterideology even within dominant culture itself, based on the grand but unrealized affirmations of the early American republic. This counterideological critique usually deploys the buried (sometimes not so buried) rhetoric of a more radical Americanism—freedom and equality for *all*—in order to criticize the ideological triumphalism of order and subordination. It can and often does, for example, generate a critique of male domination in the name of women, or of capitalism in the name of workers, or of repressive community in the name of free individuals. These counterstatements are an important element of the socially real, and, if you are trying to tell a believable story, the socially real must at least occasionally erupt into it; otherwise, the story will not be believable. Its absence would render the world of family drama, law and order, international heroics, and even drawing-room comedy or (more ambiguously) soap opera the object of derision. Even intergalactic tales are configured to look like standard contemporary adventure stories with furry-faced protagonists.

On the other hand, within these boundaries, the approach of entertainment media to authority figures, the family, and so forth, is wholly conventional. The law seeks justice as well as it can; familial loyalty is the highest value, and non-kin "families" seek to replicate it. A few rotten apples may spoil the barrel in small-town America, but communal virtue always triumphs. At the

simplest level, a deviation from a normative institution may be presented as
an instance of a social problem which exists as the exception rather than the
norm. This might be called the method of understanding deviation and
then either forgiving or quarantining it. In movies or television shows about
policemen, for example, divorce, when it occurs, is treated as a pathological
outcome resulting from a sequence of unfortunate causes which are the inevitable but unfortunate accompaniments of police work. Even in comedies, we hardly ever meet a person cheerfully divorced from an ordinary but
incompatible partner and thinking no more of it. The ideological thrust of
this kind of treatment is readily recognizable in that cinematic "happy" families are never explained as the result of their causes. All those perky,
adorable children like none any of us have ever met, wives with part-time
jobs who keep their houses spotlessly clean, and husbands with unproblematic employment records are just "normal" or, even better, they just are.
That is American life.

As for contrary solidarities of resistance, of utopianism, of institutional re-
structuring, of collective resistance rather than individual heroism, they remain as absent as they've ever been from visual culture. If they ever appear,
it will only be as part of the metaideology in which television is everything,
as in the McDonald's ad in which a raucous protest on behalf of "freedom"
turns out to be for "free fries." This is a regular trope of the system, as "rev-
olutions" turn out to be the invention of a lower-calorie beer, or "a radical
new idea" is for a new cosmetic. That is the system's politics. No doubt, content analysis will show us that political or economic authority figures are
sometimes scapegoated in Hollywood films, and this is taken as further evidence of the alleged liberal domination of media. But this kind of social criticism has always existed in Hollywood, and there is nothing specifically liberal about it; John Rambo's militaristic contempt for "government
bureaucrats" faithfully tracks Kaufman and Hart's comic satire of bankers in
the 1939 film *You Can't Take It With You*. There is no Golden Age of Hollywood; ever since the 1930s, Hollywood has been a favorite whipping boy
for the Right, which in those days allied itself with organized crime to break
strikes of screenwriters and craftspersons in the name of fighting subversion.

Rather, the regular recurrence of this kind of treatment of authorities in
visual culture is necessitated by attempts to solve a formal problem of nar-
ration, the need to resolve apparent contradictions without allowing dissent
equal time. Thus we get the ideology of the popular, in which all contradictions can be smoothed over and in which, ultimately, there is no disunity.
However, the nature of narrative in visual culture (if not in all cultural arenas) demands the appearance of conflict before harmonious resolution;

and, if conflict is to be resolved by a hero, then there must, ipso facto, also be a villain. Who is that villain to be? It must be someone who in real life is also perceived as a threat to individual happiness, for that is how ideological narrative works: it interpolates us, the audience, into a familiar scenario. Almost all popular narratives follow a common trajectory in which an original position of social or personal well-being is described. Then a potentially destructive problem is stated, and failure to resolve the problem seems inevitable. But then, at the last minute, it is successfully resolved, and the original state of social or personal well-being is retrieved. (Only movies within the horror genre occasionally escape from this framework.) The basic themes are timeless: jealousy, greed, overweening ambition, and so on. But for those who are more entertained by contemporary melodrama than classical tragedy, the perennial themes have to be embodied in some material form that makes social sense to the mass audience: thus, for example, the frequent adaptations of classics such as *Hamlet* or *Oedipus Rex* usually eliminate the problem of kingship and replace it with an updated emphasis on patriarchal inheritance in general. Narrative, in other words, always has to be historicized for a contemporary audience.

Therefore, the conventional story line, even in sitcoms, usually relies on the invocation of a genuine threat to the family, the sexual order, the community, and so forth. This threat must be serious enough to generate doubt as to the outcome but still be capable of being recuperated by the end of the hour (or half hour). "Having it both ways" is the term I use for this version of narrative in which no one can be caught unquestionably taking a controversial position—"controversial" in the sense of challenging the traditional rules of the social order without allowing any recuperation of it. Here examples are necessary to give the flavor of how having it both ways works and also to make it more easily recognizable when we are watching the system without actually paying careful attention to it.[5]

To see how the search for a universal narrative plays itself out in practice, the best way to begin is to return to the earlier brief discussion of what I will here call "policeworld," the world of cops and crime. Within the TV system's metatext, and within the American social order as a whole, the ideology of "law and order" plays a central role; it is within the workings of policeworld that national unity is confirmed and conflict disconfirmed. In this respect, what is most noticeable about television's policeworld, in particular, is that we encounter it during evening prime time, introduced by modernistic music, in hour-long segments, without a laugh track, and represented by ensemble naturalistic acting at its finest (for television). In a word, television is *serious* about "law and order"; the business of policeworld is serious business. Not only that, it's virtually the *only* serious business. What's most striking about TV's vision of urban America is that, with very few exceptions, almost nothing else takes place in it except criminal behavior. Seinfeld, for example, lives in New York, but *Seinfeld* rarely gave or tried to give any feeling of New York as a context in the way that *NYPD Blue* does. All communities, after all, are primarily places of work, but the only work that regularly goes on in commercial TV's cities is legal/police work, medical emergencies, and (usually as comedy) media work—representations of which are not about the city but about the medium itself. A show like *Boston Public* is so rare as to create a genre almost by itself. On the whole, whatever actual cities the different television programs take place in, nothing else of interest goes on in them. Except for occasional encounters with the legal system, small businesspeople, teachers, caregivers and social service providers, workers in the food industry or the sex industry or the transportation sector or the entertainment world (outside of television itself), construction and industrial workers, and so on, apparently lead lives of little interest. What this means is that, among the motives that move people to take action in the world, *fear* is by far predominant (*ER*, for example, is almost indistinguishable from a cop show in this regard). The case board of *Homicide*, while it was on the air, told it all. The number of open homicides on that board at any one time (at one point it was one hundred) is simply incredible for a middle-size city; it would be too great even for New York. That television, when seemingly serious, sells itself by selling fear (love, as in family-oriented sitcoms, being a very distant second) is a fact of the first magnitude; it helps explain almost everything else that follows. Crime—but only certain kinds of crime—is *the* problem; police work is *the* solution. A moralist might say that society must use violence to combat violence, but in fact, television puts it the other way around. We must be *shown* violence, even at the risk of highlighting it or even, occasionally, seeming to glorify it, in order to show the *suppression* of violence. This is having it both ways with a vengeance—having our violence while pretending to condemn it. This move is the essence of much of television, such as the antiterrorist narratives that have proliferated since 9/11, and, above all, the all-American cop show, especially at its most unalloyed, as in the pseudoreal *Cops* and its imitators.

We must not take this treatment of violence for granted, either; there's nothing necessary or "realistic" about it. *Batman* and *Wonder Woman*, for example, were both lighthearted, though they were both about "crime-fighting" in the city. Unlike their worlds, though, policeworld is to be understood as in some sense "real," taking place in "real" cities—New York, Los Angeles, Baltimore, Chicago, Atlanta—with actors talking about "real" things (e.g., Miranda rights, capital punishment) the way "real people" are always represented as talking in Hollywood. In actuality, this is nonsense. The make-believe world of, say, *NYPD Blue* is a lot closer to that of *Mission: Impossible* than to any real social order in which any of us actually lives, and the dialogue on *Law and Order* is so artificial as to be embarrassing. But the naturalistic Hollywood style insistently tells us that we're getting nothing more remote from reality than a heightened version of it. In sum, it's not so much that we're supposed to believe Rudolph Giuliani was a better law-enforcement official than Robert Morgenthau Jr. from some appropriate ideological perspective, but that we're supposed to understand law enforcement as vitally important *and* television as giving us an important perspective on it. Everything we see and hear we see and hear within that context. As this is also the context that the so-called news media (including television itself) emphasize above all else, the fictional narrative of television becomes most of what most people know—or, rather, think they know—about the world of law and order. Whatever the system tells us, its defense for having told us that is already built in.

Because "law and order" is ultimately about national unity, what is especially crucial in policeworld's overall narrative is the elision of class conflict and poverty as a way of life; the latter is simply written out of the script. Mass hunger, unbearable housing conditions, malnutrition, the spreading epidemic diseases of the poor, and, above all, government cutbacks in the funding of efforts to deal with all these social disasters will not be found for even a second in any of policeworld's versions of real cities. Neither will there be found any recognition of the devastating effect that these conditions necessarily have on the futures of children who, once subject to them for very long, can never become fully functioning adults. In policeworld, therefore, criminality as a way of life is fundamentally inexplicable. It has dire effects but no causes. Most shows about either cops or lawyers have at least one major character who expresses old-fashioned liberal sympathies for the hapless lowlifes they encounter (Mariska Hargitay on *Law & Order: Special Victims Unit*, e.g.), but this sympathy is given no mooring within the narrative. Such sympathies are expressed as on the one hand and on the other hand: in response to complaints (not that any will be forthcoming), the scriptwriter could say that it's there, but will never be forced to plead guilty to liberal soft-heartedness.

As for class recognition in policeworld, it has several basic components. First, wealth and independent intellectuality are suspect. This is a constant within every television genre, though *Law and Order: Special Victims Unit* is a masterwork of this kind of reverse snobbery. As soon as a snotty rich woman appears on camera, we know she's covering up some vile secret; conversely, we'd never know from watching the show that most cases of child exploitation and violent sexual abuse in the United States stem not from devious plots involving sexual slavery or stolen identities, but come from the world of the poor. We do not want to know that because, if we did, then we—not the cops and lawyers but citizens and taxpayers of the polity—might have to do something about it. Second, the most significant class division we see, not only in policeworld but everywhere on TV, is a cultural division between material and mental labor. At the same time, however, there is no social barrier between police*men* and professional *women*, who stand for the ultimate representation of complete social mobility. Above all, lower is always better, as long as it's not really poor. That familiar figure, the wisdom-dispensing waitress of shows from *Cheers* to the 1999 cop show *Turks*, is only the most emphatic reminder of this, Hollywood's favorite version of mass flattery. She reaffirms our essential classlessness. We *can* have it both ways. We don't have to actually *do* anything to be egalitarian; we just have to banter with waitresses or, in another famous instance, nannies, while making fun of our financial betters, as in *The Simple Life* or *Rich Girls* (although the satire of those latter programs would be more impressive if *males* were its target—the ditzy bimbo is a caricature straight out of traditional gender hierarchy).

The most salient point, however, is that all of this is an affirmation of a populist class *consciousness* conjoined with an implicit denial of a serious structure of class *power*. The key to this populist consciousness, as I have suggested earlier, is that it is erected on a base not of class divisions in Marx's sense but of a singular distinction between communal insiders and communal outsiders. (Thus authoritarian populism, the political philosophy of the contemporary Right, is not a deviant form of populism but is rather distinguished by the enemies it chooses). The moral centrality of policemen to the social universe of policeworld, and most especially their potential sexual access to female attorneys, happily affirms the insider status of all of us, regardless of social status, who are willing to accept the proffered moral identity. If we think of all the prime-time shows of policeworld over the years, only the sometime left-wing cynicism of Richard Belzer on *Homicide* has offered any clue that the social order might have fundamental (nonracial) conflicts at its core, and his politics is submerged in a thoroughly nihilistic persona.

The denial of *fundamental* social conflict, while seeming to show conflict all over the place, is hardly peculiar to policeworld. What is more interesting is what happens at the second level, that of interaction between policeworld and the surrounding "outside" world. Here we encounter an implicit, serious denial that policemen (and, more rarely, policewomen) form an occupational interest group, that the members of this group possess social and economic interests, authorization to use physical or even deadly force without real check, and attitudes of contempt for those they call civilians, and that these facts and circumstances often put them visibly at odds (in the newspapers, not on prime-time television) with the populace they are supposed to "serve and protect." Instead, constantly delivering themselves of casual remarks about "liberal judges" who "put scum back on the streets," the heroes of policeworld stand above the rest of us. They may (like Sipowicz) drink but they don't use dope—the one unforgivable sin in the TV metatext. They never raise employment or wage-related grievances (with the exception of Christine Cagney); they don't themselves commit crimes, harass or extort sexual favors from prostitutes, misappropriate evidence, coerce confessions, turn prisoners against each other in exchange for exculpations, or frame "known criminals" with planted evidence.

In short, we see only a humanized, idealized version of the police: their family lives, job-related stress, and mutual intimacy. In this way, too, violence is damped down, legitimated, and domesticated. So are divisive social conflicts. Again, except for *Homicide* (as it was), we rarely see gender or even racial discord among the police. Who would know from watching television that black police officers in New York actually have their own separate protective association, or be aware of the criminal justice system's legacy of misogyny?[6] As well, we never see the everyday brutality of police work, not only in racial confrontations but simply in the treatment of any persons who protest during their encounters with the police. We would never know that every large city has a significant budgetary item for settling complaints of police misbehavior, or that talking back to a policeman is probably the most dangerous activity in which any American citizen can engage. And, for all the Hollywood naturalism of policeworld, we never once hear policemen talk the way they actually talk: the constant obscenity, scatology, sexual and racial bigotry, and above all gross misogyny that constitute the way men in groups oriented to violence always converse. Except in rare instances, the culture of policeworld is not morally ambiguous, as we might think any culture of violence must be. In fact, with the single exception of its defensiveness in the face of misunderstanding and lack of appreciation, it is no different from any other subculture. There can only be one attitude toward "the law," and that is the attitude, without any hint of the irregular misbehaviors that might compromise it, that policeworld presents to us.

Perhaps even more crucially, the pretense of social realism is completely contradicted (but without letting us in on the secret) by the apparent transparency of policeworld. In contradistinction to virtually all real police work, what goes on in policeworld is almost entirely the solving of *mysteries*. The clearance rate of homicides (virtually the only crime encountered on most of these shows, except for *Law and Order: Special Victims Unit*) is incredibly close to 100 percent. It is almost always intentional and intelligent clearance, moreover, and not the result of anonymous tips, unlikely coincidences, confessional outpourings, and the other accidents and contingencies that make up the real world of case resolution (to the much lesser extent that it actually occurs). Here too, the logic of a unifying ideological narrative is followed. Policeworld only *appears* to be opaque for the moment; it is ultimately transparent. In this way, it is a world utterly without ambiguity, recycling without even a moment's thought two fictions that help sustain the criminal justice system. The first of these is the fiction that juries "find out" facts, as opposed to making arbitrary findings of "fact." The second is that what people say about themselves in the confessional mode has a necessary correspondence to what they have actually done. For this appeal to common sense, legal realism and psychoanalysis might as well not have existed. Here too, then, fantasy is at the core of the fiction, though the phantasmic quest is ostensibly a quest for "truth" rather than for the female (although more psychoanalytically-oriented theorists might question whether there is any real difference between these two types of quest.)

In one way, however, this situation is not quite as simple as it first appears. For an absolutely crucial distinction is that the classical mystery narrative is attached almost exclusively to *white* people only, white people who commit murders, scatter clues, baffle cops, and so on, just like the characters in an Agatha Christie novel. Contrarily, on *NYPD Blue*, *Law and Order* and its spin-offs, *CSI*, and so on, least of all but still noticeably so on *Homicide*, and above all on the "real" cop shows, black people apparently engage in crime as a way of life, with no manifest intention of being clever or baffling and with no "serious" motive (e.g., inheriting money, eliminating competitors, psychotic jealousy, etc.). This is no minor matter. Thus the "realism" of policeworld is purely a matter of style; its latent content is the deepest fantasy of all, namely that the *real* "heart of darkness" is black. Crimes are white and can be solved; "crime" is black and, being a way of life, it cannot be solved but can only be extirpated. How is left to each viewer's imagination, unlike Kurtz's posthumous communication to Marlow.

In other words, what is special about law and order television is its tendentious contemporaneity. Two aspects of this contemporaneity stand out most glaringly as exemplifications of the rare instances in which the system does *not* have it both ways. The first is the passing of what film historian Robert Ray calls "the unofficial hero" or "the outlaw hero," for a long time the dominant character of genre cinema and a significant presence on TV, as well (*The Rockford Files, Harry O, The Fugitive, Run for Your Life*).[7] Now the unofficial hero is observable only in his absence from prime-time television. The role has been recast for heroines, though even among these the most famous (Wonder Woman, Xena, Buffy) exist outside the realm of Hollywood's literal America, in another time or another place (and, despite being about the "CIA," neither *La Femme Nikita* nor *Alias* fits into the realist mode either). This absence of the unofficial hero, moreover, is highlighted by an apparent presence, but a significantly different presence, in those shows that were or are related but also tangential to policeworld, such as *Walker, Texas Ranger*; *Martial Law*; and *Profiler*. *Profiler* actually belonged, like *Murder, She Wrote*, to the somewhat archaic genre of "the great detective" (though Jodie Foster in *Silence of the Lambs* was evidently its prototype). The more martial-art-oriented shows often present a classic genre narrative: on *Walker*, the individual hero in the town where everyone is covering up a terrible secret, à la Spencer Tracy in the film *Bad Day at Black Rock*; on *Martial Law*, the martial artist against the mob; and, on *Profiler*, the master detective matching wits with the master criminal. But in each case, these heroes are or were *official*, backed up not only by the presumptively unquestioned moral virtue of being "the law" but also by the full panoply of legitimate armed force as well.

Thus the classical American cynicism about the law that was a constant of the private eye genre in literature, film, and television seems to have disappeared. And although this might seem a trivial matter, it in fact has major ideological ramifications, for what it really betokens is *the disappearance of the underdog as hero*. It is perhaps too strong a temptation, but one I will not resist, to say that the disappearance of the underdog hero carries with it the disappearance of Left popular culture in general and New Dealism in particular. Or to put the issue in a more precisely stated historical context, the underdog hero represented liberal individualism as a critique of existing patterns of authority—and, when "he" becomes a "she," of authority as patriarchy. Despite the Right's fanciful critiques of entertainment television's "trash" and "sleaze" that we shall see, the cop as hero stands most of the time not for liberal individualism but for authoritarian populism.

However, traditional liberalism suffers only a partial defeat here, for it is important to see that the other major aspect of contemporary policeworld is an apparent commitment to the ideology of liberal pluralism. On the other hand, if at first glance policeworld's ideology is the ideology of liberal pluralism, it is a very peculiar version thereof. In sum, the face and voice of authority are mostly white and are resolutely male. There have been

African-American men of authority on *Homicide* and *NYPD Blue*; no woman has yet achieved that position, except in the prosecutor's office where violence is not an issue. (Bonnie Bedelia on Lifetime's *The Division* was an exception, but with its all-female homicide unit that program "for women" was almost more of a fairy tale than an addition to the naturalistic cop show genre.) Instead, women (as with most black men) have now achieved the position of faithful sidekick (Mariska Hargitay in *Law and Order: Special Victims Unit*; Marg Helgenberger in *CSI*), replacing the white character actors of yore (e.g., Harry Morgan in *Dragnet*) who made a career out of that role. However, this is only an ideological interposition and, as such, is not as decisive as the nature of the narrative standpoint, which determines what it is that we see. In this respect, with the exception of *Homicide*, virtually every episode of policeworld as a unified text has a *white* protagonist. Or, put more narrowly, the narrative, and thus the moral center of these shows, is almost always that of a white man, even if from time to time he has to be enlightened about the nature of "the other," as by Mariska Hargitay on *SVU* or Andre Braugher on *Homicide*, for example.

More to the point, despite its naturalistic surfaces, policeworld is fundamentally a world of *male fantasy*. Just because this is so obvious does not mean it should go unremarked. The level of female pulchritude and glamour in policeworld is extraordinary, though more so, on the whole, in the prosecutor's (and even medical examiner's) offices than in the squad cars (think of Angie Harmon or Jill Hennessy). This is not an idle matter; it tells us that "law and order" as crystallized in television's version of policeworld is primarily a male *sexual* fantasy. The fantasy has its limits, to be sure; these fantasies, like all nonpornographic fantasy, are bounded by the most fundamental limits of the social order. In effect, the American (male) individualism that has always veered toward social anarchy is bought off by the fantasy of female availability. In this respect, for example, the ridiculous female sideline commentators of professional football's TV coverage are like the pretty schoolmarm in a traditional Western: testimony that despite the violence we're still within the bounds of civilization. The result, however, is that in most such series women appear visibly as token women, as sidekicks in a primarily male world.[8] A few series have been targeted to women: *Cagney and Lacey* and, more recently, Lifetime's *The Division* and *1-800-Missing* (both pastiches of originally male-oriented shows); but these are exceptions. Moreover, the sidekick women of policeworld are usually in one way or another strong women, whether morally or physically, and exceptionally attractive. In this way, the appeals of feminism are satisfied at the same time that yet another male fantasy is foregrounded: again, having it both ways. (This is usually true also of those series featuring genuine heroines: *Xena, Buffy, La Femme Nikita, Philly, Alias.*)[9] It is important to note, too, that, in its apparent relegation of women to the second division, policeworld is not at all exceptional; it just has a better excuse. Taken all together, prime-time television's male characters outnumber females by at least a 2 to 1 margin.[10]

From this standpoint of white male centrality, with the (usually unspoken) exception of sexual behavior (that is, homosexuality, the last "legitimate" target of discrimination), all inhabitants of subaltern positions are equal and are to be treated equally. Race, however, is really the essence of this pluralism; gender tokenism is more an expression of individual rights doctrine. So the pluralism of policeworld is really the pluralism of organized baseball—lots of black players, few managers. Because, as Stanley Aronowitz has argued, police work on television is the last venue for the presentation of male proletarian labor, we might call this also (faux) working-class pluralism.[11] As for gender, TV has recognized the cultural and occupational revolution of feminism but, again, within the limits I've already suggested. In keeping with the program of "having it both ways," the female characters are informally "feminists." But the word itself is almost never used; it is *verboten* on mainstream television. Moreover, *they* are as "tough" on "law and order" as the males. On *Law and Order*, for example, Angie Harmon argued for capital punishment against the doubts of Sam Waterston, her male boss. In short, women are now associated with male authority, even essential to its continued sway, but they remain women in a man's world. On another *Law and Order* episode about the assassination of an abortion provider, when assistant district attorney Jill Hennessy did indeed use the "f" word (in as relevant a context as one could possibly think of), she was promptly put in her place, again by Sam Waterston, who told her pointedly that the trial they were engaged in was about murder, not abortion rights.

Race creates the one major exception to this ideological confirmation of communal unity, but it is only a partial exception. The widespread destruction of black society may be the result of decades of slavery and its aftermath; self-replicating poverty treated only with "benign neglect"; the murderously violent policing of racial boundaries; long-term and continuing employment discrimination; the deliberate creation and maintenance of a rigidly segregated residential housing ghetto; and the policing of that ghetto by a mostly white occupying army. Not a single one of these putative causes, however, regularly appears on policeworld. In fact, racial polarization as a complex, carefully maintained, discriminatory way of life that benefits white people simply disappears. Instead, in sum, we are shown a peculiar, classically ideological picture of American urban life. By any reckoning, the city is apparently a place of violent crime; nothing else of importance seems to go on in it. But this hellish city has two faces. On the one hand, it is protected by policeworld, a by-and-large friendly, tolerant monoculture in which racism doesn't exist (except in *Homicide's* Baltimore) and sexual discrimination hardly at all; and the good guys, regardless of all differences in background, support each other against all comers. As in most ideologies of community, conflict is both denied and displaced. We are a community, united as one. They, whoever they are, are the other, not part of us at all. Conflict is only apparent, or, if it is undeniably real, "we," the good (mostly white) people in the audience, are not implicated in it. In short, we can have it both ways, after all.

In all this, to be sure, some cultural critics might argue that "a program provides potential meanings, which may be realized, or made into actually experienced meanings, by socially situated viewers in the process of reading." But, as the same critic adds, this "potential is neither boundless nor structureless: the text delineates the terrain within which meanings may be made and proffers some meanings more vigorously than others."[12] To see just how bounded and structured policeworld is, we would have to compare it to strikingly different versions that have been presented on British television in series such as *Prime Suspect* or (never shown in the United States) *Between the Lines* and *Blind Justice*, which show the politicization and corruption of the criminal justice system as endemic and all-embracing, or in the racially despairing HBO movie *Criminal Justice*.[13] No such meaning is ever broached in the finally complacent universe of policeworld, and it is a very rare text that could possibly be read in such a way.

Though this search for the all-embracing resolution is most noticeable in policeworld, it underlies all genres, even sitcoms. The notoriously "liberal" *Murphy Brown* was an especial repository of this technique. In one much-discussed episode, the technicians at Murphy's station go on strike. Many reporters and writers cross the picket line without any apparent qualms. Tensions are high, especially when the station's owners use managerial personnel to replace the strikers. How will the ideologically cheerful world of sitcom handle this apparently irreconcilable conflict? With no great difficulty, as it turns out. The replacement workers foul up everything they touch, and management is desperate for a solution. Meanwhile, Murphy, who has carefully taken no side beyond her own to cross the picket line, invites representatives of both sides to her house, bakes them a cake, and makes them sit there eating it until they've achieved an agreement. (It's not clear whether subjection to Murphy's culinary skills is the "punishment" they both must undergo.) The agreement's content is never spelled out for those of us in the audience who might have mistakenly thought the issues were serious. The techs go back to work, the managers back to managing, Murphy back to reporting, and everyone is happy: everything is for the best in this best of all possible worlds.

The contemporary series *Judging Amy*, supposedly another icon of liberalism, is actually another masterpiece of this kind of hedging. A 2003 episode in which the father of a seven-year-old gives an impassioned defense—described by Amy as "logical"—of pot-smoking, accompanied by a denunciation of the nation's pill-popping "drug culture" is representative in that her compliment to his reasoning precedes its repudiation by her, her mother, and her young daughter. The liberal show and its liberal protagonist have put forward the position for repealing the antipot laws, for anyone who wants to hear it, but not for long. This is a constant technique of shows about the legal system; thus, on *Family Law*, at roughly the same time, an alcoholic mother who had accidentally killed her child was acquitted of homicide, but her punishment was simply to be condemned by everyone on the show, including her own lawyers. These punishments are usually so nicely balanced that we could almost think there is a balancing act specialist at work somewhere in a secluded Hollywood office. On a Lifetime made-for-TV movie, *The Sleepwalker Killing*, a decent man is acquitted of his mother-in-law's murder on the grounds that the killing was the result of a series of unfortunate coincidences that came about while he was sleepwalking; still, we are told that, three years later, his wife divorced him. On the series *Girls Club* (created by the most famous creator of network shows, David E. Kelley), a truly vicious man who is making miserable the lives of the show's protagonists, and who appears unstoppable, helpfully kills himself. Yes and no; that is television's morality. Undoubtedly, this approach to narrative can raise the hackles of those who cannot abide even a whiff of moral ambiguity.

The kind of issue-oriented narratives that *Judging Amy* and *Family Law* regularly featured are actually rare on commercial television; they are probably most familiar from *The West Wing*, a directly political series (the only one in recent memory) that wears its liberalism on its sleeve but, invariably, finds a point of compromise or understanding of ambiguity by the conclusion of each narrative thread. However, having it both ways is most instantly recognizable in the realm of the "battle of the sexes," which, since the inception of the women's liberation movement over three decades ago, has become the battleground of visual culture most often visited. Here, we can only get a flavor of the way the system works. For instance, in a 1990's episode of *The Single Guy*, Jonathan dated a woman who demolished him in one athletic contest after another. In the midst of a round of golf, she tells him how much she likes him because he's "a great loser." He then proceeded to eke out a victory, at which point she dissolved into imprecatory shrieks and furious sobs and stalked off with an ex-boyfriend. Virtually the same narrative, in a slightly different format, took place at roughly the same time on the African-American-oriented show *In the House*, produced by and starring one of the leading creators of such shows in recent years, Debbie Allen. On this episode, her free-spirited biker sister, a world-traveling photojournalist, travels with the family and two muscular male models to a photo shoot in Mexico. In mid-flight, the pilot deserts the plane (sitcom plots must not be interrogated too closely), and the sister has to crash-land it. Having done so successfully, she faints into the arms of one of the men. Recuperation is not yet done: now she reveals that all her stories about her worldly success are lies designed to prop up her ego because, unlike Debbie Allen, she doesn't have a family to give value to her life. Again and again in visual culture, masculinity is recuperated just when all seems lost; a decade later on an episode of *Monk*, Monk is outmuscled on several occasions by Sharona, only to save her life at the end by throwing a train switch she couldn't budge.

Even if the repressed cannot be definitively prevented from returning, it can be and usually is represented in such a way that we encounter it detached from its truly serious implications. So the one time that television has directly confronted the issue of homelessness, in the 1989 made-for-TV movie *No Place Like Home*, the trials of the carefully conceived nuclear family that was the collective protagonist were caused by a fire; no homeless persons of other than impeccable work ethic need apply. We can have both our compassion and our social self-satisfaction at once, even more so in that the final family reunion is brought about by the heroics of the father. In this sense, having it both ways most prominently means, among other possibilities, that we can have feminism as entertainment without having it as meaningful politics; that remains absent. On *Caroline in the City*, also a 1995 series, Caroline's Wisconsin aunt, visiting her in the big city after recently separating from her husband, played the dual role of both the elderly woman now hungry for sex and the stereotypical relative pressuring the single woman into marriage. Get married and have good sex; the old welded together with the new; everybody wins.

Having it both ways is usually not just a joke. For example, although real priests have been associated with the Internet posting of "hit lists" for abortion providers, the person who does so on the episode of *Law and Order* referred to above is clearly identified as a *defrocked* priest, and the assassin who does his bidding is a weak-willed ex-husband seeking personal vengeance; one of the most seriously political hours in the recent history of commercial television thus turns into a detective story in which finding the characters' true motives takes dramatic precedence over exploring the actual issue. More complexly, the long-running 1980s "feminist" series *Cagney and Lacey* offered a perfect example of how this technique can work over a period of time. From one standpoint, I should not have put scare quotes around the ideological signifier in the previous sentence. Certainly the creators of *Cagney and Lacey* intended it to offer a different kind of representation of women on television, and, for a while, they indeed succeeded. Even after the network (CBS) took them in hand, they were still successful enough that, in my own household, at least, it was the only series we watched regularly and faithfully. On the other hand, we were never unaware of what was also going on in the guise of cultural innovation. Having it both ways meant that to a certain extent we were being had. In what manner becomes clear when we consider the iconography of this series after Meg Foster (known as "the dyke" in TV land) was summarily fired and replaced by Sharon Gless.[14]

Lacey, the family woman played by Tyne Daly in a frumpish mode, was also the liberal feminist. Cagney, the single woman played by Sharon Gless looking and dressing as though she'd just dropped in from the Miss Universe contest next door, was the hard-nosed (though alcoholic) upholder of "law and order" and derider of constitutional rights for accused persons. She was also the victim of gender discrimination and had at times a Jewish boyfriend from the American Civil Liberties Union. There was something for everyone; correlatively, this meant that we could not make consistent sense of these women politically. Familialism was carefully split away from conservatism, "liberated" sexuality from liberalism, and the cross-everything affair between Gless and Steve Macht told us that politics was not important enough to interfere with sex. Obviously sometimes it isn't. But often it is, and this narrative choice made an ideological choice as well. After all, it is not as though Steve Macht and Sharon Gless had an unslakable mutual passion; they were just characters in a contrived commercial fiction. Any viewer who could detect her own political stance amid this deliberate confusion must have wanted to do so very badly. In the end, "feminism" that is attached to an uncritical conception of the law and the police and detached from any critique of the nuclear family is a very particular and limited feminism. Here, to say that the show had it both ways is to say that it both had and did not have its putative feminism.

Quite differently, having it both ways can mean that a particular narrative simply embraces a social contradiction, so that we are satisfied without regard to what side of the contradiction we approach it from. On an episode of the 1990s show *Evening Shade*, a pregnant young girl keeps her baby even though she is a poor, single mother, but at her new boyfriend's urging, she gets a job working in an ice-cream parlor, as well as an offer from him to get her into a local college. At the end of the episode, a dream voice, addressing the audience, explains that "miracles really do happen." We have been told by the show's male protagonist and the boyfriend's father (played by the star, Burt Reynolds) that hard work and desire always pay off, but this was in the context of a parodied pep talk to an incompetent football team. Hard work, miracle, or both: you can take your pick. One way or the other, though, traditional morality will work out after all. (This episode will not register on the punitive radar that the conservative critics throw up to detect "religious programming," but that is exactly where it belongs.) So the young women of sitcoms and family dramas never have abortions, but they never suffer the consequences of not having them either.

In a related sense, a narrative can recuperate traditional views, even bigoted ones, by reversing our initial expectations about the other who is its object, once again having it both ways. TV sitcoms that engage in the mockery of men often turn on this narrative trope, for the essential (almost the only) subject matter of domestic sitcoms is apparent gender-bending that turns out not to be. In the hit sitcom *Home Improvement*, to take an obvious example, the "strong woman" Jill almost always had the last, usually sarcastic, word, but her last word only reemphasized the social superiority of women when they are in their appropriate environment (one could easily forget, watching the show, that she was supposed to be a lawyer). At the same time, Tim Allen was only one among a long line of television husbands who have scored moral points by gently mocking themselves—or, in many cases, beginning with Jackie Gleason, being noticeably overweight while their female counterpart is conventionally glamorous. Such husbands, obese or not, undercut the less gentle mockery of their partners by calling attention, as in *Home Improvement*, to the unmistakable hard edges of the latter. From the standpoint of female viewers, moreover, that may represent "the battle of the sexes" at its best, for, with the militarization and remasculinization of commercial culture in general since 9/11, prime-time television has been returning to the prefeminist world of Stepford wives (e.g., *Desperate Housewives*) and strong, protective men (*24, The District, The Agency*).

As for the recuperation of bigotry, the sitcom *Coach* was a particularly insistent repository of this approach. In one episode, for example, Coach made fun of a male seamster ("ya have ta wonder about a guy who makes dresses for a living"). As Coach was always obviously the buffoon on this sitcom, his homophobia was made to make him look ignorant at the same time that it was, after all, normalized. At the end of the episode, however, it was revealed that the seamster was a "real man," once a general in the British army, and Coach realized his mistake. His bigotry had been disavowed at the same time that its object had been sanitized so that we were given to think that what's wrong with prejudice is not its expression but merely that it's been directed against the wrong persons. This is a very common means of presenting, disavowing, and excusing homophobia on television generally, though in the twenty-first century its occasions have begun to dwindle. The same trope was used, though, in episodes of both the intensely dramatic *Homicide* and the satirical sitcom *The Single Guy* at roughly the same time. Just as with many liberal defenses of accused "Communists" in the McCarthy era, the accusatory stance turns out to be not a violation of moral principle but an empirical error. In addition, as Coach was always made fun of for his working-class demeanor and behavior, this episode managed to put him down not so much for being homophobic but for being, compared to the "general," a lower-class idiot. In the end, all hierarchies return to their normal state.

Today, as homophobia somewhat recedes, hypermasculinity explodes on TV and movie screens against (usually vaguely Arabic) "terrorists" and criminals: there is always an other. Moreover, even a less marginal "other" can always turn out to deserve our hostility. Again, an episode of *Coach* was far from unique in the way it recuperated misogyny. Dragooned into giving an ignominious lecture in a history class by the new female president of his college, Coach made misogynistic fun of her. Initially, as always, he was being made fun of himself. But then we discovered that she had, in fact, slept with him several years earlier and is now angry at him only because he had thereafter sexually rejected her. She had devoted her entire career toward getting herself into a position where she could humiliate him! The independent woman is independent only to secure sexual revenge for a mere slight. Compared to her, the ignorant coach and his dimwitted football players are harmless and perhaps even lovable. Here, intellectual scapegoating, the centerpiece of conventional Americana and the staple of cable's opinion shows, was brought together with misogyny in a mere half hour. This kind of reversal of fortune, in which the narrative recuperates an institution that appears to be disavowed by finally treating it as normal and natural, is a constant on television. This is especially true of gender roles; gender-bending is almost always straightened out in the end. When "Ellen," the second time around (after seasons of frantic disavowal), finally got married, the audience was carefully not shown what exactly the sex roles of the future couple would be, just as Wonder Woman and Xena invariably delivered social work-style homilies, though, in Xena's case, with a feminist twist, and Jennifer Garner on *Alias* is constantly correcting her father's misapprehensions about the requirements of "family." These recuperations of femininity are nothing, moreover, compared to those occasional sitcom episodes—for example, of *Home Improvement*, *Hearts Afire*, *Boy Meets World*—in which a "strong" wife gets her way by offering sex to her husband.

None of this is to say that balance is always achieved, for that is beyond the skills of television's internal censors. But in any event these are only examples, and, though they could be multiplied forever (there are several new ones every week on television), as I emphasized in the previous chapter, examples do not add up to an argument unless it can be explained independently of the examples. The argument is this: from the notion of "balance," there is derived a recurrent master theme. That theme is the absence of recognizable politics (*West Wing* occasionally aside) from the presentation and ultimate disavowal of opposition, dissidence, or disturbance. The television system does not just metaphorically promote alienation from the political world and thoughtful political activism; it does so literally. As Julie D'Acci notes, speaking of *Cagney and Lacey*, this is accomplished by "the displacement of issues arising from uneven social power onto the foundation of individual differences and personal style."[15]

The representative examples I have given of this tactic are mostly oblique, but TV is also quite direct when need be. On an episode of *Empty Nest* that seemed at first to be escaping the carefully guarded boundaries established by *Cagney and Lacey*, feminine caring was opposed to a conception of tough law and order, clearly coded as masculine. A snobbish professional woman hired an ex-convict in an attempt to "rehabilitate" him by molding him to her designs. She of course failed, as he won the battle of wits between them by playing on her liberal guilt. So the cynicism of "law and order" was vindicated and opposition made to seem inauthentic. This kind of disavowal can be carried to astonishing heights. One 1992 episode of *The Fresh Prince of Bel-Air* managed to delegitimize antiwar protest (by turning a judge who was once a radical into a buffoonish, cynical, sexist pig); to turn feminism into an egoistic con game (the Fresh Prince's girlfriend, far from protesting his use of her for his own status purposes, has been doing exactly the same thing to him); and to depoliticize black protest by turning it into consumerism, as the Fresh Prince happily observes that he "can be righteous and stylish at the same time." On *General Hospital* in 1995, a bartender and a businesswoman talked about their sexual relationships exclusively, and their exchange was capped by a scene in which the businesswoman says to a boyfriend who's been talking sympathetically about "sisterhood," "When you started rattling on about the feminine mystique, all I could think of was the male mystique"—at which point they kiss. Not only are the pleasures of sex clearly opposed and superior to the dubious pleasures of feminism, but the latter are put, as inauthentically as possible, in the mouth of a man.

Conversely, opposition can be deauthenticated by depriving it of its real object of concern, as in another episode of *Murphy Brown* in which the idea of liberal tolerance gets extended to short, bald, and fat men, and lawyers and dermatologists—amid many jokes about "political incorrectness"—but never to the people for whom tolerance is often a matter of life or death. This disappearance of genuine political speech can also be structured, in genres as disparate as comedy and action drama, as the disappearance of coherent opposition. Thus women (always excepting Xena, who was safely removed from current affairs) rarely right wrongs against women directly on TV. In the series *Street Justice*, one episode "dealt with" the epidemic of battering, but the narrative's lone battered woman was rescued by the series' two *male* protagonists, with help from their female sidekick (a plotline later duplicated in a Lifetime made-for-TV movie). No one in the course of the story ever mentioned the existence of shelters, which are run by women for women without any participation at all from men. Several years later, a similar narrative development, even more subtle in its implications, could be observed on the series *Hearts Afire* in which Markie Post confronts the sons of a wife-beater but not the man himself. The sons will presumably straighten him out; no women from the battered women's movement need apply.

Several comments need to be made about these examples. First, the denial of politics means also the denial of meaningful political alliances. This is only necessary if we are expecting them: not on *Homicide*, for example, but very definitely on *Cagney and Lacey*, whose producers always had to work to appeal to viewers other than feminists (and at one point even lost their original network).[16] In general, this denial of collaborative politics is such a commonplace on television that it has become almost a reflex to have accused rapists defended by women, accused blacks prosecuted by blacks, and so on. In particular, whenever there is a socially sensitive trial, casting is carefully arranged so that white men are not seen oppressing women or minorities in the role of judge or district attorney (unless, rarely, the idea is to make exactly that point about a particular, unrepresentative judge), an astonishing number of whom therefore turn out to be black, Latino, female, and so forth. (On the short-lived *Kate Brasher*, in 2001, a black male judge presides over a trial of Asian-American defendants.) On the one hand, this could be viewed as a laudable effort to overcome stereotyping or to give minorities roles other than as criminals. But its latent function is quite different in that, on shows such as *Law and Order* and its various spin-offs, lectures about "law and order" are seen being given by the very people who are actually the object of its worst oppressions and discriminations. So we can be sure that, if a woman claiming justifiable homicide is suspected to be misusing the battered woman's defense, she will be prosecuted or judged by a woman. The one outcome that is not to be permitted is the appearance of political solidarity among the victims.[17] This kind of disavowal perhaps reached its height in *Serving in Silence*, a TV-movie about Colonel Marguerite Cammermeyer, the first field-grade officer to be court-martialed for being a lesbian, who in the movie faces a board headed by a black colonel (did anyone watching believe this really happened?), or an episode of the seemingly hard-hitting series *China Beach* in which a working-class black soldier, who has confronted a middle-class black woman with her supposed class privilege, leaves her at the end of the episode with the remark, "Free love, baby, that's what the movement is all about", or above all, in the 1994 TV-movie *Shadow of Obsession*, in which a female judge, mimicking many male judges in both Britain and the United States but not, to my knowledge, a single female judge in real life, frees an accused attacker because his victim had been dressed "provocatively."

Second, these descriptions mostly emphasize gender wars because they comprise the most recognizable form of ideological conflict in the TV world, if not the only one. Just as in policeworld, but more generally, class conflict simply does not exist. Although in the most thorough study of "what America is watching" (see chapter 3, note 8) businessmen are allegedly scapegoated, in fact they are mostly shown as powerful individuals who, for reasons I've noted, have incidentally committed dastardly crimes. They are hardly ever shown as deceivers of consumers or conspirators against the public interest (the made-for-TV film *Barbarians at the Gate* and one or two depictions of pharmaceutical malfeasance about sum up that vision of big business), and they are never, ever shown in what is after all their primary social function as employers, and exploiters, of human labor. And, as for racial conflict, it exists only as an occasional point of reference. Black people are seen either as token good guys in the white ghetto that white Americans call "American society," as figures of familial or clownish fun in their own television fantasy ghetto, or as an anonymous criminal class, but never as a fractured community whose membership in and exclusions from "society," and whose internal fissures as well, are determined by the (not always) informal system of American apartheid. Again, national unity—much too fundamental to be undermined by clueless fat men and sarcastic women—is the touchstone.

Third, the repudiation of politics in general is a central component of the narrative technique of having it both ways: We might think, for instance, of the episode of *Beverly Hills 90210* in which a torturer from a Central American nation who's being attacked by "campus activists" turns out to be a nice guy who resigned for "health problems" in order to save his friend, the college president, embarrassment; or the episode of *Boston Public* in which Jeri Ryan, playing the teacher who is closest to being the show's moral center (by virtue both of her iconographic status outside the series and the back story that places her as a public school teacher within it), responds to a question about teaching creationism, first, by comparing it to astrology (as, presumably, a nonscience) but, second, by back-tracking into a generalized and quite ridiculous defense of the possibilities of nonrational knowledge; or of the famous episode of *L.A. Law*, a series which by virtue of its subject matter necessarily specialized in a kind of liberal/conservative cut and thrust, in which Kuzak successfully defends a murderer by using what opponents of civil liberties call "a technicality": that is, the police failing to present evidence properly. As Kuzak and his client leave the courtroom, the client tries to congratulate Kuzak, who turns away just as the victim's widow steps forward and assassinates the acquitted killer. Justice is served, after all, and no one need have any divisive thoughts about anything. This is the ultimate step in the kind of law-and-order balancing act described above: a plot line so apparently attractive that it was repeated on *Law and Order: Special Victims Unit* almost twenty years later..

Here, however, the system is caught in a dilemma, and we can see why it should be so that, although the Right claims millions of adherents in its one-sided culture war—the Kulturkampf identified by Patrick Buchanan at the 1992 Republic Convention—its distinctive voice can rarely be heard on prime-time network television, just as the critics of "liberal" Hollywood assert. (I prefer "Kulturkampf" to the English "cultural warfare" because, as the humorist Molly Ivins said of Buchanan's speech, "It sounded better in the original German.") The haters of liberalism can appear as marginal characters only, never as the kind of authoritative protagonists who provide direction and ideological closure for viewers. Even when they are protagonists, like the conservative African-American prosecutor in *For the People* (2002), their character must be softened and their positions balanced by some other character or alter ego. The talk show and the politicized sermon are the Right's appropriate métier, for these permit, as fiction does not, the intimidation, bullying, and excoriation of enemies that its ideology requires; and commercial television can permit them to proliferate as a specialized genre outside network prime time because then they do not cost it any potential audience. The rage, the hatred, and the frequent political paranoia of gun culture, virulent homophobia, neo-Nazism, and ultraconservative Christian fundamentalism can indeed be found all over the independent cable channels of the United States, especially outside of the Northeast, as well as on the talk shows which are dominated by the ultra-Right—but not in prime time.

The problem is that, like the producers of hard-core pornography, the storytellers of the Right have only one story to tell: the permutations of hypocrisy and betrayal by the enemy within are to their fantasies what the permutations of intercourse are to hard-core porn. Like pornography, therefore, their narratives, if unalloyed by the kinds of contrary tension that create ambiguity and uncertainty, must soon tire all but the obsessed. When Rush Limbaugh becomes "Rush Limbaugh," though, he cannot be assimilated by mainstream visual culture. Only as that epitome of ideological neutrality, a sportscaster, could he find an alternative television role, and even that did not last long. On fiction television, what role could he possibly play as a substitute fictional hero: a rising young conservative politician who defeats an aging liberal hack? An antiabortion activist who firebombs family planning clinics to prevent the new "Holocaust"? A heroic army chaplain who denounces Islam as the work of the devil? A social scientist who persuades a young mother on welfare that she will become part of "the dependency culture" if she doesn't take care of the home of an abusive ex-boyfriend so he can be inspired to become an entrepreneur? A stubbornly committed scientist who is persecuted for proving that black people have genetically inferior intellects or for teaching creationism instead of evolutionary theory? A teacher who gets a group of schoolchildren to ostracize a victim of AIDS? A post-Rapture resistance leader in an adaptation of the *Left Behind*? Oddly enough, no one seems to have taken these ideas to any recent story conferences. But, then, these would have to be partisan political persons on one side of a self-defined ideological and sometimes violent civil war, and the entire raison d'être of Hollywood's ideological self-presentation is to *avoid* divisive politics at all cost. When, in 1994, Rush Limbaugh did play "Rush Limbaugh" in *Hearts Afire* (a production of that Clintonian and alleged "liberal" Linda Bloodworth-Thomason carried on the same network that carries his talk show), it was as a cuddly and jokey teddy bear with virtually no angry political views at all. Somewhat later, there was a short-lived series, *Ned and Stacey*, in which—to quote *TV Guide's* apt but mis-leading description—a "Left-Wing reporter" managed to get along quite well with a roommate of the opposite sex, who was a self-centered ad agency hot-shot. However "Ned" might have been described (and note the "having it both ways" reversal of the expected politics of gender), Alexander Cockburn he was not. But this is as it must be; the narrative logic that requires taking coun-terideological sentiments and behaviors into account is the same logic that re-quires that they seem as apolitical as possible.

The central point about this depoliticization is that it is easily explicable no matter what theoretical view one takes of cultural causation. To the ex-tent that, as the network spokespersons insist, market considerations do hold sway, divisive politics is to be avoided because it makes a poor mass market commodity. To the lesser extent that, as elite theory claims, manip-ulative communications elites have independent power, they must draw our attention away from any counterideologies, right *or* left, that might question their position; the same is even truer of their bosses, the real power hold-ers according to the class/structural thesis. And, as for the ideological struc-ture of national unity that is Hollywood's ultimate prop, it is maintained only by suppressing serious attention to any political views that might destabilize the historic compromise it is based on, which means virtually any political views at all.

Even religion, the supposed absence of which from the screen is lamented by Michael Medved, Stanley Rothman, and *TV Guide*, under-standably falls afoul of this structural necessity. Unless it is limited to cer-emonial functions (cinematic weddings and funerals have always been re-ligious, usually Catholic), or to fantasies about angels or miracles (*Touched by an Angel, Joan of Arcadia*, e.g.), religion has to be identified as *some particular* religion, and this is dangerous. Religious people who take their own doctrines seriously are not always charitable to those out-side the tent. Millions of Americans (as opposed to the populations of every other advanced industrial society) believe that Satan is real and does his evil works in civil society—works that are not only denounced by their religion but that are practiced by creative artists themselves and by the elite populists, as well. Is Judge Roy Moore a popular hero, as Brent Bozell would have us believe, or a dangerous demagogue? That is a ques-tion that no one in the world of entertainment television wants to have to contemplate.

Viewed in the light of all the considerations identified here, the absence of contemporary right-wing ideology from dominant culture becomes eas-ily understandable. It cannot be assimilated by an institution that aims to speak for and to everyone. Traditional conservatism could, and plenty of that can be found in mass commercial culture. Unless the private enterprise of Hollywood could be replaced with an all-powerful cultural commissar, it is hard to imagine how visual culture could be *more* familialist, or patriotic, or reflexively oriented toward "law and order" or could more complaisantly present America as a "classless" society.

Seen in historical context, then, contemporary conservatism is finally a counterhegemonic project: nothing less than, as Stuart Hall argues, an attempt to change the very meaning of "(liberal) democracy."[18] Regardless of how many people identify themselves as "conservative" in response to public opinion polls, this conservatism's stance is revolutionary, especially in the sphere of culture and ideology. In the United States, its spokespersons have the manifest intention of overthrowing, or at least short-circuiting, what has been for some time the dominant American public philosophy of equal rights and pluralistic incorporation of minorities. (The same people who once opposed civil rights legislation now "support" civil rights but say that racial equality has been attained and that current demands "go too far.") American pluralism has its limits, and Hollywood's does even more so, as one might expect of an institution whose methods of finance, distribution, and management are themselves more monolithic than pluralist. But, at the very least, Hollywood's ideology, like that of the dominant culture it attempts to speak for, is inclusive. Everyone, it is hoped, will be addressed by it and no one deliberately ignored. To ignore or exclude an audience segment is potentially self-destructive; some competitor may pick that segment up. For example, knowing that middle-class black people have money to spend, Hollywood fills the airwaves (relatively speaking) with black families, not to mention judges, police chiefs, and the like. Often these conform to familiar stereotypes, though many of the stereotypes are thought by their expositors to be positive—for example, the dignified black man, the nurturing black woman. But the effort is there, and, even as the United States slides toward a new form of racial apartheid, with white communities locking themselves into fortified apartment complexes and sending their children to newly segregated schools, the effort redoubles, just as (on commercial television) timid glances at same-sex love occur in the midst of nationwide sexual panic.

The right-wing culture of authoritarian populism and patriarchalist theocracy, contrarily, cannot easily be included on its own terms. The ideology of contemporary visual culture would be unproblematic for, say, liberal Republicans of the 1950s. For today's very radical conservatives, Hollywood is Sodom and Gomorrah, and television is a battleground to be captured rather than a medium of entertainment to be enjoyed . Thus, at first glance, it might seem strange to see televangelists denouncing television and asking their constituents to "turn off your sets," surely a self-defeating injunction. But the apparent contradiction disappears once we understand television not as a technology but as a subculture—a system—to which they do not belong. They believe that they are not part of that system; they have a point. But this is because of the *exclusivist* character of their ideology. The Right does not demand simply that Hollywood show America functioning two-parent families or ennobled upholders of law and order, for cinema and especially television are full of these; it demands rather that that be all it shows.

What these critics are really after is an updated version of Soviet theorist Zhdanov's socialist realism, with the allegedly good news of American small town family life substituting for the happy peasants and workers of Stalinist art. The dominant ideology's narrative fictions tell us that violence is a cause rather than an effect, that religion creates unity rather than disorder, and that truly dysfunctional families are rare rather than all too common; they therefore invert reality (as Marx said ideology always does) to some extent. At least, however, they do show us a fairly accurate version of the disintegrating phenomenal world before coming up with a spurious account of its ultimate integration: that is the task of ideology. The Right, though, often seems to want to turn ideology into propaganda—turn the pictures of despair to the wall and paint happy faces on their backs. Its spokespersons seem to think that visual culture should remain immune to, for example, the domestic violence of the world's most gun-crazy nation, not to mention the mass destructiveness of its most imperial one. (With 665,000 guns purchased *legally* in California in one year, 1993, are Bruce Willis and Mel Gibson really fantasies after all?) Nor do they ever criticize the proliferation of "true" police stories, in which constant police brutality, most of it directed against nonwhite young men, is presented without pause or irony as the proper response to life on the mean streets.[19] The continuing legacy of slavery and its offshoot, the horrific and unique, for such a rich nation, poverty and despair, are visible on every street corner as is, in a much different way, the perennial American obsession with fantasies of lustful sex conjoined with a repressive terror in the face of its actualities. These are the reality check of American visual culture. And visual culture in the naturalistic mode, however it evades and however it fantasizes, can only in the end be a report on, or a reworking of, the visible. As we have seen, Hollywood also gives us good news aplenty. If there were a market for more of it, we should surely get it, though one wonders how network television could possibly find room for it. Shall we have a procession of films in which Patriot missiles and "smart bombs" never go astray, female soldiers are never harassed by their male counterparts, there are no symptoms of mass poisoning from the Gulf War, terrorists are foiled weekly by the CIA, and American soldiers are greeted with strewn roses now that Iraq is at peace and Saddam Hussein has been overthrown? Tales about the triumph of simple virtue are hard to come by.

The cultural Right wants what it cannot have: to turn false consciousness into a culture so that the Iraqis who are believed by uninformed persons, under the Bush administration propaganda barrage, to have been involved with Osama Bin Laden or even the attack on the World Trade Center somehow become denizens of the real world. It wants the denunciation of enemies who either don't exist or are too weak and marginal to be a real roadblock to national progress: Satanic cults, "outside agitators," an unending threat of "Arab" terrorists, anti-Christian educators, and predatory perverts. And it wants the sanitizing of what is irrevocably dirty: instructional morality plays for children passed off as entertainment for adults (though children themselves, their imaginations as yet unconstrained by the moralizing of adults, will opt for the kinesthetic delights of cartoon violence every time). Certainly, re-creations of *The Brady Bunch* or *Leave It to Beaver* are imaginable, but, in the age of AIDS and teen pregnancy, how could they be possible? Nor need we be so time bound; if unproblematic families were interesting (or existed), we can be sure that Tolstoy and Dreiser and Lawrence would have written about them. Not "anti-Americanism" but the complexity of life and, thus, of the literary imagination is and always has been the object of the Right's cultural detestation. Lawrence and Dreiser, for example, were as hated in their time as Steve Bochco is today; cultural conservatism always proceeds by comparing "trash" to "classics" that its forebears once attacked just as vigorously.

Still, though, we have to account for the fact that some symbols within the arena of public discourse will be recycled by the forces of ideological dominance while others are left to fend for themselves. Ideological crisis, after all, can be confronted from different political standpoints without the dominant ideology of family, community, and nation being intentionally traduced in any case. To pursue this question further, let us suppose that the right-wing critics of Hollywood may have a point: that Hollywood's products may, on the average now (whatever they were in 1946), be "more liberal" on some issues, such as gender, race, and sexuality, than the attitudes of the populace as a whole. Although there is no real reason to believe this, it is surely not an indefensible observation. And it is even less indefensible to

observe that hard-core conservative views, of the kind that dominate the
talk shows and especially the airwaves, are much less frequently visible in
film or on fiction television. To be sure, all the themes of the new (post-
Reagan) conservatism are available in Hollywood productions of the last
two decades, both on film and television, especially its emphasis on military
(or militaristic) heroism since 9/11. From the standpoint of the conservative
critique, though, these are apparently mere tokens: why is not Hollywood
suffused with the political views of a (supposed) plurality of the American
people? It is true, furthermore, that fiction television has remained dominated by a kind of reflexive liberalism of tolerance even while stereotyping
minorities and certain "aliens" and naturalizing the "urban jungle" from a
policeman's point of view. To the extent that this mild cultural liberalism has
resisted the conservative takeover of political economy and other instru-
ments of ideological indoctrination both, why has it been able to do so?

Let us therefore proceed by asking ourselves an obvious question. Within
the framework of popular narrative as I have described it, the structural requirement of "having it both ways," can we explain the behavior of those who
create popular cultural commodities without resorting to ad hominem accu-
sations of deviant intentionality or without asserting, having previously described Hollywood elites as substantially unrepresentative of the general populace, that "they are not in it just for the money and that "they also seek to
move the audience to their own vision of the good society"?[20] Any answer to
that question must proceed from the recognition that we are analyzing an institution for the production of cultural commodities intended to have a universal appeal and, more and more, even a genuinely universal appeal, not just
limited to their nation of origin. The best way to approach this question is to
ask, how did universal appeal come to entail what it now appears to entail?

What we find over time, in brief summary, is an expansion of the historical American polity marked by ideological continuity amidst partisan strife
and profound social change, as well as by a general ideological crisis that has
to be reflected in visual culture if it is to be reflected anywhere. American
consumer capitalism, relentlessly expansionist since the end of World War
II, remains American consumer capitalism—"the envy of the world"—but,
for some time, a deep sense of unease and insecurity has accompanied it.
American pluralism also remains (uniquely) American pluralism, but the
scope of the social groups that are now included within it as formally equal
partners has also greatly expanded even as—the paradox incarnated so com-
pellingly by policeworld—a divide amounting to a chasm continues to separate some of them from each other. The sense of crisis in the expanding
economy and the apparently unstoppable expansion of the polity together

generate a feeling in many people that they have lost control and also promote the expansion of what can be said and done without sanction by traditional authorities. This is the historical outcome that conservatives decry
from one perspective as "sleaze" and from another as "moral relativism"; but,
right or wrong, there is nothing they can do to reverse it.

At the same time, it is a particular version of this outcome that appears
on commercial television. Cinema and television both developed as mass
production industries, but, perhaps because of its earlier appearance on the
historical stage, cinema incarnated a paradox perfectly apprehended by
Godard in the remark quoted in chapter 1. The mass-produced product of
cinema was, by the time of the earliest silent feature films, intended for the
consumption of masses of consumers *who were also isolated individuals*.
Hollywood, in Hortense Powdermaker's evocative phrase, was a "dream
factory," and dreams cannot possibly be contained within the confines of
public space.[21] Another way of putting this point is that early capitalism's
ideological promise to promote the self-fulfillment of the free individual
remains the promise of Hollywood cinema, however dubious that promise
may have become. In contrast, the later variant of capitalism of which television and the auto industry were together emblematic (as is now computer
technology), and which has today taken over a good part of Hollywood
movie-making as well, has completely freed itself from the antiquated
moorings of Enlightenment individualism. Late capitalist organization aims
not at capturing production opportunities but at capturing consumer markets; the self-fulfillment of the liberated and productive individual, which
was John Stuart Mill's vision as well as Karl Marx's, is replaced by the "happiness" of the nakedly utilitarian consumer. This is happiness as conformity
to a universal role; in this new worldview, any real individuation might lead
to an escape from mass consumption and is, therefore, a threat. Advertising
and public relations were the avant-garde of consumer capitalism, but it
was in American television that the concept of the infinitely manipulable
consumer reached its apotheosis. The peculiar nature of television narratives, their combination of multiple viewpoints and ideologically balanced
trajectories, cannot be understood outside this context.

As Godard suggests, commercial television, as opposed to classical Hollywood cinema, aims at *obliterating individual response*. Evoking dreams
and fantasies lets the creators of movies think that they are contributing to
the conquest of the dull workaday world by creative individualism; but, for
the producers of television, any hint of dream or fantasy is the deadliest
possible threat to the very lifeblood of their medium. Structurally, the centrality of television to mass consumer capitalism (in the United States and,

more and more, everywhere else) is a function of advertising. In contrast, until the fairly recent takeover of Hollywood production by multinational conglomerates that use movies as advertising promotions, movies did not sell anything but themselves.[22] Commercial films are meant to have mass appeal, and, in that sense, the film world is different from, say, the world of oil painting, where value is determined not by popular taste but (in the past) by patrons or (today) by wealthy connoisseurs. But, in principle, every film also exists in its own right as an object of aesthetic consumption. Although some creators of network television programs—Norman Lear, Barbara Corday, Steve Bochco, and Diane English, for example—are incipiently every bit as much creative artists as the best directors and writers of cinema, their structural role is different, for their work exists *only* as conduits for commercial sales. When studios kill a financially unsuccessful movie, it goes right on existing in many forms; when a network kills a series, it's gone.

This means in practice that television popularity is purely competitive. A movie is a success for someone if it recaptures its costs and makes a slight profit. In fact, there are movies that have never been seen except on cable television or video cassette that are financial blockbusters for their producers; and an independent like Hal Hartley can make his mark and even become well known without ever venturing off of Long Island. Network television shows, however, do not exist to be watched at all; *they exist to be watched instead of other television shows*. (So, in January 2004, CBS, to take just one of many examples, rescheduled its number one hit *CSI* to place it opposite NBC's popular new reality show, Donald Trump's *The Apprentice*.) If a program is less popular than another program on at the same time, or even if it is *more* popular with the wrong people—that is, with relatively low-spending people—at that time (e.g., the elderly, African Americans), it may come to be considered a relative failure no matter how popular it is in an absolute sense. This will be seen as the case even if its production costs undercut the competition, for it is networks and not sponsors who pay immediate production costs and then must try to recover them.[23] From this perspective, any potential distraction from immediate reward in the name of idiosyncrasy or nonconformity, no matter how momentary, poses a threat to the sponsors who foot the initial share of the ultimate bills (the rest must be recovered, if at all, from syndication and overseas sales) and, thus, to the producers who depend on the sponsors. To return to where we began, addiction—or at least habituation—is the physical state sought by commercial television.

There are certainly all sorts of group sociological reasons—maleness, whiteness—for the various emphases of dominant visual culture, such as the ubiquity of violence or the nature of afternoon soap operas. But, if we ask what is the primary *social* value that these commodities, taken as a whole (as a metatext), must over all be seen to manifest, the question, seen in the lens of this history, surely answers itself. For those who produce commodities for a mass market, the idea of commodity consumption itself is their fundamental orientation. This is not a matter of selling out, or being philistines, or failing to understand the pleasures of difficult art, but rather of basic assumptions about the meaning of life. And television is quite different from the traditional cultural milieus in this regard. To the editors and hands-on publishers (not today's conglomerate entrepreneurs) who created the modern book-publishing industry, reading books (and, preferably, buying them) was an immense pleasure and therefore a "natural" human activity. Moviemakers often, if not always, have the same kind of bias. They have self-interested reasons for hoping that audiences continue to attend cinemas, and certainly, in recent years, much of moviemaking has degenerated into the business of franchising (*Men in Black I* through *15*), giving the big studios more and more the aspect of television networks. Still, most of the individuals involved actually have some devotion to the art or skill of what they do and intellectually have very little to say to people who don't watch movies. Even the producers and directors of the most worthless action movies, such as Jerry Bruckheimer or Michael Bay, really believe that there is aesthetic value to be found in the purely formal editing techniques that make their films so visually fast-moving and so substantively worthless. Commercial television, however, is oriented not toward the actual content of programs but, exclusively, to their sales value—which is the value of selling products other than aesthetic pleasures. Thus television elites occupationally assume the value of *consumption in general*, whether the goods consumed be artistic or intellectual, or indistinguishable brands of beer. To them, therefore, whatever forwards consumption in general is good, and whatever retards it is bad; they will always favor the production of whatever saleable product they can get away with selling as long as they can get away with selling it—just like the board of directors of, say, Enron. In other words, their primary value is toward a version of market freedom—sell whatever you can to whomever is willing to buy it—that has nothing to do with liberalism of any kind. Or as the chair of Fox Entertainment Group put it, "I just think it's an inexorable conclusion. The audience is never wrong."[24]

The other primary value of dominant visual culture, again following from the historical development outlined above, is an at least lip-service version of *tolerance*, for tolerance is nothing other than the normative aspect of universality: of treating everyone, regardless of race, creed, or color, as a potential consumer. There have always been immense historical pressures against this tendency, of course, and its development is the result of courageous struggles by particular persons, not some automatic version of history. Still, Mill, though premature, was prescient when he remarked in 1859 that "the entire history of social improvement has been a series of transitions, by which one custom or institution after another, from being a supposed primary necessity of social existence, has passed into the rank of an universally stigmatized injustice and tyranny."[25] A perhaps apocryphal story about Samuel Goldwyn, from the 1940s, encapsulates this historical tendency well. Told that there was difficulty with the screenplay for Lillian Hellman's play *The Children's Hour*, as it was about lesbians, Goldwyn is said to have replied, "No problem; we'll make them Americans." This is today's right-wing ideology stood on its head. With the final and official repudiation of state racism in the Civil Rights Act of 1964, all versions of outright discrimination have gradually gone on the defensive and can only be asserted by claiming they are their opposite: "color-blindness," opposition to "special privileges" or "quotas," and so on. As illustrated by the Bush administration's brief in the University of Michigan case, with its careful reference to "quotas" and avoidance of any criticism of "affirmative action" such as might offend minorities, the idea of diversity, in its earlier guise of pluralism, is in the American grain, as commentators from Gunnar Myrdal to Robert Dahl have noted; it is at the heart of what Dahl called "the Creed."[26] That is why Bernard Goldberg, in his allegations of liberal bias at CBS News, could find plausible instances only where issues of race or gender were at stake. Liberal pluralism is exactly the default stance for newsgivers who wish to appeal to the widest audience possible, to be popular without being unprofessionally populist. Even homophobia tends to be repudiated by official conservatism when expressed too vitriolically, let alone violently.

Once liberal tolerance has been institutionalized, the would-be universalist does not know how to treat his opposite number, the closed-minded sectarian, at all and certainly not how to treat him sympathetically. On the BBC, with its near monopoly of British television and a traditionally elitist orientation encouraging its controllers to put "culture" ahead of "democracy," the 1960s series *Till Death Do Us Part* could present without apology and without compromise, in the figure of Alf Garnett, an unmitigated and unrecuperated bigot as its protagonist. Brought to the United States in *All in the Family*, he could only become that figure of fun Archie Bunker, his bigotry recuperated week after week by a dotty wife and an exasperated daughter. How could it have been otherwise?[27]

However, the national consensus (to the extent that there is one) on tolerance breaks down at the point where it meets up with the authoritarian populist or theocratic identification of "evil," of a noncriminal deviation, usually involving sexuality, that yet on some ground or other is alleged to go outside the bounds of what "the people" ought to be expected to tolerate. It is around this gray area of what is to be tolerated that major cultural struggles take place—including today's Kulturkampf. And here then the issue becomes not what is to be *included*—the traditional concern of liberalism—but what is to be *excluded*. Thus the cultural Right does not complain about censorship: there are no stories of soi-disant conservative film or television scripts being abandoned or distorted due to pressure from liberals, Leftists, feminists, or others. It's much more likely to work the other way around, as the authors of the "controversial" teleplay about Ronald Reagan could testify or the victims, some years ago, of Proctor & Gamble's decision to withdraw sponsorship from shows that had "controversial" subjects. There are certainly pressures on Hollywood from the representatives of minority groups working to overcome the results of decades of stereotyping.[28] For example, aside from vaguely Arabic terrorists, or drug-runners from Colombia, it is hard nowadays to make a television episode about gangsters (as opposed to youthful African-American and Hispanic drug addicts) if they have *any* obvious ethnic identity, so that we are occasionally treated to the unbelievable sight of multicultural criminal gangs. (Hollywood still produces films and television programs about Italian gangsters, but they are mostly conceived and directed by Italians themselves, as with, most famously, *The Sopranos*.) These antistereotyping pressures, though, are all directed at the same "liberal Establishment" that the Right harasses. They are not directed at the production of conservative scripts because those are apparently in such short supply. Yet there is no hue and cry to open up Hollywood to conservative writers; the outspoken conservative Lionel Chetwynd (*Hanoi Hilton, Ruby Ridge, Kissinger and Nixon*) has been writing television as well as theatrical movies for thirty years without interruption or complaint from the Left, most recently scripting the hagiographic presentation of George W. Bush in Showtime's *DC 9/11: Time of Crisis*.

At the same time, there is an understandable reason for the relative absence of the Right from Hollywood's (or New York's) creative writing community. Certainly the conspiratorial and even paranoid style of political belief is not in principle incompatible with the production of literary fiction, even great literary fiction, as the example of Louis-Ferdinand Celine attests. Yet the two do seem to be incompatible in contemporary America. Even with the plentiful, potentially productive resources of the televangelical church behind it, the cultural Right settles for Walt Disney reruns and "family television" (yesterday's children's shows) on its own cable channels and has no higher hopes than to create "Christian-friendly" entertainment, whatever that might be, for its own cultural network. Otherwise, it makes no attempt to generate, let alone distribute, the same kind of cultural commodities that Hollywood produces, preferring instead to dominate, as it does, the arena of *talk*—of propaganda. For this version of conservatism, ideological interpellation of a creative kind, even at the low artistic level of ordinary television scripts, is apparently too complex to be of interest. It is quite probable that the Right's desire for cultural control is too feverishly immediate, too total in its ambitions, to lose itself in the delays and devious trajectories, the immersion in disunity only ambiguously recuperated, that characterize the most enjoyable narrative fictions.

Even in policeworld, where the ideology of a united community would seem to be fertile ground for the Right, an unyielding ideological stance comes up against the realities of both history and visual culture. The police, and prosecutors, can only be cultural heroes if they are presented as representatives of the culture rather than as its inquisitors. That representation entails a more or less honest approach to the facts about American violence and occasional acknowledgment, rather than complete dismissal, of known facts about the arbitrariness of the judicial system, its racism, sexism, and so forth. From the standpoint of a liberal viewer, that acknowledgment might well seem begrudging, or half-hearted (as it must always be offset by a restatement of the hard-line view); and stereotyping remains omnipresent in formula narratives no matter how hard cultural producers might be trying to avoid it. But from the point of view of a steadfast contemporary conservative, all efforts to achieve balance and representativeness, to acknowledge imperfections and injustices even in a limited manner, are just more examples of "moral relativism" or "political correctness" at their insidious work: denigrating the good guys and exculpating the evildoers. The Kulturkampf is satisfied only with condemnation; and, from this standpoint, the obsession with balance, the commercial need to appeal to all potential buyers, comes across precisely as the overly tolerant *liberalism* that authoritarians see as their mortal enemy. This is why casual viewers of television might be baffled when they see the dedicated no-politics of programming, and the contentless titillation of commercials, being characterized as "liberal." In the Kulturkampf, anything that is not for me is against me; anything that is not morally correct is the work of the (liberal) devil.

To return, then, to my earlier distinction between ideology and propaganda, in its treatment of television entertainment as liberal propaganda, the right-wing critique of entertainment television betrays a lack of under-standing of how narrative fictions, especially visual narrative fictions, actu-ally work. Even in the absence of network censorship and prescriptions of balance, and even assuming that authors have unmixed motives (as is only rarely the case), there is an immense distance between author and audi-ence, filled by cinematographers, directors, composers, editors, producers, potential distributors, and the psychic ambiguities of audiences themselves. Without a formal voice-over to tell us the exact meaning of what we are seeing—and perhaps even then—it is extremely difficult to pass off propa-ganda, or even firmly rooted and unambiguous ideology, as entertain-ment.[29] All interpretations of what the audience is "really" seeing and accepting, therefore, must pass through a theory of the social order and the psyche that connects them to the formal structure of narrative. There are brilliant examples of such critique available; the right-wing critique con-nects a crude, even ignorant, version of structure (that visual fictions have the structure of an argument) to an equally crude political theory of "elites" versus "the people" and, finally, to an even more crude theory of the audi-ence that, viewing it as an anonymous, manipulable mass, totally elides de-cisive distinctions between genders and social classes.[30] It is the critique, not its subject matter, that deserves the label of "agitprop."

Can we say then in more detail what is the real standpoint of commercial entertainment television as opposed to this demonizing version of it? It is, to begin with, no different from what I have described as the standpoint of information television in chapter 2; it is simply more detailed, more in-flected with aesthetic choices. Ideologically, the deep desire of those per-sons who control television production is always *to be* conventional while seeming to be daring or original. Convention, of course, is a constantly mov-ing target, which even the most traditionalist among us rarely hit directly even while steadfastly aiming at it. Ideologically, the system's response to this unmistakable dilemma is its attempt to be both acceptable *and* norma-tive at the same time: a constant conjuring trick in which audience and in-stitution feed back to each other what each can pretend has originated with the former but is embellished into narrative formulas by the latter.

In practice, then, the overarching themes of commercial television's worldview—national unity, individual competition, the ultimate goodness of the social order, and the sovereignty of commercial television itself—reiterate certain story lines and types of visual presentation over and over again. The world consists of good guys and bad guys, and violence by the good guys is almost always acceptable (on entertainment television, violence by the bad guys, like serial killers or terrorists, tends to be more aesthetically stylish). However, actors (in both senses of the word) engaged in productive social action or social amelioration are suspicious of all collective or cooperative attempts, *other than police work*, to ameliorate social ills. Meaningful group cooperation and action—as by trade unions, grass roots political organizations, and so on—which rarely appears on the news, is even harder to come by in the world of entertainment. It is replaced by the centrality of cynical and competitive individualism, most recently the essence of so-called reality television. (No one seems to have taken notice of the bizarre narrative line of *Survivor*, on which people, who in almost any imaginable circumstance would bend all their efforts toward cooperation, are induced by the programmers to betray each other in every possible way.) Concomitantly, entertainment television, like its junior partners at the news desk, promotes a vision of politics as a spectator sport, insulated from the normal daily life of most people, with an absence of meaningful social class boundaries and class conflict. It also promotes a peculiarly American version of pluralism that combines disdain for the very rich and very intellectual, as well as a self-congratulatory but also very stereotypical ethnic, racial, and sexual egalitarianism, with a narrative frame in which white people, usually male and usually youngish, are taken as the norm for purposes of viewer identification; whereas nonwhites (as well as any easily identified ethnic types), women (not always but often), elderly persons, and those who engage in nonnormative sexual behaviors are readily identifiable as a stereotyped other (even when the stereotype is allegedly beneficent, as on *A Queer Eye for the Straight Guy*). To resolve narrative dilemmas, television always features the utility of a problem-solving approach to a largely beneficent world from which, for most people, any serious anxiety about the meaning and nature of human life (as opposed to fear of street crime or "terrorists") is absent, together with the attribution of undeniable social misery or unmistakable injustice to the activities of a few "rotten apples." Perhaps most notably, the system demonstrates an absolute preference for "good looks" as the linchpin of both female and (especially) male sexual fantasy that trumps all other values: trumps them over and over and over again in, for example, the demeaning treatment of women on reality dating shows, the omnipresence of gender-specific commercials, and the contempt shown by newspersons for independent women such as Judith Steinberg,.[31]

Above all, capping this conglomeration of mostly abstract ideological positions is what we might well call the metaideology of the television system itself: that it is and ought to be, more than any other system, central to our lives. Put simply, television's standpoint is to *be* the world, to replace the world with itself. This is most especially true of the political system, much of which, developed over a century and a half, television has simply eradicated and replaced with its own hierarchy of values, including the cult of celebrities as their true incarnation, its voracious appetite for money, and its unyielding preference for the ad and the sound bite in place of the public address. But the metaideology also helps explain less consequential developments as different as the subordination of the legal system (or at least our expectations of it) to its various fictional and pseudoreal televised versions; the refashioning of therapy into rituals of public humiliation and redemption à la Oprah or Jenny Jones; or the transformation of team sports, not only and most notably professional and collegiate football and basketball, all unrecognizable compared to how they were played forty years ago, but even the more conservative baseball (with the addition of the designated hitter rule in the American League and the destructive prime-timing of postseason games). Sports indeed offers the most instantly recognizable instance of how the television system attempts to absorb the outside world into itself and then justify itself as an integral part of that world, as most obviously by the turning of the Super Bowl (a usually uninteresting game of no interest to the rest of the world) into a rite of national integration and celebration so delicately centered in the nation's (real or alleged) psyche that it can be destroyed by the momentary exposure of a woman's breast.

The metaideology also explains the craze of reality television, in which television replaces more traditional narratives with a direct relationship between the vicarious experience of audiences and the medium itself. Whether functioning as the big casino (*Survivor* and its successors), pimp (*Joe Millionaire*, *The Bachelor*, etc.), creator of social mobility (*America's Next Top Model*, *The Apprentice*), or fairy godmother (*Extreme Makeover*, *The Swan*), the medium becomes the sole referent (displacing literature and cinema) for the ultimately American story of "rags to riches," now transformed from any kind of narrative of ambition or talent into a narrative of audience popularity. Donald Trump's *The Apprentice*, introduced in January 2004, achieved its instant acclaim by representing a refreshing deviation from all this fake "democracy." No popularity votes here; The Man himself makes all the decisions about who wins and who loses. But in the end, of course, he too represents democracy of a paternalistic, authoritarian variety: just what the contemporaneous political regime stands for. This "democratic" narrative is the only narrative the metaideology recognizes as legitimate, and it is a narrative which the audience (once known as "citizens" or "voters") now consumes more avidly and, for millions, with more sense of participation than with the activities of the political system itself; for many, quite likely, this has become the only vote that really counts. Just as the sense of national victimization met television's unparalleled technology of entertainment in the aftermath of 9/11 and the invasion of Iraq, so the ideology of Americanism has met the socially unifying qualities of television-watching in the specific genre of made-for-television reality. Or, as that same Fox executive nicely put it, "I am excited by the notion that this form of programming, over which there has been a lot of hand-wringing, can galvanize a huge audience to come back to network television."[32]

Although television's worldview is neither specifically conservative nor liberal, the ideology and metaideology taken together are not without a vague but sweeping social content. In the end, they compose a worldview of not just conventionality but also complacency. It is complacency on behalf of all those whose view of the social world or life in general could not be described as "alienated" or "extremist"; and it is conventionality from a standpoint that generally accepts the norms of the present and does not devalue them in comparison to some image of the past or some putatively better future and that excludes all varieties of moral ambiguity or irony. By "moral ambiguity," I mean something distinguishable from unhappy endings, such as good people dying young, which occurs, on television, when actors are being written out of the script because they have another job or got tired of their role (e.g., Lesley Hope as Kiefer Sutherland's wife on 24). Rather, moral ambiguity exists when good people turn out to be not so good, or bad people not so bad, and we, the viewers (or more likely, readers), cannot decide which side ought to be taken: there are three sides to every question, and they're all wrong. As for irony, in context it suggests "a discrepancy between what might be expected and what actually occurs." Neither of these is found on commercial television, except for the easy irony of sitcoms.

Put yet more sharply, this is an ideology constructed with the specific end of making the audience feel good about itself: "Morning's at seven/Evening's dew-pearled/God's in his Heaven/All's right with the world." No doubt this characterization is still rather abstract; its substance can be made more concrete, perhaps, by reference, for comparison's sake, to a work of serial narrative fiction, HBO's Six Feet Under, that is not a product of the commercial television system. (With the passage of time, and the flagging of invention that comes to all series over time, the show began to lose its narrative power, but these comments remain largely applicable.) On Six Feet Under, for example, gay men are not an occasion for either comedy or the superficially warm fuzziness that characterizes a commercial show such as Will and Grace. The gay partners on the show are a couple like just about every other it depicts. That is, they have a fraught, often failing, relationship, and they make us think not about the pleasingly democratic possibility of letting the normative familial order be more pluralistic but, rather, about the possibility that *any* familial order encompasses a world of pain. Similarly, the matriarch of the extended family that is the center of the show's world is a grandmother with the desire for independence, sexual drives, and occasional adventures that is usually attributed to much younger (and more glamorous-looking) women. But, once again, where the habituated viewer of commercial television would expect comedy and belly laughs (e.g., *Caroline in the City*), her pains and lusts are played straight, and her warped but real emotional liberation is central to the show's development. This is the ambiguity about life itself that the system, in its need to placate all potential consumers, cannot give us. That "sleaze" and "violence" may disaffect millions from the product is not a contradiction of this purpose, but a failure to achieve a level of real universality; nobody's perfect. And, in any event, the people for whom the conservative culture critics speak feel self-righteous and superior to television—feel, in fact, quite good about themselves. Holy terror, despair, anger at unrecuperated injustice, suspicion that this world is the only world there is and as such is irredeemable and unsalvageable: these are the emotions that the system does not allow to be expressed; it survives as it is only by holding them at bay.

NOTES

1. Althusser, *Lenin and Philosophy, and Other Essays*, trans. Ben Brewster (New York: Monthly Review Press, 1971), 162. By "ideological," I mean the collection of symbols, institutions, and beliefs that together describe the supposed unity of a community or group that is not truly unified; the unity that is, is (partially) spurious: it is an illusion. If the description were of a real rather than illusory unity, we might call it "scientific," or "empirical," or "factual"; "ideological" always implies that we are subjected to an illusion. The New York Yankees, for example, really are a team; the U.S. military may be but is also riven by various concealed divisions; the United States most definitely is not. For an elaboration of this definition, see my "I Have a Philosophy, You Have an Ideology: Is Social Criticism Possible?" in *Massachusetts Review* 32, no. 2 (Summer 1991).

2. It is not, for example, elites of any kind who have made *Lady Chatterley's Lover*, once banned in every English-speaking jurisdiction, Penguin Books' all-time best-selling publication.

3. For an entertaining account of how "balance" on TV is actually achieved, see Tad Friend, "You Can't Say That," *New Yorker*, November 19, 2001, 44–49.

4. See my "Recuperating the Social Order," chapter 4 in *Cracks in the Pedestal: Ideology and Gender in Hollywood* (Amherst: University of Massachusetts Press, 1998).

5. Judith Mayne calls this narrative technique "the door that swings both ways." See her "*L.A. Law* and Prime Time Feminism," *Discourse* 10, no. 2 (1988): 30–47.

6. A rare exception, in February 2000, *NYPD Blue* had a series of episodes that recognized racial disharmony in the police force.

7. Robert Ray, *A Certain Tendency of the Hollywood Cinema, 1930–1980* (Princeton, N.J.: Princeton University Press, 1985). Rick Blaine in *Casablanca* can stand for all these heroes.

8. As Allesandra Stanley reports in the *New York Times* of March 3, 2005, it took years of pressure on the creator and producer of the *Law and Order* franchise before one of its spin-offs (*Law and Order: Trial by Jury*) was finally allowed to cast women in lead roles.

9. On the double consciousness of Hollywood's "feminism," see my *Cracks in the Pedestal*, chapters 8 and 9.

10. For an up-to-date report, see *TV Guide*, November 15, 2003.

11. See Stanley Aronowitz, "Working Class Culture in the Electronic Age," in *Cultural Politics in Contemporary America*, ed. Ian Angus and Sut Jhally, 135–50 (New York: Routledge, 1989).

12. This is the quality known as "polysemy" or "multiplicity of meanings." See John Fiske, *Television Culture* (New York: Routledge, 1989), 15–16.

13. For a detailed discussion of those programs, see Philip Green, "American Television, Crime, and the Risk Society," in *Crime, Risk, and Justice*, ed. Kevin Stenson and Robert R. Sullivan, 216–19 (Portland, Ore.: Willan Publishing, 2001). This essay also appeared under the title "American Television and Consumer Democracy" in *Dissent* (Spring 1998): 49–57.

14. For the history of the show, see Julie D'Acci, *Defining Women: Television and the Case of Cagney and Lacey* (Chapel Hill: University of North Carolina Press, 1994).

15. D'Acci, *Defining Women*, 150.

16. They finally gave up the battle for good in the last episode of the show, a hysterically paranoid two-parter in which Cagney and Lacey were on the run from just about every large corporation, government agency, media conglomerate, and criminal organization in sight. Faithful watchers had no difficulty in decoding this barely concealed commentary on everything that had gone before. But by then the show had already been canceled. Some years later, when Daly and Gless were brought back for two TV-movie appearances as "Cagney" and "Lacey," the premise of that last narrative was wiped out of existence.

17. To see what I mean here, one would have to see the movies *Salt of the Earth* or *Sweet Sweetback's Badasss Song* or *The Question of Silence* or the Australian *Shame* or *Matewan* or *Norma Rae*—or one of a host of low-budget rape-revenge movies in which a band of women hunt down a rapist. See my *Cracks in the Pedestal*, chapter 8.

18. See the essays in his *The Hard Road to Renewal: Thatcherism and the Crisis of the Left* (London: Verso Books, 1988).

19. For a description of these shows, see Robin Andersen, "That's Entertainment: How 'Reality'-Based Crime Shows Market Police Brutality," *Extra!*, May/June 1994, 15–17.

20. Linda S. Lichter, S. Robert Lichter, and Stanley Rothman, "Hollywood and America: The Odd Couple," *Public Opinion* (December/January 1983): 58. This article is really a précis of what was to become their full-length book, *The Media Elite* (Bethesda, Md.: Adler and Adler, 1986). A decade later, in Stephen Powers, David J. Rothman, and Stanley Rothman, *Hollywood's America: Social and Political Themes in Motion Pictures* (Boulder, Colo.: Westview, 1996), 4, this thought was rephrased more strongly as "the desire of elite groups to control images and stories *without necessarily converting them to monetary advantage*" (emphasis added).

21. See Hortense Powdermaker, *Hollywood, the Dream Factory: An Anthropologist Looks at the Movie-Makers* (Boston: Little, Brown, 1950).

22. See Mark Crispin Miller, "How TV-Ad Techniques Are Reshaping the Movies," *Atlantic Monthly*, April 1990, 41–68.

23. See Betsy Sharkey, "The Secret Rules of Ratings," *New York Times*, August 29, 1994, for an explication of the difference between numerical popularity and popularity with appropriate consumers.

24. Quoted in the Business section of the *New York Times*, January 25, 2003.

25. See John Stuart Mill, "Utilitarianism," in *Utilitarianism, On Liberty and Considerations on Representative Government*, Everyman's Library edition (London: J. M. Dent & Sons, 1984), 66.

26. Robert Dahl, *Who Governs?* (New Haven, Conn.: Yale University Press, 1961), chapter 28.

27. At the time *All in the Family* opened, Laura Z. Hobson, author of the most famous American novel about anti-Semitism, *Gentleman's Agreement*, remarked that she would not take the show seriously unless it used the word "kike"; only then—in the aftermath of the Holocaust—would we know that Archie Bunker was for real. It never did; and he never was. In fact, *All in the Family* even elided the word "Nigger," for which Archie substituted the solecism "Nig-Nog."

28. See Linda Holtzman, *Media Messages* (New York: M.E. Sharpe, 2000), for a thorough discussion of television's stereotypes.

29. In television, the most obvious exception would be *West Wing*; yet approaching it with the expectation of a uniquely political (and "liberal") approach that its publicity had aroused in me, I found even that show to be irritatingly uncertain and fussy in its narrative conclusions, always taking one step back if it had taken two steps forward. In cinema, the most famous example of agitprop is *Salt of the Earth*, which does have a voice-over by its female protagonist and was made for propaganda purposes with financing from the trade union whose strike it was heroizing. Even while wanting to call it a "great movie," I would have to concede that a

viewer has to be fairly strongly committed to its point of view going in, in order to enjoy it.

30. To see what intelligent interpretations of visual fictions look like, see Linda Williams, *Hard Core: Power, Pleasure, and the "Frenzy of the Visible"* (Berkeley: University of California Press, 1989); Carol Clover, *Men, Women, and Chain Saws* (Princeton, N.J.: Princeton University Press, 1992); and the essays on "reading television" in Robert C. Allen, ed., *Channels of Discourse, Reassembled*, 2nd ed. (Chapel Hill: University of North Carolina Press, 1992).

31. On this last point, see Diane Clehane, "Does Reality TV Hate Women?" *TV Guide*, Dec. 20, 2003, 46–48. Diane Sawyer's treatment of Steinberg and Dean during the Democratic primary campaign in January 2004 is typical: Interviewing a woman who devotes her time to caring for sick children, Sawyer could only condescendingly chastise her for her lack of clothes sense and time spent on the campaign trail with her husband.

32. See note 24. For an analysis of "reality programming" as our new social "reality" itself, see Mark Andrejevic, *Reality TV: The Work of Being Watched* (Lanham, Md.: Rowman & Littlefield, 2004).

5

DISTRACTIONS:
"SEX" AND "VIOLENCE"

The realities of the American television system, in other words, are that it is ideologically stifling as well as culturally monopolistic. These realities, however, are hardly ever discussed in public. Instead, conventional discussion pursues two phantoms designed to distract attentive citizens from the real business of understanding media. One of these, the lie of liberal domination, we have already discussed. The other, which in the end is difficult to separate from the phantom of "liberalism," is the imaginary specter of "sex and violence" at the heart of visual culture. Here the conservative critique takes a normal aspect of entertainment and builds on it in a tendentious direction. Both of these distractions must be dealt with and understood for what they are before we can get to the crucial issue—for democrats—of monopoly ownership and control.

Regardless of their stated intentions (to "protect children" or to preserve "culture" from "degeneration"), all the conservative attempts to stifle one form of cultural production in favor of another ultimately forward a particular version of political struggle (the Kulturkampf). The political goal of these cultural warriors is to pursue a shift in cultural power without effecting any change in the monopolistic nature of that power. At the moment, to be sure, the Bush administration's desertion of populism for naked corporate oligarchy, as epitomized in the FCC's attempt (discussed in chapter 2) to loosen constraints on cross-ownership, has fostered an alliance in which such opponents of "liberal media" and "sex and violence" as Brent Bozell, Donald Wildmon, and the leadership of the National Rifle Association (NRA) have joined forces with more typical left critics of media monopoly to oppose the relaxation of rules. Preventing the further expansion of Disney or ABC, however, is a far cry from actually democratizing media ownership and attacking television's cultural imperialism. On the ground, the cultural war remains in full force. Its method is the dispersion of propaganda in another form, that of a so-called research methodology that mimics the methods of social science while in fact subordinating them to an ideological agenda. In the absence of a critique that will name it for what it is, this ideologically driven research, in the form of partisan propaganda, comes to dominate the cultural arena and is often treated respectfully by mainstream journalism. Recognition of the ways in which this ideological discourse disguises itself as social science is, thus, a necessary precondition to understanding the symbiotic relationship between the commercial system and the right-wing critics who, posing as its enemies, are actually its shills.

There are four infallible signs of this ideological media discourse; taken together, they illustrate the way in which what looks like analysis can actually be a front for propaganda. The first of these is the deployment of what I have discussed above as the elite domination, or better, elite manipulation, paradigm, albeit in a very different context. We've seen the shortcomings of this paradigm in the field of propaganda—"news" and "information." There it seems to have at least some connection to reality but here, though, none at all. With regard specifically to the creators of visual culture—the world of (ideologically tinged) fictional narratives—this paradigm implausibly suggests that we can be cozened about the nature of the visible world by a handful of cameramen and actors; there has to be an especially strong theory of public opinion formation to make it work, and, in fact, there is. The nature of that theory of public opinion, however, is less revealing about that opinion than it is about the theorists and political activists who propagate it, for the elite manipulation paradigm reveals a fundamental contradiction at the heart of conservatism.

Conservatives pursue power by, among other tactics, deploying the rhetoric of capitalist market freedom in opposition to both liberal reformism and socialism, but they hate the actual results of capitalist market freedom in modern society: a general (though far from complete) democratization of the upper class's penchant for conspicuous consumption; private indulgence of relief from monogamy; profligacy, sexual deviance, substance abuse, and immersion in erotic literature; and so forth. Agreeing with Justice Oliver Wendell Holmes's remark that "Every idea is an incitement," they invert his irony and turn his plea for freedom of speech into a prop for repression. *Our Bodies, Ourselves* will incite lesbianism by showing how to do it; the videos of Annie Sprinkle will incite sadomasochism by graphically depicting it; *Playboy* will incite rape by objectifying women; *The Satanic Verses* will incite blasphemy by mocking Islam; *Murphy Brown* will incite single motherhood by glorifying it. In other words, the elite manipulation paradigm of the Right and its few (perhaps unwitting) feminist collaborators presumes that people are only targets for indoctrination into one or another variety of dogma or perversion; it neither expects nor values independent moral or intellectual behavior.

In this respect, the important thing about ideology—as the spurious reconciliation of opposites—is that the delineation of partially spurious unities requires, above all else, the policing of boundaries: to make certain that those who are with us belong with us and those who are against us can be defined away and excluded as an illegitimate minority. Between the end of the Cold War and the apotheosis of the terrorism threat on 9/11, sexual panic became the most obvious response to the problem of maintaining boundaries in the partially spurious community of Americans—the problem of separating members in good standing from outlaws. Politically, this hysteria has manifested itself in a growing demonization of an alleged underclass as hideously brutish; of its female members—single mothers on welfare—as avatars of rampant, destructive sexuality; and of same-sex lovers or would-be spouses as destroyers of the family. With respect to the commodities of visual culture, though, those topics are too painfully real to be tenable as narrative themes. Instead, boundary maintenance work focuses variously on "pornography" and "obscenity," on the excesses of "radical feminism," on supposed glorifications of criminality and sexual deviance, and on rhetorical defenses of "the family" and other authoritative institutions.

Let us look again, for example, at that critique's most notorious instance: ex–Vice President Quayle's criticism of *Murphy Brown*, a criticism which reflected assumptions about the "Left-leaning" media. Implicit in his attack was the assumption that any apparent endorsement of undesirable social behavior by a mass media role model would potentially lead to an increase in that behavior: the elite manipulation paradigm in a nutshell. As the much more sophisticated Stanley Rothman puts it, writing about movies rather than television, "The new elites enjoy a power . . . until recently unimaginable in scope and size. It is . . . a power . . . (that) could best be characterized as cultural, in the broad sense"; and later, "(O)ur study assumes that motion pictures affect the opinions of many of those who view them to at least some extent over the long haul. . . . There is little evidence that a single film or even group of films significantly affect audiences' views over the long haul. However, if large numbers of motion pictures portray businessmen or Jews as thieves, blacks as violent or stupid, women as weak or clinging, and the military as corrupt, as a matter of course, it is reasonable to believe that such presentations will impact audiences to a significant extent, especially if the other mass media tend to characterize such groups similarly."[1]

Sophisticated or not, the ways in which that passage obscures reality are stunning. To portray the military, the most popular institution in the United States, as corrupt, or businessmen, the most successful individuals in the United States, as thieves, is simply to fly in the face of most people's perceptions; it can accomplish nothing. Worse, in the former case, if a corrupt officer is not in the end counterposed to a basically healthy institution, the studio or network will lose the absolutely essential endorsement of the military for any future filmmaking involving their weapons, troops, etc.; and we might try to imagine what would happen to sponsorship if any TV series regularly suggested that drug companies rip off the public or that the cosmetic industry brainwashes women into unnecessary expenses. Actually, as newspaper business sections become versions of the police blotter, it appears that *real* businessmen are considerably more likely to be "thieves" (and to go unpunished) than the media have ever begun to suggest.

On the other hand, there is truly a culture war in the United States about the proper role of women, and thus to hint, as do so many commercials, sitcoms, daytime talk shows, and family dramas, that women can gain the rewarding financial and sexual attentions of men by being weak or clinging is to take a potentially influential position in that struggle, on behalf of well-established mores and institutions that remain firmly in place after decades of rebellion by millions of women. As for blacks, to portray black men as violent is one of the things at which TV (and Rothman's "other mass media") in its various formats excels, and the social effects of *this* portrayal are comparable to that of portraying Jews as thieves in 1920s Germany. To put "the military" and "blacks" or "Jews" in the same sentence about the ideological effects of mass media is shameless.

In any event, there is no "evidence" to speak of that any "large number of motion pictures" (or, as Rothman and Lichter argue in later books, television) portray businessmen as thieves or the military as corrupt (or single motherhood as desirable) or systematically propagate any images of the kind that agitate the Right. That is, as opposed to the presentation of "news," there is no reason whatsoever to believe that movies (or fictional television) function as propaganda. They are *ideological* narratives and—to repeat—ideological narratives are almost always about latent imaginings of unity and harmony that survive or grow out of an initial threat. *Counterideology*, if unqualified, suggests the existence of disunity and cacophony. For the neoconservative attack on visual culture to be taken seriously, we would have to accept that a "large number" of cultural commodities are counterideological. No one can seriously believe this. If we think, again, of the cultural sphere of "law and order," we can see immediately that most of the threats to the integrity of community that it portrays come from criminals, whose appearance on screen or tape, however, immediately raises the issue of violence that so exercises television's critics. Alternatively, but much more rarely, such threats emanate from the powerful: persons in positions that enable them either to reward *or* to punish the average citizen and who also, in policeworld, have the resources to rearrange clues, suborn witnesses, and generally make murder plots more complex and interesting. This is why "so many" (actually, very few) films and television episodes seem to criticize political leaders and big businessmen: who else is there? Thus, for about a decade beginning in the late 1960s, an occasional made-for-television movie or series episode would be about a plot to take over the government by some right-wing industrialist or military figure (often played by the actor Andrew Duggan). This was Hollywood's studiedly evasive way of hinting at the real politics of the time: secret invasions, White House conspiracies, and the pervasive political influence of big money. That the genre disappeared just as an unmistakable secret and extraconstitutional government surfaced under President Reagan speaks much more to the Hollywood elite's timidity than any conspiratorial agenda. Government is sometimes oppressive; business is often exploitative; representatives of both occasionally lie, cheat, steal, and kill to attain or keep their power. Everyone knows this, and most people know this more than visual culture lets on.

For this reason, the cultural products that criticize "big government" cannot be called either liberal or conservative. Americans generally have always been suspicious of government. Conservatives and liberals are simply suspicious of different kinds of governmental activity (interference with economic activity versus interference with civil liberties, e.g.), and Hollywood is usually canny enough to limit its criticisms to the one category common to both: the resentment of "bureaucracy." As for traditional Left criticisms of the capitalist political economy, they are virtually nonexistent. I cannot think of a single recent telefiction offering a view of "the market" or "government regulation" that the most dedicated libertarian could criticize. Interestingly, the episode of *Murphy Brown* that was made so notorious by Dan Quayle resolutely avoided any mention of the problems created by a free market approach to child care.

What is surprising, in other words, is not that Hollywood produces so many anticapitalist film or television scripts but that it produces virtually none; it is not too surprising, though, because, regardless of who writes or directs them, all Hollywood films and television episodes are produced by capitalists.

The other crucial aspect to the critique of (nonexistent) counterideology is the assumption that some unstated number of images of disunity effectively undermines or subverts existing social harmony. This too is not believable. What is evidently missing from this reasoning is any real theory of precisely what is at stake: the psychology of communication. Are "role models" accepted or rejected, and if the former, why? We note, for example, that seventy years of the most intensive indoctrination and manipulation imaginable had almost no effect on the underlying beliefs and dispositions of the peoples of the Soviet Union. Was this due to communicative ineptitude, the strength of traditional culture, or the blatant lack of fit between what propaganda and ideology described and the lives that Soviet citizens were actually leading? Are American women single mothers because they want to be or because they can't help themselves? When they encounter a positive portrayal or even many positive portrayals of single motherhood, do they read that as an encomium for their own behavior, an accurate portrayal of an equivocal social position, or a joke to be viewed with the utmost cynicism? Does graphic sadism send men out looking for victims, satiate whatever sexual urges some of them might have in that direction, turn them off the whole idea, or simply pass most of them by? The safest answer to all these questions is probably that no one knows for sure, but what is absolutely certain is that a theory which doesn't even recognize the necessity to confront them has nothing to say about "impact." The social science and popular literature of manipulation and indoctrination, instead, concentrates on the allegedly deviant or elitist beliefs of professional journalists and other communicators without bothering to explain how these are not only communicated to, but also impressed upon, the minds of the mass audience.

Thus liberal communications elites are dangerous because they mold the minds of the masses who would otherwise, according to this particular narrative, be good conservatives (or nonviolent men?). The position of these elites, in the Right's version of populist political theory, is therefore undemocratic in that the ideas it espouses from its privileged position are unrepresentative. But, if all of this is true, where did those naive, weakminded, and credulous masses get their original, allegedly more conservative, ideas from in the first place?

Either public opinion in the age of mass media is created by indoctrination and manipulation, or it is not. If it is, as this analysis suggests, then there is no "genuine" or "real" or "authentic" version of popular beliefs; all are or were the outcome of indoctrination or manipulation. What is really happening in this kind of argument is that it is always *the other fellow* who is being manipulated: "You are being brainwashed, but I see through the deception to the truth; you are part of the 'general climate,' but I analyze it." This kind of theorizing is conceptually and morally bankrupt. It proceeds, as Marx put it in a quite different context, "by dividing society into two parts, one of which is superior to society."[2]

Thus the first characteristic of the ideological research agenda is its abject failure to analyze (or even notice) its own premises. Its second characteristic is a tendentious historical narrative that sweeps serious analysis under the rug by replacing it with what is best understood as fantasy thinking. This is what Stephanie Coontz calls "the nostalgia trap": the comparison of contemporary social behaviors to imaginary behaviors in an invented past. There was a Golden Age once; now society is fallen, and in recent times the decline from "the way we never were" has been steady.[3] Right-wing media studies all proceed from some alleged baseline in either the recent or the distant past (preferably Victorian times), when there was allegedly less of whatever social behavior is being targeted and most importantly when the social order itself supposedly was a more moral and stable place. Of course, the fantasy, being a fantasy, is historically mutable; it can be located anywhere (or, perhaps, anywhen).

If projected backward far enough in time, the nostalgia trap supports a call for a return to what is usually called traditional morality. Traditional morality in the United States included slavery and the violent disciplining of free blacks that followed it; the suppression (also often violent) of women's individuality, civil rights, and freedom of expression; the brutal treatment of the children of the poor; religious, ethnic, and racial intolerance; and so forth. These were not accidental accretions to "traditional morality," but its very essence, as the simple rule of traditional morality was everyone in her or his place. If, on the other hand, the fantasy is treated more realistically by, say, removing it only as far as the 1950s, it requires that anyone old enough to have lived in that period have amnesia and, therefore, fail to recall the hysteria about mass media, sex and violence, "rock and roll," comic books, movies, and the other seductions of innocent children that were supposedly rife during that period. In either case, explicitly or implicitly, this decline in social morality is traced, in part, to the increase in the targeted behavior, which is practiced by the villains of the story: the scapegoats.

Consequently, a third sign of the ideological research agenda is *scapegoating*. Instead of a pluralistic appreciation of differences, this agenda, like the attack on liberals, is based on a moralistic division of the social order into "the people" and their enemies. There is a righteous community of the concerned to which right-wing media investigators and a vaguely defined audience—is it a "popular" audience?—belong; it is frustrated by an alien or ill-willed minority. Right-wing media studies all carefully divide the social order into "us" and "them." "Us" is everyone who is properly concerned with the ills diagnosed by the critics; "them," like Jews in Weimar Germany, or "criminals" in NRA propaganda, are the outsiders solely responsible for social ills: the scapegoats. Sometimes this move results in sheer bigotry. This is evident in a contemporaneous report issued on March 30, 2000, "What a Difference a Decade Makes," from L. Brent Bozell III's "Parents Television Council," a report that highlights "declining standards" as manifested in "sexual subcategories: the more bizarre the better." Chief of these, other than oral sex, turns out to be homosexuality: "The largest increase was in homosexual references; for every one in '89 there were 24.1 in '99." The report, though, gives only two examples of "declining standards" at work: "A cop asks a man if another man had been 'your lover.' The man answers, 'He was my husband.'" "A closeted action-movie star tells a film executive that he wants to be open about his sexual orientation: 'My life is a living hell. The shame, the hiding. I want to be able to walk down the street with my man and say to the world . . . 'This is the man that I share my bed with.'" These are the only two serious "references"; the rest are bad sitcom jokes of the kind that, ever since *I Love Lucy*, have tried desperately to keep up with the real sexual milieu that keeps spiraling out of control around them and us.

One might think that there could not be a better message for children about adulthood than these two variations on the same theme: that true love supersedes convention and that we ought not to be ashamed of our loving selves. With suitable amendment for differing attitudes toward emotional expression, this is one of the major statements of the classical novel from *Pamela* onward. We might easily argue, in fact, that one good measure of the progress of "civilization" is the spreading of the protective umbrella of "true love" over more and more of its genuine protagonists. But then the real message of the Bozell report is that no serious thought such as this one should ever cross the minds of "our children." In the recurring litany of those cultural conservatives who always long for the old days when men were men, women were excluded from public life, people of color were brutally oppressed, and the lower orders knew their place, the Bozell report complains that "Broadcast television no longer serves a broad public interest," as it did, presumably, when it could be described by Newton Minow as "a vast wasteland," Elvis Presley could be seen only from the waist up, and none of the black musicians who had taught him what he knew could be seen at all. But the key to this notion of the public interest comes in the following explanation: "Concern over raunchy content airing in time slots traditionally set aside for family programming was one of the factors that led to the formation of the Parents Television Council in 1995." We can only understand the real significance of this sentence by transposing it into some of its possible alternatives: for example, "Concern over the dominance of television in time periods that could be set aside for reading, schoolwork, artistic creation, or family discussions, led to the formation of. . ." Or perhaps, "Concern over the distorted view of the world that lowest-common-denominator programming-for-profit breeds in the psyches of habitual televiewers led to the formation of. . ." What, indeed? Or better yet, "Concern over the fact that a handful of giant corporations determine the presentation of those images that monopolize the visual world of our children" led to the formation of Parents for the Democratic Organization of Mass Media. Instead, the scapegoating tactic insures that "them" is seen not as the monopolistic sector of corporate capital that actually controls and censors virtually all mass media outlets but rather as "media elites" behind whom stand "liberals" or liberalism. The actual press releases of such outfits as the Center for Media Public Affairs, with their nutty empiricism and their risible counting of f-words and s-words, pretend to stand on a "social science" underpinning of theoretical "studies," but these are conducted by the same people who do the media analysis. Ask Lichter and Lichter who is responsible for the allegedly sorry state of current media affairs, and they can refer you to the Center's own publications: publications that pull no punches about the Hollywood scapegoat.

The last and most crucial sign of the ideological discourse, therefore, is that it is supported by *pseudoscience* or junk science: the one-sided use of research hypotheses to isolate a targeted variable rather than to test alternative explanations. Generally, it is important for observers of commercial mass culture to understand several things about such "research." First, whenever a particular behavioral stimulus is isolated for study, and the target group's responses are neither compared to those of a control group nor observed in the presence of other, potentially competing stimuli, then it will invariably be found to have an effect on them. Moreover, not only do we in fact have zero knowledge as to how broad cultural phenomena impinge on individuals, we don't even have real knowledge of what we call a "culture." That word is just a metaphor, the handy shorthand for a set of observations strung together to make some (but not very much) sense. Given the metaphorical nature of culture, cause-and-effect is a very poorly chosen schema for studying it, being derived as it is from a field of observation and study that is not metaphorical but has an observable material reality. The metaphor of an organic whole (in a very weak sense) is much more sensibly related to the metaphor of culture, and, while it suggests interrelationships between different arenas of behavior, it precludes calling one the cause of another. Above all, scientists—even social scientists—proceed by developing a hypothesis as to how some measurable or at least observable state of affairs is being brought about by an antecedent cause or causes or how it fits into a structure of relationships in a particular way. They then attempt to test the hypothetical relationship, most importantly by eliminating or failing to eliminate competing possible explanations of it. Pseudoscientists, contrarily, exhibit no interest in the material world—for social scientists, the world of life expectancies, incomes, educations, and the like. Nor do they test their own causal assumptions against possible alternatives. Instead, in the social realm, they issue moralistic fiats that are neither measurable nor observable; they then purport to show or at least suggest cause and effect by demonstrating that whatever they're studying has risen while "morality" has gone down.

In addition to its easy assumption of relationships that do not necessarily exist, the ideological research agenda also crucially depends on arbitrary operational distinctions, as between depictions of authorized and unauthorized violence or between normative and nonnormative versions of sexuality, as well as on a notion that avant-garde or outlaw productions are culturally and morally threatening compared to whatever is socially normative. This also is totally arbitrary and tendentious. Any serious observer (say, Alexis de Tocqueville, John Stuart Mill, or Max Weber) would emphasize the possible risks of conventionality in comparison to the risks of creativity; other aesthetic or moral philosophers would assert the value of what they would call authenticity versus inauthenticity. This line of serious analysis simply disappears to be replaced by what the sociologist C. Wright Mills called "common sense empiricism" that is "filled with assumptions and stereotypes of one or another society," as though taking one's own prejudices for granted could somehow give them objective substance.[4]

A democratic culture, however, should be reflective not of majority attitudes—a charitable description of authoritarian populism, which demands not just reflection but strong identity—but of the social diversity and the genuine social conflicts that characterize all contemporary societies, not least the United States. Oligopoly—the most accurate description of the economy of mass media—makes this impossible, for (as discussed earlier) it can only produce conformity and uniformity. This condition should lead democrats to search for ways to break the stranglehold of both conglomerate ownerships and giant advertisers on media, but the conservatives instead put forward intellectually dishonest arguments about the allegedly elitist control of production—dishonest in that artistic skill like any other must always be the preserve of an elite; and this kind of scapegoating distracts from the real issues of power and accountability.

If we look at some concrete products of the right-wing propaganda machine, we can see how this culture war operates on the ground. The Center for Media and Public Affairs, now almost two decades old, is perhaps the most prominent purveyor of ideology in the name of research. Though it is funded by the John M. Olin Foundation and the Sarah Scaife Foundation, the most important and powerful explicitly right-wing foundations, and came into being with accolades from conservatives such as Pat Buchanan and President Ronald Reagan, it is allegedly "nonprofit" and "nonpartisan" as compared with such compeers as Reed Irvine's Accuracy in Media or L. Brent Bozell's Media Research Center. It exists, however, solely to demonstrate a so-called "liberal bias" in the mass media of communication. That, at least, is its observable purpose. Its real purpose, however, is to be an instrument of cultural warfare—to help secure institutional control by conservative ideologues on behalf of conservative ideology. It does this not simply by demonstrating liberal bias in the media but by implicitly associating this "liberalism" with a supposed predilection for gratuitous sex, violence, obscenity, and general disdain for the mass audience. The liberal as mind-poisoner: what could be more classic?[5] Does the media's supposed liberalism make any contribution to the public good such as, say, less sympathy for various forms of intolerance than might otherwise be the case, or a not completely uncritical view of power and authority? The Center is not interested in such questions, but only in condemnation. And, above all, as all this is wrapped in the mantle of "objective analysis," the propaganda machine has become a regular source for the world of so-called serious journalism, such as the *New York Times*. In a perfect case study of how "consent" is manufactured, ideology enters the world of opinion manipulation in the guise of objective analysis and, if successful, eventually comes to be the common sense of busy and underinformed reporters who have little knowledge of the world of idea creation and even less of ideas themselves.

A recent intervention by the Center illustrates this process perfectly. As part of an "ongoing study of sex, sleaze and violence in popular entertainment," the Center in 2000 released three studies on "Sexual Imagery in Popular Entertainment," "Violence in Popular Culture," and "Profanity in Popular Entertainment," about the last of which they note that "foul language is where the action is in the popular culture's ongoing descent toward

the lowest common denominator." Here all the characteristics of the research agenda—the nostalgia trap, scapegoating, and junk science—are
combined. To begin with, the adjective "popular" goes completely uninter-
rogated, and yet almost everything follows from the definition one chooses
for it. Does "popular" mean how people in the mass behave, so that the "ongoing descent" is an indictment of the masses as slobs? Or does it contrarily refer to the mediated world of *commercially* created culture; and, if so,
does "popular" then refer to all for-profit cultural productions or only to
those that are successful in the marketplace of communications? One can
presume, I think, that the authors' refusal to address these questions is deliberate rather than accidental, for they can then indict whomever they
choose without having to address the question of whom, exactly, they are in-
dicting or, especially, what position on the spectrum of social knowledge
they themselves represent. After all, if the people who do "media research"
are not "knowledge elites," then who is?

But rather then ask who "the people" are and what they think, the re-
searchers, whenever they might have to confront the issue of exactly why
they are engaged in the apparently pointless enterprise of counting up
scenes of bloodshed, uses of the word "fuck," flashes of female breasts, and
the like, retreat instantly to the pretense that they are only doing the will of
"the majority," as evidenced by public opinion polls that show disaffection
with the system's content and declining audience size. Here, though, they
offer a proposition incompatible with their other basic proposition about
the effects of "repeated portrayals" of businessmen as thieves, and so on.
Both these propositions cannot be true at once: either audiences are really
disaffected and thus haven't been taken in by any programming or they've
been taken in, but then why should they be dissatisfied? Ignoring this in-
compatibility, though, let's assume that audience cynicism is what the critics really believe to be the case. In that event, I have already addressed the
problem of declining TV audiences; they demonstrate nothing but commercial television's loss of its monopoly on visual culture. As for polls themselves, they are actually evidence of nothing at all, as the Center's studies
quote only those that asked the question its authors are interested in and
gave the answer they were hoping for; how many other polls might have
given opposite or different results we will never know. On the other hand,
that doesn't matter either because if the results were truly indicative of anything, the polls would nonetheless be pointless. If 80 percent of viewers really think there's too much violent programming (as claimed by the only poll
the studies actually reference), then the most watched programs would be
relatively nonviolent (and sexually or asexually conventional, as well), the

most violent ones would quickly go off the air, and no one would have to worry about TV violence. As it is, sponsors often censor programs that they think have gone too far; when this doesn't happen, we can safely assume that the audience size for their programs and their likely future in syndication and foreign sales, as discounted by the costs of producing a particular program compared to the costs of buying time on it, is satisfactory to the people for whom commercial television is really created.

In the same way, to the extent that wrestling and crime shows and action/adventure series and violent made-for-TV movies are "popular" (or relatively inexpensive to produce, as in the first and last-named cases), we can safely conclude that, as far as audiences are concerned, the polls are just one among endless examples of "don't do what I do, do as I say." As D. H. Lawrence wrote in another context, we should trust not the teller but the tale. The tale is straightforward: audiences watch violence and sex. As for the teller, who comes to life only when being interviewed by pollsters, what is astonishing about the 80 percent figure is not that it's so high but that it's so *low*. Who could possibly reply negatively to the leading question, "Do you think there's too much violence on TV" (or any of its variants)–especially as, in answering the question, most people are probably thinking, is there too much violence *for children*? On the questions you ask depend the answers you get.

This is just one example of what goes wrong when research consists of asking a specific question intended to produce a specific answer, instead of fully testing a hypothesis.[6] There's always "too much" of anything, anywhere, that's known to be "bad" for us; if we asked whether there's "too much" criticism of the president on the broadband, we'd probably get a similar result, although, as of this writing, there's hardly any. As though recognizing how weak public opinion polling is as evidence of real behavior (could they really only find *one* poll that gives the right answer?), the report at other times resorts to the evasive language of "public concern" over the extent of "sleazy sex" or "profanity" on TV. But of course there's "public concern"; there ought to be "public concern" about *everything* related to commercial culture precisely because it is commercial and, thus, never ascends from the status of being in production to that of being in distribution—the only status that counts—with the good of anyone but its sponsors in mind. If there is anything about the system that is not a matter of "public concern," then public opinion is a poor guide to reality.

But then it isn't quite their guide either. Among television shows (as opposed to feature films shown on TV), HBO's "critically acclaimed" *Oz* and *The Sopranos* lead the pack in "hard-core" profanity. These programs are not from the commercial system at all but are available only to subscribers who pay for the privilege of viewing them. Are these people who pay for the pleasures of profanity making a mistake? Is there a theory of false consciousness at work here? Do these programs, which aren't even part of the basic commercial system and are seen by far fewer people, represent the threatened "descent?" Or is that the politically serious movie *Primary Colors*, which, after having been shown on TV, led in all categories of "profanity"? If these cultural commodities are actually "sleazy," if the critical acclamation the Center studies acknowledge (or emphasize) is leading the descent rather than attempting to counteract it, we'll find no hint of that either way from the Center's reporters. The framework of the report is one giant value judgment about "the antisocial connotations of entertainment that uses epithets and vulgar expressions to legitimize incivility, boorishness and mutual disrespect"; but only when an entertainment is what they consider to be safely beyond the pale (say, the movie *Something about Mary*, which actually also has its critical defenders) will the Lichters venture to link it directly to their conclusion.

Furthermore, though the studies criticize the media for "antisocial" behavior, they never bother to ask serious questions about the nature of fictional narratives and their relationship to social reality—whatever that may be. Perhaps, for example, criminals and politicians actually use *more* profanity than those shows allow; and perhaps such popular entertainments tend to "legitimize" incivility more, the less realistic they are about the profanity and violence of their subjects. Thus, the studies, having turned up *NYPD Blue* languishing in eighth place among broadcast TV series, are unable to confront the possibility that the most "antisocial" aspect of TV's ever-popular cop shows is how terribly they *lie* about the language of men in blue, concealing rather than revealing the police force's obsessive recourse to obscenity, scatology, sexual insult, homophobia, and racial bigotry. Perhaps, conversely, some resort to profanity conveys deep truths about the social order. The authors of the studies, for example, are righteously disturbed by the first broadcast appearance (in 1999) of the phrase "Shit happens" (or, as they helpfully put it, "S— happens"). It does not occur to them that this useful phrase, to be found on the lips of men and women from all walks of American life, perfectly encapsulates the contemporary attitude of resignation in the face of a world manifestly out of most people's efforts at control. There are arguments for, contrastingly, a fairy-tale approach to telling stories, just as there are arguments for a serious realism that is genuinely faithful to its subject matter according to the temper of its times (e.g., to criticize Charlotte Brontë for not writing about sex à la Nora Roberts would be anachronistic, to put it mildly). But there are no arguments except artistic slackness, or a deliberate intention to deceive, for using apparently realistic surfaces to cloak a whitewashing of social relations or community mores. Perhaps we should cheer anytime reality breaks through.

The Center's study on violence is similarly distorted to a point that calls its intentions into question. "Violence that is a routine part of contact sports" was excluded, but professional wrestling, the most routinely violent of all contact sports, was grimly included, lending added weight to every measurement of TV violence the study could manage to create. Also excluded were "verbal threats or emotional abuse that did not rely on physical force," though again for no plausible reason. Every protocol about battering firmly states the contrary, and any experienced woman could give horrific examples to justify that inclusion, as could the victims of bullies everywhere. The commentators also prefer that "serious violence" show "direct harmful results" and generate "moral judgments"; they also "give the devil his due" by awarding respect to works of popular culture with "artistic value," such as the movies *Saving Private Ryan* and *Schindler's List*. All the studies are full of table after table, meaningless percentages and measurements laid on top of each other, that treat these arbitrary inclusions and exclusions as though they represent some material reality. This gives the whole finally an indelible air of common sense empiricism that, in another context, Mills called "crackpot."

But why all these judgments? If consequences are what interest us—and why else endlessly troll the screens and broadbands for scenes of degradation—isn't the portrayal of legitimated violence in real-life sport or real-life war or police work just as likely (or more likely) as make-believe violence in fantasized fictions to warp the attitudes of we the audience? A dozen years ago, the late Neil Postman pointed out that newspapers and television news probably have a much greater impact on children's vision of the world as a violent place than do cartoons and even nighttime television programs.[7] As it happens, the Center for Media and Public Affairs lumped "together violence in news coverage with violence in entertainment programming" in one of its reports of an increase in television violence.[8] But, like good propagandists everywhere, it did not ask the most pressing question, whether news producers had changed their coverage criteria (thus perhaps deserving the implicit criticism of the study) or whether there really had been more domestic and worldwide violence of the kind TV news always covers. Of course, to raise such a question would be to suggest that perhaps some kinds of violence could profitably be covered less as compared with others, not to mention making it less possible to find scapegoats in the media. In the end, the study really has nothing to say other than that violence is bad—except when it isn't. And portrayals of violence are dangerous—except when they aren't. But, while saying nothing, it has managed to imply that something terribly important is being said and that it is being said about matters that are truly an object of our "concern."

The observations of the Center's studies are as totally arbitrary as its definitions. For example, if an increase in the portrayal of violence is truly pernicious, truly desensitizing, then it ought to result in an increase in real violence. Generally speaking, though, historically "the correlation between violent crime rates and intense entertainment violence is the opposite of what the usual hypotheses would suggest." And as one might expect, "The entertainment industry's bloodiest peaks come *after* real crime has come to dominate the news media and national conversation." In fact, there is not the faintest reason to believe that television has increased the level of violence in American society and some reason to disbelieve it. In the television age, violent crime rates have gone up and have gone down and have not been noticeably higher than they ever were. So, during the 1990s in the United States, the portrayal of acts of violence apparently increased (if we are to believe the Center) as their actual commission diminished.[9] The same phenomenon had appeared in the 1930s, when actual crime diminished as its portrayal in movies and newspapers peaked. Moreover, the available data suggest that, long before the invention of visual mass media, in the 1890s for example, violent crime rates were considerably higher than they are now. Conversely, modern crime rates began their secular increase in the 1960s, a period during which television violence was minimal compared to its appearance in the 1990s. All these facts appear to contradict, or demolish, the assumption upon which the anti-TV propaganda is based, and their existence cries out for greater complexity and imaginativeness in our attempts to understand our own society and the nature of individual consciousness-formation. Perhaps we receive these images as fantasies, and, thus, they have a different salience than the literal-minded think. In truth, we really have no explanation of the data. Perhaps the extent of violence is wholly demographic and economic—how many footloose young men are there at any time? Perhaps the apparent bellicosity or lack thereof on the part of political leaders is the key; perhaps President Clinton's unease about resorting to acts of military intervention during the 1990s was socially valuable. But the propagandists peddle only ideological simple-mindedness.

For that matter, why exactly does the Center for Media Affairs or any of the other right-wing propaganda agencies issue a study on profanity, sex, and violence? Why not one on homophobia, racism, and ethnic stereotyping? On the growth or decline of tolerance for the "other"? On pluralism or exclusiveness in social representations? Margaret Thatcher, when she was Minister for Education in a conservative government three decades ago, understood the possibilities more fully: she banned the importation of *Sesame Street* by the BBC on the grounds, among others, that it overemphasized social pluralism and diversity (was "too American"). Turning her emphasis around, we might ask if, for example, taking the cause-and-effect model seriously, a violent but multiracial children's cartoon might be healthier for child development than a whites-only less violent program or a nonviolent cartoon with homophobic stereotyping?

The chief excuse for the emphasis on ill-defined violence is that there are studies purporting to show the pernicious effects on children of televisual "sex and violence." Here, too, it has to be emphasized that junk science, with its dedication to the "study" of isolated abstractions that have no materiality except the researcher's obsession with them or ability to use them politically, never really studies the potential "effects" of television on children. As all serious social scientists know, being studied while you watch TV is a totally different experience from just watching it; the latter experience is much more likely to produce couch potatoes than rapists or killers. There are also reports in which young people acknowledge an increased propensity to violence or hurtful sex because of their television watching, but these too clearly offer versions of the Twinkie Defense to be taken seriously. It's a very naive young man who doesn't instantly realize the wonderful opportunity afforded by such investigations: "Look, ma, it's not my fault, the TV made me do it!"[10]

The unfortunate truth is that some children are angrier or more aggressive —whatever is actually being measured—than others. Their predisposition to act out these feelings is strengthened by whatever cultural products, mores, or patterns are available for them to seize on. If there were no television to fill this role, something else would, as has always been the case: *for there is no possibility that, in a violent society, art and commerce will not reflect the omnipresence of violence.* Focusing on one product or another simply enables us to blind ourselves to the reality of the way we are. Television is a symptom, not a disease. Like all symptoms, it can have its own negative effects, like a fever that rages out of control if not treated properly. But reducing the fever merely allows us to address the underlying problems; it doesn't eliminate them.

"Disease" and "symptom," of course, are only metaphors, though conservatives often use them as though they represent a reality, just as antidemocrats have always done. The body politic is neither sick nor healthy; it just is what it is, and we have no idea what makes it so—only guesses. To turn away from misleading metaphors and ineffable causes, then, the material problem posed by the television system is that, because of its (apparent) virtual cost-lessness, it became and remains the built-in child-sitter of choice for parents everywhere (except when replaced by computer games that are hardly violence-free in their own right). It is also, and at the same time, the primary means of communication for the producers of consumer goods. In this re-spect, it may very well not be good for character development for young chil-dren to watch *any* kind of television at all. Why aren't they reading instead, or going bowling, or doing homework? The critics constantly complain that "family hour" programs (i.e., from eight to nine p.m.) are being contami-nated with "adult-type" content. But why should *families* be watching TV to-gether? Surely they are not being manipulated into excessive television watching by devious or subversive liberals. On the contrary, adults watch, and children watch, because the consumption of commercial television is not only part of, but the essential core of, the American model of consumer capitalism. As I argued in chapter 4, the essence of commercial television's approach to the world is *to become the world; watching is being.*

Perhaps, in truth, what the ideologues of the culture wars call "the sleaze factor" in American society is simply consumer capitalism in its pure, un-regulated form, for which children's television is then the very best training. These obvious possibilities are never considered by the sex and violence doomsayers, whose intention is not to raise serious issues but to distract us from them; to criticize their ideological enemies, but never to bite the hand that feeds them. As they want to clean up television, it is clear that they want us, whoever we are, to go on watching it—perhaps even more than we already do—as one of the criticisms of the networks is that their audience share has gone down and, accordingly, they must not be giving people what they want. Thus, they cannot ask what would seem to be the most obvious question in this day and age: what factors were responsible for the unparal-leled militarization of American policies abroad and in Americans' attitudes toward the rest of the world, following 9/11? This would seem to be a con-siderably more important issue than comparative crime rates and their mo-ment by moment fluctuations, but these critics not only have shown no in-terest in this question, they don't even recognize it *as* a question. The TV images of the attack and its aftermath seem to have increased feelings of na-tional unity, but that was turned into violent militancy by the opportunistic Bush administration, not by any spontaneous groundswell of public feeling. Public opinion for preemptive war had to be prepped and cajoled by a bar-rage of lies emanating from the administration, a campaign that was en-dorsed and undergirded by a propaganda campaign emanating chiefly from opinion commentators on cable news programs. Did televisual violence, or any other aspect of the system's performance, pave the way for this distortion of consciousness, a distortion that in the summer of 2003 resulted in more than one-third of the respondents in a nationwide public opinion poll either believing that, or not sure whether, Iraq had used weapons of mass destruction during the American invasion? Here we have the substitution, by millions of adult persons presumably in their right minds, of fantasy for reality. Were ninja turtles, violent cats and mice, and cartoon superheroes responsible for this mass breakdown in rational thinking? Or, rather, was the causal factor the availability of a nationwide communications system at the fingertips of demagogic leaders? And what of the leaders themselves? As the destructive occupation of Iraq wore on, one observer noted that "much of what comes out of the mouths of Pentagon officials these days is utterly undisciplined and deeply unprofessional. From comments that we're fighting a holy war against the evils of Islam to the presidential invitation to 'bring 'em on,' there is a kind of giddy, hopped-up-video-game quality to the way our top brass discusses things."[11] Who has watched "too much violence?"

The same problems arise when "sex" rather than "violence" is the issue. This is true even of the more careful Center, whose study on "Sexual Imagery" (packaged with the studies on violence and profanity) is not limited to the inflammatory categories of "family" and "children" and is not bigoted in the mode of the Parents Television Council. The study begins once again with a reference to "public concern" and continues with the claim that it is based on a "scene-by-scene scientific content analysis of 248 broadcast and cable television episodes . . . the 50 highest-rated made-for-TV movies . . . 50 top-grossing movies . . . and 495 airings of 189 different music videos." It ends with its authors portentously intoning, "Whether this profusion of sexual fantasies is also free of consequences for American society is something we will soon find out."

Here again, the study is a classic case of how hidden presumptions turn junk science into what passes for analysis. To begin with, several things are noteworthy about this air of dire foreboding, not least the fact that the overall three-part study, published in March 2000, starts (in the section on profanity) with a quotation from then-President Clinton decrying "the banalization of sex and violence in the popular culture." To any reader who could stop laughing, this just might suggest the possibility that what people *say* about sexual behavior has nothing at all to do with how they *act* and that the public opinion polls the study so heavily relies on as expressions of "public concern" are utterly meaningless. (How did the Lichters imagine the millions of consumers of pornography would respond to a poll question about whether television has "too much" emphasis on sex?) Second, and much more consequentially, it is now four years later, as of this writing, and even in that short time period, sexual imagery has exploded all over our TV screens, mostly during the course of explicitly sex-oriented reality TV shows on which the networks pimp for men or women who pretend to be looking for fame, or sex partners, or both. (Unlike the minor-league pimps who hang out around, say, the Port Authority building in New York, the network producers have no fear of arrest or of being compelled to make payoffs to the police.) Momentarily, at least, these shows have become tremendously popular, even while "public concern" over their content has been striking only in its absence.[12] Yet nothing has been "found out" about the social effects of sexual fantasies, and nothing is likely to be. If an increase in impersonal displays of sexuality for commercial purposes is pernicious, then *something* bad ought to be happening somewhere as a result. But as part of their deployment of the nostalgia trap, the propagandists assume a decline in "morality" without any demonstration of, or even any show of interest in, what it might mean in the material lives of people. This is the same kind of reasoning that led to Justice Scalia's hysterical homophobic outburst in his dissent in *Lawrence* v. *Texas*, as though just naming an outcome the speaker doesn't like is enough to justify an indictment of it. The reasoning is circular: bad sexual behavior on television will bring about bad sexual behavior in the real world (what could be more "real" than television?). Oddly, as is suggested by the strange choice of "profanity" ("the condition of . . . showing contempt or irreverence toward God or sacred things") for a report that is actually about "obscenity," the official moral theology of the Catholic Church seems to have been adopted wholesale here, but without the excuse that it is the word of God. It is in fact only the word of Brent Bozell and the Lichters and those people responding to opinion polls, many of whom, when not giving those opinions, spend much of their time avidly consuming the "sleaze" that their opinions allegedly decry. To be sure, this is undoubtedly the true opinion of millions of Americans, many of whom, especially evangelical Christians, are so disenchanted with the state of commercial television that they are attempting to create their own television network, although PAX Television, already attempting to be just that, makes only minor inroads on the networks. That is their right, certainly, and anything that causes harm to the commercial system is probably for the better—but not the morally better, for there is no reason to believe that the Christian view of sexuality (it is actually only one "Christian" view among many) is in any way preferable to the pagan or libertine view. Here commonsense empiricism becomes moral bullying, from which it is often indistinguishable. My desire to have television programming I like, instead of simply turning off the set, becomes instead my desire to deprive you of television programming that you like.

In any event, it is the implicit claim to be social science that is special, and especially false, about the Center's study. Again, its procedures are arbitrary and tendentious. The precise claim of the study is that "each scene was examined for both visual images and dialogue or lyrics containing sexual content." "Scene" is then carefully defined, but "sexual content" is not at all; the very subject matter of the study is a subjective free-for-all. The dictionary definition that is apparently closest to what the study has in mind (there are four definitions in the American Heritage Dictionary entry) is "implying or symbolizing erotic desires or activity," but how on earth is this to be measured? The only possible answer, evidently, is by determining whether these scenes provide a certain kind of pleasure for the viewer(s), and, short of hooking up a large sample of the audience to some kind of arousal-measuring device, we cannot possibly know this for anyone but ourselves. What the study illuminates, then, is the propensity of its paid-by-the-hour watchers either to be aroused by who knows what or, more likely, to presume (because that's what they're being paid to do) that other people have been aroused by images that they themselves are carefully *"analyzing,"* without permitting themselves any response to them.

The invocation of "public concern" suggests that, in the minds of the critics, a frequent response to these images is, rather, repulsion. However, if repulsion was the major response, there would be nothing to worry about; the culture wouldn't be "descending into sleaze" but resisting it, and the producers of popular culture would be losing money by the bucketful instead of happily inventing (or, actually, imitating) one reality show after another. Thus, no matter what the critics say about public opinion, their real concern—their only concern—is that too many people are *liking* what they're seeing. "Too many" for whom is not clear. In any event, once we grasp how indeterminate both the presentation and the reception of "sexual content" are, we must see that there may be much more or much less of it on television than the study indicates (perhaps both). Erotic pleasure being central to life itself, the former is probably the case.

Thus, again the Center's study hopelessly botches the first step in a scientific study, definition and observation. When we investigate the next step of classification—the specific ways in which "sexual content" is attributed, especially what it calls "hard-core" material—then the aura of science dissolves even further into tendentiousness and sheer falsity. In Linda Williams's standard formulation of what most people mean by "hard-core"—that is, what is relegated to the adults-only back rooms of video stores—it presents itself "as the unfaked, unstaged mechanics of sexual action"; privileges "close-ups of body parts over other shots . . . sexual positions that show the most of bodies and organs"; and has created "generic conventions such as the variety of sexual 'numbers' or the externally ejaculating penis."[13] Needless to say, none of this has ever been observed on such conduits as *Ally McBeal*, *Friends*, or *Love Boat: The Next Generation*, all of which were identified by name in the Center study, or the Lifetime Channel, which supposedly had the most "hard-core material" among basic cable channels, though only the series *Any Day Now* is named. "Of course," the study adds, "most hard-core material included on broadcast television involved talk (92%) rather than action (8%)."[14] That is to say, most "hard-core material" wasn't "hard-core" at all or even soft-core; it was just raunchy conversation, primarily among women.

The classificatory tendentiousness of the study also extends to a supposed paucity of "consequences" and "moral judgments" in the "Hollywood version of sexual activity." But just why, say, "sex without consequences"—the study's particular bête noire—is bad goes unspecified. One would think that women have been fighting precisely for the possibility of sex without consequences ever since Margaret Sanger first began distributing free condoms to poor young females in New York City, not to mention the fact that, from Hester Prynne onward, most moral judgments of sexual activity, whether actual or fictional, have been judgments of *women*. But, then, it is instantly obvious that most conservative media-watching is a straightforward attempt to roll back the achievements of the feminist revolution and gay liberation. We can't have either of those cultural movements without "sexual imagery in popular entertainment" because one of their primary goals has been the proclamation of sexual self-definition on the part of women (and, later, gays), rather than quiet submission to the definitions of others. And although sexualized music videos are still mostly about the sexual fantasies of adolescent males, it is indicative that among the regular network shows the Center finds most "sex-saturated" were *Friends*, *Ally McBeal*, and *Any Day Now*, all aimed primarily at a female audience.

So what the study disapprovingly calls an overwhelmingly "nonjudgmental attitude toward sex" is in fact overdetermined. In the first place, it is precisely what one would expect in an era when traditional sexual authority has been challenged to the core. More crucially, the study does not consider the possibility that these are the very core of a consumption-oriented culture that television both encourages and reflects. Thus, when in its habitually prim tone the study calls on television to be "emotionally complex and aesthetically satisfying," we have to pause to remember that any

such programming would be simply incompatible with commercial television's institutional purpose of addicting viewers to passive pleasure. Do
these critics think that, with proper encouragement, the networks or The
Family Channel or Disney might show Bergman's *Face to Face* without
ads? (Perhaps they would think it encourages adultery or divorce.) Do the
Lichters, for example, want there to be more shows like the (violent, pro-
fane, obscene, and sexually graphic) *Sopranos*? Is the honest representation
of violence in a horrifyingly violent world "aesthetically satisfying" or not?

The intellectual evasiveness that supports this kind of moralism is revealed even more sharply by a recognition of what the study on "sexual imagery" does *not* cover at all, namely, television *advertising*. If it is true that
depictions of violence breed violence, and depictions of sexuality breed sexual misbehavior—if images enter into our minds as symbols and come out
as corresponding behaviors—then the first question we would think should
be asked is, what kind of communication is commercial advertising, and
what corresponding behaviors might it breed? The answer is that most ads
are either serious exaggerations (at best) or outright lies. If messages we receive from mass media result in corresponding behaviors, then the most
ubiquitous messages of all will surely have the strongest possible effect. And
what they will bring about, by application of the logic the conservatives
bring to the messages *they* analyze, is the inability of the citizenry at large
to distinguish truth from fiction: which as we have seen is sometimes the
case. Moreover, these are not trivial or incidental lies, but they are the most
important messages we receive in a consumption-oriented society: how we
ought to spend our money. Specific content aside, television advertising
teaches us that we should pay no heed to the injunction to tell the truth—
to the very essence of what might be called moral behavior. As this is also
the very message of the Bush administration and its cable news supporters,
perhaps the conservative disregard of "truth in advertising" is not accidental; perhaps its ideal citizen is a couch potato spending hours viewing inoffensive trivia *en famille* and believing any nonsense that is uttered by governmental or corporate authorities.

As to their specific content, television commercials are by far the most sexualized medium in all of American culture. As every hour brings new illus-
trations of this obvious fact, it would be pointless to multiply them; however,
one charming exemplification, in that it performs so many tasks at once, is
Nescafe's 2003 ad for the nicely named Fleche, with an emphasis on its female model's cleavage that perfectly replicates the cleavage of young actress
Elisha Cuthbert in the segment of *24* that immediately precedes it. If we
want to engage in a soft-core hunt on commercial TV, the place to look is in

commercials for jeans, cars, beer, diamonds, lingerie, batteries (?), and even various types of insurance, all of which depend heavily on the invocation of "sex without consequences." As for the writers, commercial artists, and other functionaries who create these ads, they are the one group of persons, above all others in American society, who are not susceptible to the witch-hunting charge that they are liberals trying to subvert the culture; they are just frantic income-earners trying to make a buck by making many bucks for their clients. If they and their employers imagine that the best way to do that is by attaching scantily clad models having mud fights with each other, or making karate attacks on men, to every product they can think of, they probably know much more about the social order than do the authors of these studies.

As selling products is the actual purpose of commercial television, the so-called programs are merely hooks to get viewers to watch the titillating ads. Yet the Center shows no interest in sex-saturated advertising. To do so would be to challenge the legitimacy and perhaps the very existence of the people who pay its own bills, the corporate elite of America. Thus the accusatory formula, "Hollywood's tendency to glamorize sex without consequences," contains both a superficial truth and a profound lie of omission. It is Madison Avenue's tendency that is at stake here, for, to the extent that "Hollywood" really means "television," Hollywood is only the piper; the man who pays the piper is calling the tune. Commercial mass culture—a term which comprehends almost all of "free" television and much, but much less, of filmdom—is an institutional complex with one overriding function: to encourage persons to be passive consumers while at the same time demobilizing them as active citizens. Steve Bochco or David Kelley or Rosie O'Donnell or other paid-up members of the creative elite may willy-nilly, despite their clearly contrary intentions, be carrying out that function; but they are hardly the parties responsible for the main outlines of twenty-first century capitalist culture. For that matter, even the Murdochs and Michael Eisners are, as Marx put it in the preface to *Capital*, primarily "the personifications of economic categories, embodiments of particular class-relations and class-interests." It is a total way of life we live; to turn that incredibly dense and powerful juggernaut into the product of sleaze merchants (or "liberals") is like imagining Weimar inflation as the work of Jewish bankers. In the prose of such nightmarish hatemongers as Ann Coulter, the simile is so exact as to be terrifying.

In the end, conservative flak-throwing is a serious *political* exercise in distraction, but intellectually it is trash, much more so than, say, *Beavis and Butthead* or *South Park*, the creators of which know what they are doing and are actually quite knowledgeable about the aesthetic and moral categories they play with. To try to make sense out of the reports of the Center for Media and Public Affairs (or the Parents Television Council) is to find only nonsense. Their message is, apparently, that there are too many representations of sexual activity and pain-inducing behavior on television (and in films), but if we ask "too many for whom?" or "too many for what?" we get no answer. Because the people who control the television system are in the business of making money and selling goods, and would stop doing whatever they are doing if those two enterprises failed, a much simpler conclusion is that the invisible hand is doing what it's supposed to do—amalgamating the pursuit of private profit into a publicly unavoidable way of life—and the right wing doesn't like the result; or pretends not to. Adam Smith himself would not have been surprised, as his point was that the invisible hand only produces public *good* if certain antecedent conditions are met, chiefly that society is bound together by "moral sentiments" that constrain both rich and poor alike. Most of the sentiments he concretely had in mind are disdained by the governing class and economic elite in the United States, who neither feel nor take any sense of personal responsibility for the condition of the poor, the outcast, the young, or the weak and whose chief aim in life seems to be to avoid paying taxes, even inheritance taxes, for the built-in ameliorative costs of a vastly unequal society. Once again, perhaps this is because *they* watched "too much sex and violence" on television; or perhaps it is because they listened to too many talk shows from which sex and violence, but not pure selfishness, were totally absent. Given that, on a large scale, the most destructive members of any society are often not its violent criminals but its criminal leaders, it would be interesting to know what television programs *they* watched as children, but that question is of no interest to pundits and sociologists who walk around, as the sociologist Martin Nicolaus once remarked, "with their eyes cast down and their palms turned up."

For that matter, one has to wonder why the Lichters and Brent Bozell and all the people who do their research for them have not been numbed, desensitized, and so forth by the endless moral trash they force themselves to watch. Quite obviously, like the sociologist who goes to the porn palace purely for scientific purposes, they know it's not going to have any effect on *them*. They are apparently better than the rest of us. But their seeming outrage at the system is only a pretense, anyway. Because they have no creative ability themselves, and despise so many of those who do, the diagnosis of sleaziness is their only possible path to cultural power. They would be totally bereft without the television system to attack and would starve to (cultural) death, like a predator without any prey. Their intervention is solely about power; it has nothing at all to do with "standards" or "values."

But in any event, if the right-wing cultural critics really believe that the people should get what they want out of the system, they have set off down a conceptual and practical blind alley. How many people have to be willing to pay how much money for a specific good for us to be able to say that people want it? And how can we ever find the answer to that question if we distribute the good, whatever it is, to them virtually for free? If satisfying a majority is supposed to be our goal ("the fictional world of prime time can be sharply at odds with public sentiment"), does this mean that popular narrative fictions should be constructed in accordance with the ideological divisions of the population?[15] If that is the case—and it is hard to see how anything else can be meant by "public sentiment" or "the majority"—then apparently we have given up on the whole enterprise of discovering and applying the objective standards that so entrance conservative thinkers in other contexts. (See chapter 6.) If there is anything majority or popular sentiment does not do, and makes no effort to do, it is to arrive at objective standards or moral truths. Popular sentiment is exactly what the Lichters and Rothman call it—a sentiment. It is about as subjective and amoral as a standard can be, being nothing more than the likes or dislikes, often applied coercively, of a particular group of people at a particular time.

That public sentiment can also sometimes be called traditional morality adds nothing to its inherent subjectivity but merely locks us into the nostalgia trap. It is certainly possible to make an antiliberal or antiprogressive argument about the course of history. But these critics don't and can't make it, because they want to expound a politics that takes credit for the massive economic and military progress of the United States while denouncing the social and cultural changes that accompanied it; they want to separate the elements of "progress" out from each other and pick and choose among them, just as they do with "traditional morality." This cannot be done; major historical change is not a show horse that can be ridden around the ring under the rider's control. It is always revolutionary, and a revolution, as has often been remarked, is not a tea party. In the American case, the onset of the social, cultural, and political revolution (and counterrevolution as well) and the inspiration for everything that followed it—the political radicalism of the 1960s, women's liberation and feminism, gay liberation, and the startling cultural and pedagogical changes, including the ideological death of patriarchy that accompanied these—was the Civil Rights movement, a movement that, in turn, had its birth in the 1950s that is now central to the conservative nostalgia trap, and that itself, in turn, was inspired, even mandated, by the New Deal of the 1930s. The conservative critics do not have the courage to say that, if they could, they would reverse the course of

American history, but that is what they would have to do to bring about an end to "trash," "sleaze," and "degradation." It is this contradiction that has led them into one intellectual cul-de-sac after another.

NOTES

1. Stephen Powers, David J. Rothman, and Stanley Rothman, *Hollywood's America: Social and Political Themes in Motion Pictures* (Boulder, Colo.: Westview, 1996), 2, 10.

2. From Marx's "Third Thesis on Feuerbach," in *The Marx-Engels Reader*, ed. Robert W. Tucker, 2nd ed. (New York: Norton, 1978), 144.

3. See Coontz's devastating account of nostalgia passing as history, *The Way We Never Were: American Families and the Nostalgia Trap* (New York: Basic, 1992).

4. C. Wright Mills, *The Sociological Imagination* (New York: Oxford University Press, 1959), 123.

5. The Center for Media and Public Affairs *Archive*, as of July 2000, contained at least half a dozen publications (most of them coauthored with the political scientist Stanley Rothman) that develop this proposition. The ugliest of these works, Michael Medved's *Hollywood vs. America* (New York: HarperCollins, 1992), while not a product of the Center, relies heavily on the work of Lichter and Rothman for its "data."

6. The methodologically correct approach is usually to test what I've referred to earlier as the "null hypothesis"—that is, to try to establish that there is no effect from whatever variable is hypothesized as strongest. When the hypothesized effect keeps turning up despite our best efforts to discard it, then we know that we have a good working hypothesis on our hands.

7. In 2003, the BBC released a long-term study finding that, as reported by the *New York Times* on September 23, "Children know the difference between actual and fictional violence and find violence on television news more disturbing than anything else they see on the screen."

8. *New York Times*, August 5, 1994, A13.

9. The quotation is from Gerard Jones, *Killing Monsters: Why Children Need Fantasy, Super Heroes, and Make-Believe Violence* (New York: Basic, 2002), 97. All subsequent remarks about rates of violence are from this book. Inter alia, Jones notes, on page 75, that the popularity of televised wrestling, the most prolific source of violent images according to the flak-throwers, has also periodically increased during, not before, violent crime waves.

10. To be sure, in 2003, the American Psychological Association finally officially considered the correlation between exposure to violence on television and character development to be unassailable. The APA's conclusion followed the publication of the study by L. Rowell Huesmann et. al., of the University of Michigan's Institute for Social Research, "Longitudinal Relations Between Children's Exposure to

TV Violence and Their Aggressive and Violent Behavior in Young Adulthood: 1977:1992," *Developmental Psychology* 39, no. 2 (March 2003): 201-21. Although this was certainly not an example of what I've called "junk science," its limitations are immense in that it makes no attempt (nor could it have) to decipher the causal connection between the two, a crucial omission since the already unimpressive "statistical significance" disappears completely when the causal arrow is reversed. (Compare tables 5 and 9, on pages 212 and 214.) Worst of all, the investigators think that they are testing the hypothesis that one kind of viewing among several causes aggressive behavior later, but in truth they only test half of their hypothesis. They properly vary types of TV viewing but totally forget that "aggressive behavior" is also variable and describes the soldier, the athlete, the politician, and so on just as well as the criminal. Above all, the period of the longitudinal study (1977–1992) was a period of allegedly increasing "violence" on television, and yet, as we have seen, *it was followed by sharply decreasing rates of violent crime in the United States*.

11. See Patricia J. Williams, "Death and Discourse," *Nation*, December 22, 2003. It's not coincidental that it takes a woman to ask this question.

12. For a relatively detailed account, see Patricia Leigh Brown, "Hey There, Couch Potatoes: Hot Enough for You?," *New York Times*, July 26, 2003. An FCC spokesman told Brown that the number of formal complaints to the Commission about sexual displays has not gone up in recent years. In fact, for a population of almost 300 million people, the reported figure of roughly one complaint *per day* is astonishingly low.

13. Linda Williams, *Hard Core: Power, Pleasure, and the "Frenzy of the Visible"* (Berkeley: University of California Press, 1989), 48-49. *Hard Core* may be the best book ever written based on the methodology of watching visual culture and then classifying what one has seen. Reading it before one reads the various media "studies" of the Center for Media and Public Affairs affords an object lesson in just how terrible, how false to their subject matter, they are. Its viewing panels don't *look at* what they see; they just label it with pointless signifiers ("liberal," "conservative") that have nothing to do with the actual visual material.

14. I must admit, embarrassingly, to never having seen or even heard of the series *Desmond Pfeiffer*, which supposedly led all series in hard-core scenes, though whether they were "talk" or "action" is not vouchsafed.

15. See S. Robert Lichter, Linda Lichter, and Stanley Rothman, *Watching America: What Television Tells Us About Our Lives* (New York: Prentice Hall, 1991), 4.

6

MATTERS OF TASTE

In sum, the problem of entertainment television is not some conspiratorial or deleterious behavior on the part of media elites, but the dominance of a comprehensive worldview, as described in chapter 4, a worldview that is difficult to resist. What attitude ought we to have, then, toward these media representations of ourselves and others? Here I will offer two guidelines. First, we should and need have no interest in the abstractions offered by the right-wing cultural warriors. There are no such things as "sex" and "violence." There are only people injuring each other in various ways or not. Nor is there any virtue in being inoffensive; to make that a criterion of legitimacy in discourse is to cede control over that discourse to those who are or—usually—pretend to be the most easily offended. The distinction between "injuring" and "offending" is crucial, furthermore. As John Stuart Mill said, "There are many who consider as an injury to themselves any conduct which they have a distaste for, and resent it as an outrage to their feelings . . . But there is no parity between the feeling of a person for his own opinion, and the feeling of another who is offended at his holding it; no more than between the desire of a thief to take a purse, and the desire of the right owner to keep it."[1] Anyone who does not understand this distinction need only leaf through the most obnoxious publication they know of and then put their hand on a red-hot stove burner. Abusive men understand the difference: when they want to terrorize women, they don't make them read *Hustler* or *American Psycho* or watch *Henry: Portrait of a Serial*

Killer; they hit them. And they were doing that in massive numbers long before mass-market porn or visual media were invented.

Of course, a case has been made out, by some feminist theorists and activists, that pornographic portrayals of sexuality do harm women as a class
by leading men to engage in violent sex acts that they might otherwise, presumably, not have engaged in. Conservatives are often tempted to hijack
this argument and extend it to cover "rampant" or "degraded" or other portrayals of sexuality of which they disapprove. The spectacle of watching
them try to establish, in a court of law, under the usual rules of evidence,
that *Ally McBeal* encourages men to do physical harm to women, or is part
of a movement to extend the sway of patriarchy and thus of male violence
against women, would certainly be entertaining. However, this is a direction
conservatives would hardly want to move in, for the feminist critique of
pornographic depictions of sexuality is part of a larger critique of patriarchy
of which the linchpin is, in this view, "compulsory heterosexuality." Unless
"emotionally complex and aesthetically satisfying" television is supposed to
scorn even tastefully portrayed heterosexual relations as a bastion of patriarchy, the propaganda machine will find no help from feminism for its authoritarian puritanism. Radical feminist theory is not based on the premise
that society would be more orderly and humane if only pornography were
abolished but, rather, on the premise that pornography is a central practice
of an inhumane, male-dominated society: a society that looks very much
like the one the conservative critics wish to preserve (or return to). In practical politics, any alliance is plausible, even between conservatives and radical feminists, but it is impossible to find any common theoretical ground
between the two.

At this point, however, a second question demands to be answered. How,
if at all, does Left ideological critique, such as what I am offering here, dif-
fer significantly from its conservative counterpart? Does it also not constitute an attempt to substitute one elite for another, the critic's aesthetic and
moral standards for those of the mass audience, the censor for the market?
Or, to rephrase a question that is often asked of critics of commercial television, does your criticism of television programming depend on some *aesthetic* theory that distinguishes among "better" and "worse" programs or on
an *ideological* standpoint that discriminates among programming that is
somehow good or bad for the free development of people's thoughts (presumably, in each case, in order to generate policies favoring production of
the former)? The short but complicated answer is this. In order to say anything intelligible about any fictional television program, one must be able to
make aesthetic distinctions, as all such programs are acts of creativity and

the imagination; and one must have and articulate an ideological standpoint, as all such programs are imbued with ideological assumptions that give coherence to their narrative resolutions. Similarly, in order to say anything intelligible about information television, one must have a political viewpoint that both enables and requires the making of distinctions about what is true and what is false, as otherwise "the news" is just a dull wash of words with no inherent meaning. But, on the other hand, criticism of television as a system for delivering either popular commercial entertainment, or statements about the world that are allegedly factual and informative, does not depend on, and absolutely ought to avoid, any substitution of the critic's aesthetic or political values for those of the audience. Criticism of the *system*, such as I am offering in these pages, is intended as an indictment of how the system is organized to deliver the goods; my occasional criticism of the goods themselves is intended solely to demonstrate the *narrowness* of the goods being delivered, and the *barriers* the system sets up against the delivery of any other kinds of goods, but it is not intended to substitute my demands for anyone else's. My ideological critique is not that programming is procapitalist, or materialist, or religious, or irreligious, or socialistic, but that it is exclusionary rather than pluralistic; and my ideological standpoint is that pluralism is always preferable to conformity, and any increment to pluralism is for the better (leaving aside for now the question of marginal media products such as pornography and hate speech).

That is the simple answer, and I have already made the point directly in writing about news and "liberal domination." With respect to entertainment television, however, this simple statement obviously requires elaboration and clarification. To begin, we have to first distinguish among varying types of cultural critique, which proceed from sharply differing criteria and encourage entirely different kinds of discussion. Thus, there are certainly standards of aesthetic criticism, but the aesthetic question is itself much misunderstood today. The idea that "Marxists" or "feminists" or other categories of cultural critic created entirely for purposes of dismissal don't believe in "standards" or "values" is both false and inane (though given more credence than it deserves by the straw man occasionally erected in the name of postmodernism). Of course, there is good art and bad art; Marx himself was notoriously a cultural snob. By any standard, Ernest Hemingway was a better writer than Mickey Spillane (and so was Raymond Chandler); by any standard, John Ford made better movies than Edgar Ulmer; by any standard, *The Sopranos* is richer fare for the mind and the eye than *Arliss* (and Spillane, Ulmer, and the head of production for HBO would almost certainly agree, as would cultural critics otherwise separated by their political beliefs).

However, what has to be emphasized about this recognition of aesthetic standards is that nothing follows from it; there is no reason why any particular person should read Hemingway instead of Spillane or watch *The Sopranos* instead of *Arliss*. The world of aesthetic judgments is self-contained; as Jeremy Bentham famously remarked, "Prejudice apart, the game of pushpin *is of equal value* with the arts and sciences of music and poetry."[2] The pleasures to be gained from detecting a difference, real or imagined, between "great," "good," and "bad" art are real enough but are limited in their scope (e.g., the possibility of being able to have fruitful discussions about individual artistic creations with persons who share one's general aesthetic standpoint but may have interestingly different comments to make about particular applications of it). In any event, the cultural argument about aesthetic standards is irrelevant for judgments about the commercial television system in that, within it, aesthetic values are approached, if ever, only by accident; the kinds of reasons sophisticated viewers typically give as to why they prefer one program to another ("ensemble acting," "moments of social realism," "real wit on occasion") are from the realm of purely subjective preference, not trained aesthetic judgment.

This then leads to a second, quite different, sociological perspective on cultural commodities that takes the standpoint of the audience and, rather than asking "how good is this?" asking how and why is it, or is it not, likable? This perspective is especially applicable to television programs, most of which exist primarily to cater to the desires of their expected audience. From that perspective, there are neither better programs nor worse programs; neither more entertaining ones nor less entertaining ones: only the diner can judge the feast. Audience appreciation is separate from, and has nothing to do with, aesthetic judgment, although it is possible to offer complex analyses as to how such programs do or do not work. It is, however, the especial delusion of cultural tyrants of all political persuasions that their appreciation of what *is* good somehow translates into a statement about what the audience (other than themselves) *ought to appreciate* as good. But it doesn't. For example, various persons may believe that there are tasteful (*Masterpiece Theatre*?) and tasteless (*Beavis and Butthead*?) programs, or morally virtuous (*Judging Amy*?) and morally disreputable (*Ally McBeal*?) programs; but those adjectives are just euphemistic ways of saying, "I like," and thus those distinctions supply no reason to prefer the one over the other. To establish that they did supply grounds for preference would require a linking metaphilosophy—a philosophical analysis that explained why having certain kinds of aesthetic standards is ethically or socially better than not having them, *and* ought therefore (contra Bentham) to be legislated, if only symbolically. As aesthetic knowledge and judgment could not be further from political knowledge and judgment, the soi-disant literary critics should, as Socrates would have advised, stick to their last.

The attempt to convert one's private viewpoint into a social requirement is what we generally call moralizing, and moralizing is what the conservative propaganda machine produces. It is also, most of the time, synonymous with hypocrisy, in that none of us (saints aside) is really any better than the rest of us, but moralizing requires precisely the insistence that better is what I am: I have standards; you're a sleazy couch potato. In this respect, the culture wars have had an especially pernicious side effect. By hitching their political agenda to the star of objective moral (or aesthetic) truths, modern-day conservatives have blurred, if not corrupted, the public discussion of ethical life and aesthetic value. If there are some kinds of discernible (if not objective) truths, then they can be discovered only by reasoning about them, not by announcing them by fiat before discussion has even begun and not by fabricating hypothetical relationships between mediocre cultural commodities and the decline of Western civilization or between a predilection for the passive enjoyment of visual junk food and the active intention of committing rape and murder. Moral philosophers from Immanuel Kant to Thomas Nagel and Peter Singer have reasoned about morality. The Lichters, Brent Bozell, and their political compadres (Bob Dole, Dan Quayle, Joseph Lieberman) simply engage in loud-mouthed ranting, hoping that, if they pronounce dogmas at the tops of their voices, no one will notice that that is all they are doing, and thereby fatally misleading anyone who listens to them about how the serious business of discussing morality should take place. And their moralizing is no less useless for its pretense of discussing supposed causes and effects, given that, as I have pointed out, we are always totally in the dark as to which way causation runs in large-scale social affairs. Nor, in this particular case, could we obtain definitive answers even if it were possible to study social causality, as accusatory but contentless labels like "public morals," "sleaze," "degradation," and so on, are arrows pointing nowhere. It may be possible, as the sociologist Emile Durkheim urged, to study indices of social morale, such as rates of suicide or mental illness. But whether we would be studying the effects of entertainment media as opposed to, say, the incidence of poverty and inequality or the paranoia of talk radio, no one could possibly say; and, in any event, the right-wing propagandists have never shown the faintest interest in considering such real, observable corollaries of a way of life they benefit from so nicely while pretending to criticize it.

Third and last, it is also possible to study the ideational content (*not* the consequences) of cultural creations; that is the kind of ideological critique

I tried to articulate in chapter 4. This kind of critique aims at interpretation and searches for explanations, as I have done there. It is, or tries to be, about not how the audience receives messages from the mass media, but about the nature of the messages; and not whether we approve or disapprove of them, but what they are; and not what is being heard, but what is being said. Unlike flak-throwing, ideological critique seeks no influence over the arena of cultural production but, rather, tries to suggest, to anyone who might be interested, that we are often not, or not only, seeing or hearing what we're told we're seeing or hearing (by the system's exegetical machinery of *TV Guide* and the like) or what we might think, at first glance, we are seeing or hearing. The goal of this critique is a better understanding of the kinds of programming the system encourages overall, its usually hidden political and psychological implications, and its built-in limits. If would-be media reformers such as myself and others referred to in these pages want to do something to broaden the limits within which commercial programming operates, it is out of a theory of the relationship between free speech and democratic possibility, not from any desire to squelch one kind of programming and substitute another. Nor could it be, as none of us has any idea what kind of visual culture would emerge from a freer, less monopolized media system.

There are certainly standards of judgment that, if not wholly commensurable, are at least susceptible of reasoned discussion and, often, consensus among informed persons. These are the criteria of analysis that are internal to a particular field of artistic creativity and are ultimately based on an intimate knowledge of the components that make up works in that field: how colors cohere and contrast in an oil painting, when "free verse" becomes conventional prose, why lengthy political speeches tend to fall like lead weights in the middle of a fictional narrative, what differing kinds of kinesthetic statement are made by a close-up, a two-shot, or a pan, why louder is not necessarily funnier, and so on. I call these "neutral truths," meaning by this that they are, and remain, true regardless of the intentions or values of any particular person. Contrarily, for example, the truths of Christianity are not neutral truths; there is no reason to believe them if one is not a Christian. On the other hand, the general truths of evolutionary theory are neutral truths because, whatever fundamentalist Christians would like to believe to the contrary, they remain true (that is, capable of scientific demonstration pertaining to the fossil record for instance) and cannot be falsified by external (e.g., religious) criteria.

In the world of aesthetic judgment, there are certainly no neutral truths of the scientific kind, but there is a kind of neutral truth; that is, there are standards based on the kinds of knowledge I have described above, standards that no person who knows anything about the field can deny the validity of (although he or she can always refuse to apply them). The elaboration of such standards is once again an attempt to arrive at Nagel's "view from nowhere." These standards all together compose what the late Pierre Bourdieu called "the rules of an artistic field." The rules are known to all who enter the field, left, right, or center, and the game of critical analysis— as opposed to saying "I don't know anything about art, but I know what I like"—cannot be played by anyone who doesn't know them.[3] On the other hand, in the eternally gray area where "art" meets entertainment, or edification, or belief, the so-called "objective standards" or "neutral truths" lose most of their relevance. They lose their relevance because the other, external criteria for judging the value of a work of art (or of any good) are not only incommensurable with each other but have to be so. Does it move me? Does it express beliefs or ideas or feelings I can take seriously? Do I desire to gaze on "beauty" or do I find deeper meaning in what others would call ugliness? None of these or other similar questions can be answered authoritatively; there is no Platonic realm out there in which any answer is particularly "true."

At the same time, it is possible to show that there are consequential differences between some types of creative expression and others. One of these is the attitude the creator takes toward the audience: there is an art that flatters and cajoles its audience and an art that defies its audience to face potentially unpleasant truths. To return, then, to the distinction between commercial and noncommercial television, it is the unwillingness to leave the audience with an uneasy sense of itself for more than a second that distinguishes the commercial television system from other modes of entertainment. In this respect, the faux populists, with their ostentatious indulgence of "the majority" and its far from artistically coherent standards, partake precisely of the value relativism (if not emptiness) that they otherwise criticize.

A very brief account of several well-known episodes of *The Sopranos*, which distinctly does not flatter the audience, may clarify this distinction. In one already famous episode, Tony Soprano's psychiatrist has been raped. Suspecting what has happened, he asks her if she'd like him to "take care of it." She sits and stares at him. We see her thinking: she is envisioning Tony brutally killing the man who has raped her. She hesitates; she says, finally, no. In another episode, a high-school soccer coach has sexually abused one of the players; on hearing about this, the Soprano mobsters fly into a rage, and, shortly after, they savagely beat up the coach. In yet another episode,

Tony, playing the good father to the hilt, is taking his soon-to-be-graduated daughter on a tour of northeastern colleges, when he spies a man who had once testified against the mob and then gone under cover. While the daughter is interviewing at Bowdoin, Tony garrotes the man to death. Finally, in an astonishing scene, Tony's wife Carmela, on learning that the daughter's high-school counselor has written her a rather unhelpful letter of recommendation, confronts the man in his office and quietly blackmails him into rewriting the letter by letting him know who she is and to whom she is married.

In the first two of these episodes, we see vicious career criminals—for that is what the Sopranos are, without exception—as enthusiastic enforcers of traditional morality, the kind of morality so beloved by law-and-order conservatives, with no interference from "moral relativism" or "situational ethics." The rape episode is especially significant, in that Dr. Melfi—played with so much dramatic conviction and integrity by the actress Lorraine Bracco that psychiatrists have invited her to speak at their conventions—is throughout the series (at least its first two years) the moral surrogate for the audience. That she has to think hard about whether to send a vigilante off to kill her rapist means that we too are thinking about it. We are contemplating fighting fire with fire, an approach that is the very opposite of the respect for law and order that makes us conceive of the Sopranos as criminals in the first place. We are not being flattered; we are being interrogated. As for the other two episodes, together they force us to confront the possibility that just as, in Aristotle's famous argument, a good man might not be a good citizen, so a good parent might not always be a good citizen either. And again, as is the case with Dr. Melfi, Carmela Soprano has been another moral surrogate throughout the series (though more ambiguous because more complicit), so that her total desertion from the cause of moral decency is all the more striking.

All in all, *The Sopranos* confronts us with the unpleasant reality of the moral world rather than the complacent substitute we get for it on commercial television. To be sure, viewers can have different opinions about the social or moral problems highlighted by an issues-oriented program such as *Judging Amy*: for example, do social workers do good, necessary work or do they make social problems worse? But what we can never have any doubt about is who is supposed to be our representative in the narrative field, and, if we reject the choices of that representative, we simply substitute our own judgment for hers without calling into question that we are now making the "right" choice. Ideological television's narratives, that is, are always about what the good person should do, never about whether we the viewers are ourselves good persons in the first place. Thus, Tyne Daly, the narrative protagonist of all social work subplots on *Judging Amy*, is presented and defined as a good person, as a person who makes moral judgments to which we the viewers should attend, even if her overbearing personality grates on our sensibilities and even if on specific points we might disagree with her. No one watching the program can possibly mistake this. In the same way, no one can possibly mistake that Amy's courtroom judgments are the conclusions, even if again we might disagree with some of them, that follow from a highly intelligent, thoughtful, and well-intentioned reasoning process (and, on those very rare occasions when that is not the case, Amy herself is the first to let us know she has erred). In total contrast, the narrative protagonist of almost all the action on *The Sopranos*, Tony Soprano, is clearly a malevolent, destructive man who has no intention of putting any other moral or social end before his own (or his own family's or gang's) self-interest. Thrust into the position of identifying with him as our narrative surrogate (even though, in the background, actress Lorraine Bracco is, as I've noted, our troubled moral surrogate), we can rarely watch the program for more than a few minutes without confronting the reality of our own divided selves. For most of us, one part of the self will identify with Tony (even if only for a moment) and thus root for his triumph, while another part of the self will try to reject that identification because it wants to "do the right thing.[4] In fact, many viewers-to-be of *The Sopranos* were at first unable to watch it until word-of-mouth and the machinery of cultural hype overcame their initial reluctance, precisely because it was so painful to realize that we were being asked to take pleasure in watching brutal and totally unjustifiable violence.

Nor, once we begin to think about it, can we easily avoid the equivocal position the show puts us in. For the truth is that we do live in a material world where, like Doctor Melfi, we compromise with criminals and criminality every day, having our garbage disposed of by them (the Soprano mob is, quite realistically, in the business of garbage disposal), our restaurant linen and the cash we get from our banks laundered by them, and our "recreational drugs" supplied by them; and we also know that our police forces break the law every day to get convictions against the criminals who really bother us but make very little serious effort to break up entrenched mobs like the Sopranos. We also, like Doctor Melfi, live in a world where, because we have compromised easily and often, situations will arise in which not only is there no obviously correct course of action, but all possible courses of action may be wrong, and we can only choose, perhaps, the least worst; and, conversely, the "right" thing (e.g., helping one's children get into college or supporting the arts) is often being done by morally loath-some people. Nothing even faintly like this has ever been seen on com-mercial television, for in the world of television every apparently insoluble dilemma can be resolved by a morally appropriate solution; and, when bad men do good things, it is because they're not really so bad after all, if only via a death-bed repentance or some other means by which conventional melodrama sentimentalizes the realities of moral choice.

Note that I have made the above comparison without suggesting here or elsewhere that anyone should watch *The Sopranos* instead of, say, the banal and visually empty *Once and Again* or, to repeat a point made earlier, that anyone who can't afford the monthly charges of HBO, and thus can't watch *The Sopranos* (or *Angels in America*, or *Six Feet Under*, or documentaries such as *Murder on a Sunday Morning*), is being deprived of a basic human need. What I have rather done is to suggest simply that there is a noticeable, structural difference between some of the programs available on pay chan-nels and all of the programs available on commercial channels and that this difference is consequential in a particular way. (The people who run the commercial networks are aware of this: they all turned down *The Sopranos*.) Again, to return to an earlier formulation, commercial television only nar-rows our experience. On the entertainment side, with very rare exceptions (the first season of *24*, perhaps), it presents stale visual material as though it were fresh (compare any episode of *Star Trek* with films such as *2001* or *Alien*, or any woman-in-peril movie from the Lifetime Channel with *Psy-cho*); and it presents familiar narrative resolutions as though we hadn't al-ready encountered them a half dozen times this week. And what makes this a narrowing of experience is that the familiar resolutions are familiar pre-cisely because they're ideologically safe and, thus, false. The commercial tel-evision system offers easy ways out of hard problems, moral dilemmas that turn out to be not really dilemmas, implausible separations of the good guys from the bad guys, and reconciliations that ignore everything that's gone be-fore, as when, on several courtroom dramas over the years, a defendant who is clearly guilty gets assassinated by one of his victims after securing a ver-dict of acquittal because of some "legal technicality."[5]

In contrast, there are no moral dilemmas on *The Sopranos*, as the possi-bility of entertaining them has been precluded by having a really immoral man as our protagonist in the first place; instead, there is only our own in-escapable double consciousness. And there are no resolutions to assure us that all is right with the world because all isn't right with the world, not for a minute. Tony Soprano stays out of jail even though, before our eyes, he has committed enough crimes to be put away for several lifetimes. (He will probably come to a bad end, but only because the series itself must end.) He does so not through some rhetorical trick that lets ourselves off the hook, such as reference to "soft" or "liberal" judges or a "technicality"-based system rigged in favor of the guilty but because our social world is much too complex and our values much too ambivalent for it to be seriously possible that the criminal justice system could deliver justice on a regular basis, especially when criminals serve a public function. Even the recent series *The Shield*, which shows brutal cops at work behind the back of the law that ought to restrain them, cannot offer what *The Sopranos* does because its protagonists, being cops, are doing what must ultimately be seen as good work, and we are never in any doubt about that. We are forced to identify with good men doing bad things, but that is an argument that defenders of the military have always made. We are most definitely not forced to find our way in a landscape with no good men at all and nothing good being accomplished by anyone on either side of the law. In a 1950 movie, *The Asphalt Jungle*, a businessman who finances a criminal gang remarks that crime "is nothing but a left-handed form of business enterprise." It isn't that John Huston's anarchism tells a simple truth that we all should believe, but it does offer a critical thought that we all should at least entertain seriously— a thought that is brought before us once again by *The Sopranos* and that has never, in any form, been brought before us by commercial television.

Does any of this matter? If the contrast I am making between a conventional ideology that offers easy ways out and a tougher-minded look at our social world is not an evaluative judgment, then what kind of judgment is it? Before attempting an answer to that question, let us note that the conservative propagandists, rather than confronting this issue, sedulously avoid both rigorous criticism and serious questions. In their fake moral world, the only thing that can be said about *The Sopranos* is that it's littered with "bad language" and "violence," although admittedly it might be said to be more "artistic" than network products. But what they can neither acknowledge nor, probably, understand is that they are asking an entirely irrelevant question: a question that has nothing to do with the quality not just of art, whatever that may be, but of any popular entertainment in general. Popular entertainment is designed to be popular and serves its function if it accomplishes that for enough people to enable it to continue in operation. As the media guide *Time Out New York* put it at the end of 2002, "Here's a preview of the lowest, most degrading shows you won't be able to tear yourself away from in the next few months." To reject popular entertainment's way of delivering itself is to reject not the entertainers but the audience. As the postmodern critic and philosopher Umberto Eco once asked rhetorically, "Is the audience bad for television?"[6] His suggestion was that such is the case, but a more nuanced answer is that audience and medium are bad for each other, in that both (at least during their interactions) unquestioningly partake of an enveloping social system that privileges certain kinds of communications while proscribing others. Whether we can imagine a different, more open, way of organizing the system so that more honest and serious addresses to the audience may sometimes be broached is the real question that needs to be addressed and not whether we can keep actors from saying "shit" in front of the women and children. Beneath their attention to "Hollywood elites" and "sleaze," the real animus of the conservative critics is against the expressed tastes, however they may be derived, of a large part of the mass audience. This is not a matter of aesthetic interpretation. It is political partisanship passing as both aesthetic and moral judgment to suggest that preferring *Beavis and Butthead* to all the programs of The Family Channel put together somehow makes me or anyone else (many millions in fact) a less good American than those who have the reverse opinion. Indeed, we might well want to argue that, when, after the capture of Saddam Hussein in December 2003, Paris Hilton in a miniskirt outdrew George W. Bush's interview by Diane Sawyer, the mass audience received its ultimate vindication, preferring simple fun (and putting down the rich) to another hour of mendacity and obfuscation by the Supreme Court–appointed president.

Thus, the question of how the mass audience is to be represented to itself—and not the question of taste—ought to be the framing question of all considerations of visual culture. Film studios and television networks are, in the mythology of the American way of life, private enterprises responsible to no one but their shareholders. The networks, in contrast, have actually been awarded public franchises, and it is possible to make out a case for government regulation (including censorship) of them on this score. But, if this is what the Right wants, it will have to bite the bullet and opt for state socialism instead of free enterprise capitalism as its preferred political economy in the realm of communications. This is unlikely. I have had colleagues who were far to the Right of the overwhelming majority of their students, but we all know how they would respond if told they must assign more radical feminist literature because that is what their students want. They would reply quite correctly that the students can take some other course; however, pay them by the student, and they might change their tune. Then they would be in the same position as are film studios, networks, and advertising agencies, who already labor under the stringent discipline of the consumer's market. If "the people' don't like visual culture, they argue, we don't have to buy any. Why should we be able to tell its creators what to put into it, any more than painters should have to produce realistic representations of kittens because that is the visual art that viewers most prefer? If the audience likes sentimental pap or dishonestly resolved narratives, give that to them.

This is the *partial (but only partial) truth* of what, in contrast to the class/structure model of mass media, or the elite domination paradigm, we might call the democratic market paradigm. But its truth in turn is only partial. In fact, against criticisms of programming stemming from the elite domination thesis, the film and television community, which we call "Hollywood" as shorthand, can only offer a defense that is riddled with bad faith. To complaints as to violence in children's cartoons, sexual license in prime-time series, the exclusion of certain voices from discussion shows, the absence of serious drama from the airwaves, from wherever on the political compass they derive, the network owners and the producers of commercial mass media entertainment reply that they do nothing but attempt to give "the people" what they want, and the success or failure of any show is the only relevant index of whether the people have or have not wanted it. That is, they answer the *populist* complaint with a *marketplace* defense. We are all free to flick the dial, or punch the remote, or turn off the set altogether. If millions of people watch it, whatever it is, then it must be good—until they stop watching it or until *advertisers*, the real decision-makers in television's version of the consumer marketplace, stop paying for it. In this way, one spurious populism answers another, the "democracy of the marketplace" versus the "democracy of majority opinion."

Reflecting an inherent ambiguity in the ideology of democracy—and not just a play on words—democracy, in this formulation, is defined merely as a culture and not as a set of institutions. As I have emphasized, the *institution*, American cultural commodity production, is purely oligarchical and entirely dominated as it is by advertising agencies, network executives, and the owners of cultural monopoly capital; not the faintest hint of democracy attaches to it. Ted Turner, Rupert Murdoch, and the top managers of Sony\CBS, Time Warner, and so on, are the people who in fact determine what we see, when we see it, and how we see it. The analysis of the market paradigm, however, suggests that the oligarchs do not really have oligarchical power; they, or rather their corporate underlings, may propose a new series or a movie or a budding star or a new genre, but consumers ultimately dispose: ours is the real power. It would be terribly misleading to conclude that there is no truth in this version of how mass media work; surely there is. Not even in the most traditionalist European society would television managers be allowed by the general public to feed it a steady diet of classical tragedies from Euripedes, Racine, Goethe, Shakespeare, and Ibsen; dramatic proletarian fictions about the miserable lives of the dispossessed, the homeless, and the down-and-out; Marxian exposés of the iniquity of capitalism; avant-garde, nonnarrative, or sexually esoteric dramatizations from the likes of Godard and Fassbinder; and nonviolent, intellectually subtle animated cartoons demonstrating the virtue of tolerance and the evils of discrimination. The truth of the matter, however, does not lie "in between" the extremes of elite and marketplace theories. Rather—and here again the class/structural analysis serves us better—neither of those models incorporates a satisfactory theory of *representation*: the actual heart of the matter. If the mass media are to represent us to ourselves, then, in a democratic, pluralist society, the "us" who is represented surely ought to be a democratic, pluralist "us." But neither the apologists for the monopolized market nor the populist opponents of the "arrogant cultural elite" can meet that criterion. Each relies on a false, even antidemocratic, model of the polity. The former rely on a pseudomajoritarianism based on spending power and willingness to be attentive to a forced diet of mediocre entertainment and pseudoinformation; the latter rely on an authoritarian majoritarianism that falsely portrays "the people" as a cultural and ideological monolith.

To adopt a truly representative stance toward the media would require not just that fundamentalists, right-to-lifers, bigots, and sexual authoritarians be portrayed more regularly, as would certainly be both realistic and fair. It would also require, with equal justification, that the same opportunity for visual representation be available to, say, striking workers, African-American community activists, nonwhite immigrants resisting monolingual education, women's movement activists, mothers on welfare, homeless people (as in Charles Burnett's film *Sidewalk Stories*), and all those others who operate at the margins of society without succumbing to right-wing populist self-pity or neofascism. It could also mean, more conventionally, celebrating family stories in which dedicated mothers (Carol Burnett in *Friendly Fire*), or widows (Laura Dern in *Afterburn*), take on the forces of the State to salvage the honor of the men they've lost or tales of individual heroism in which a conscientious civil servant blows the whistle on a gigantic cover-up (Alfre Woodard in *The Agent Orange Story*).

Here again, though, while the media moguls provide little enough of such entertainments, the Right's authoritarian patriotism and identification with the powerful rather than the powerless rejects these and similar fictions (or semifictions in some cases); ideology as historic compromise is inadequate to its wishes. So we will find not a single voice raised from the Right to ensure this kind of representation of difference, nor to praise it when it comes. (Where was conservative welcome for any of the above telefictions or for such prounion feature films as *Norma Rae* or *Matewan*?) Nor can we find any right-wing version of John Sayles, year after year putting together the financing necessary to produce his own left-wing scripts about urban corruption, corporate malevolence, racism, marginal sexuality, and the like. Far from asking that visual culture be opened up to its own talents, the Right's real demand is that Hollywood *not* show what its constituents dislike: one-parent (female-headed) families, sympathetically portrayed homosexuals, sexually active teenagers, divorcées, or abortions (except to condemn them). This is a call for repression rather than representation; more than just a version of cultural warfare, it is a politics based on a political theory as well.

Here again it is useful to quote John Stuart Mill (who is made into a nonperson by the antiliberalism of the Right): "On any of the great open questions just enumerated [for Mill, belief in God is the chief of these], if either of the two opinions has a better claim than the other, not merely to be tolerated, but to be encouraged and countenanced, it is the one which happens at the particular time and place to be in a minority. That is the opinion which, for the time being, represents the neglected interests, the side of human well-being which is in danger of obtaining less than its share."[7] It's not that Mill is necessarily right and the neoconservatives wrong; in principle, they have a counterargument. As exponents of majority sentiment, they do seem to believe, contrary to Mill, that "neglected interests" ought to continue to be neglected or, at least, relegated to the dustbin of permanent minority status. Michael Medved, for example, is fond of quoting certain television producers (a very small number, in fact) to the effect that they want to influence public opinion, that they have a message to send on behalf of certain "neglected" ideas or persons; he makes no attempt to conceal his hostility to this avowed aim. But this is hardly a counterargument he can comfortably make. Theirs is exactly the same goal that he has in mind (together with the Lichters, Bozell, Irvine, and Rothman); he merely wants to send a different message. His message is, among other things, that if television goes out of its way to present positive images of gays and blacks, why shouldn't it equally go out of its way to present positive images of the neglected majority, middle Americans? In a revealing passage from *Hollywood vs. America*, he asks: "Why is it inherently less valid for the American Family Association to try to pressure the networks for *fewer* homosexual characters on prime-time TV than it is for the Gay and Lesbian Alliance Against Discrimination (GLAAD) to try to pressure the networks for *more* such characters? Both groups are engaged in totally legitimate efforts to influence major TV producers to broadcast images that correspond with their own views of what constitutes a good society."[8]

Once again, we encounter the peculiar version of moral relativism to which the contemporary Right retreats every time its own activities are criticized. "Totally legitimate" substitutes a *formal legal* category—constitutionality, First Amendment rights of free association and petition—for a *moral* or *political* category: what ought, or ought not, to be done. The two have nothing to do with each other; they are apples to oranges. I have a legal right to do many things that it would be *wrong* for me to do, that are cruel or hurtful to others, that go against the grain of democracy, that discriminate unfairly, or that make life harder for people who already have a hard life. I have a right to be homophobic, but I am a disgusting human being if I knowingly take advantage of that right. Medved is perfectly aware of this distinction, as (in one of many similar instances) he follows a lengthy criticism of the allegedly offensive film, *The Last Temptation of Christ*, with a First Amendment rejection of calls for censorship and a plea for Hollywood instead to reform itself, to treat religion respectfully rather than contemptuously. If it is *wrong* to treat Christians disrespectfully (his quite erroneous characterization of the film), why is it not *wrong* to treat homosexuals disrespectfully, as GLAAD alleges of mainstream television? (Perhaps they are incorrect, but neither he nor any of the groups he is defending claim that.) The fact is that it is perfectly consistent for a group like GLAAD to demand fairer treatment of homosexuals on-screen, and yet defend the makers of *Last Temptation* (including its Catholic director Martin Scorsese) from the charge that it is offensive to Christians to depict Christ as a sexual being. To return to John Stuart Mill's distinction, it is wrong, when speaking in public space, to be unfair or discriminatory toward people who can suffer as a result, not necessarily legally actionable, but *wrong*. Gay persons, for example, *are* victims of society-wide bigotry that regularly eventuates in harmful behavior. On the other hand, in this nation at least, Christians need fear neither institutionalized bigotry nor any of its material results, and, if some of them choose to be offended by an expression of deviation from their beliefs, that's their own choice; no harm to them can or will result.

This is the context—the struggle between authoritarian populism and minority rights, between the defense of intolerance and the defense of liberal tolerance—within which we always have to evaluate the right-wing assault on the media. Christians are not a stigmatized minority (in the United States at least), nor victims of hate speech. Like other majorities, they are never truly "neglected." In contrast, the voices of gay persons and blacks, for example, are rarely heard when compared to those of their more normative counterparts (talk-show hosts? news anchors? syndicated columnists? stars of action series?). In fact, genuinely pluralist democracy is the last thing that groups such as the Parents Television Council are interested in. Democracy would mean real cultural conflict in place of our false choice between cultural monopoly and cultural warfare: false because the free market in images that brings us oral sex and bloody vampires is brought to us by the same people who bring us the free market in world trade, environmental carcinogens, and fundamental health care. Not wanting to admit this truth, and therefore resorting not to a serious political theory but instead to scapegoating, conservatives can only repeat their "liberal elite" mantra.

As it is impossible to imagine a non-elite system for producing mass cultural commodities, the real complaint is not about elites but about liberals. The media elites are evil, subversive, and malignant; they desire to destroy "America"—of which, it appears, they are not truly a part. In the ominous title of Medved's *Hollywood vs. America*, we can see the authentic hand of the commissar and smell the deadly whiff of grapeshot. Describing a Hollywood elite, both in movies and television, who are allegedly losing the battle of the marketplace by defying conventional American morality, he and his like can only explain this seemingly irrational behavior by postulating an ideological takeover by liberals, who would rather promote their anti-American ideas than make money. This would be truly extraordinary behavior and suggests a frightening degree of ideological dedication on the part of burrowers from within, much like that which was attributed to "Communists" in the 1950s. But, then, Hollywood, in Medved's phraseology, is "the poison factory" with "a sickness in the soul" and a "bias for the bizarre"; it promotes "promiscuity" and "illegitimacy" and "maligns marriage," has an "addiction" to violence and has "motivations for [its] madness" that are "driven by some dark compulsion beyond simple greed" and that seem to be nothing more nor less than the destruction of all values "America" holds dear; the sickness of the soul, he tells us on several occasions, is "pathological."[9] This use of the language of ill health to describe one's enemies is all too familiar; it inevitably implies that treatment, not criticism, is what the offenders deserve.

All this has nothing to do with sex, profanity, and violence; it has everything to do with an apparently unappeasable lust for cultural power. For we must note that Bozell, Medved, the Lichters, and Rothman wrote their most inflammatory attacks on the media toward the end of a period during which conservative Republicanism had won three consecutive presidential elections and been in national power for almost twelve years. All of this despite the domination of mass media by mind-poisoning liberals! Diane English, Linda Bloodworth-Thomason, and the other purveyors of television's liberal sleaze must surely be forgiven for wondering where they, and Murphy Brown, went wrong. Primarily, they did not understand what was at stake. When Dan Quayle attacked Murphy Brown for her deleterious approach to family values, we remember that he himself was the heir to a major media monopoly which owns exactly the same tools for manipulation and indoctrination as do, in his mind, the writers and producers of television programs. His deployment of the elite manipulation paradigm, therefore, told us much less about *their* intentions, whatever those may be, than about his own expectations of communicative power and control. Diane English should be not an independent writer/producer for national television but, rather, an employee safely under the thumb of an editor who knows which side the boss's bread is buttered on. It is not that the marketplace of ideas should be free but that he and his class, and not anyone else, should control it.

If television writers do really have the nefarious intentions attributed to them, it is very likely that they're in the wrong profession. "Sex," "violence," and "profanity" probably accomplish nothing but to appeal to some people's likes and inflame other people's dislikes and, possibly, to sell the goods they're designed to sell. But if mass media does not poison minds, why should we care what it does? As I have already suggested, it certainly monopolizes the space for public discourse and alienates the persons who ought to be engaging in that discourse from the terms and venues in which it takes place, but that does not bother the authoritarian populists either; they are all for monopoly. Here, rather, we come to one final variant of "the people" deployed by them, and it is as bizarre, to use Medved's word, as his version of Hollywood. In this incarnation of the people, they become at one and the same time not only "the majority" but also *the true victims,* victims of both manipulation and subversion.[10]

This notion of the majority as victims of culture prefigures the strange turn of events by which, after 9/11, the most powerful nation in the world somehow became an entire nation of "victims." There are all sorts of emotional reasons why, in the aftershock of an unprecedented event, millions of people should have had that response; but there is no excuse for intellectuals whose chosen milieu is rational thought. Not getting enough family-friendly programming in prime time is surely the strangest sort of victimization to which a vast majority has ever been subjected. After all, no matter how strenuous or angry the Left critique of television might be, it has little or no punitive content. If I say that there is too much depiction of normative heterosexuality, or American patriotism, or uncritical "family values" on television, I will be taken as a failed comic by most people outside the arcane field of cultural studies. Or, if I claim that various minorities are stereotyped as criminal or mob-ridden or oversexualized, or that women are patronized by the television system, this has the effect of interest-group lobbying generally. It will be taken as self-defensive and self-interested and will achieve even the mildest of changes only if it is thought to have the strength of at least some numerical force behind it. Most of all, such efforts will be thrown into what is now (due to the efforts of the flak makers) the historical dustbin of political correctness, where they will remain even if an occasional nervous network executive attempts to respond to them. A few scriptwriters will lose the liberty to tell the political equivalent of dirty jokes; no one and nothing, except perhaps creative integrity (if one believes that it exists on television in the first place), will be hurt. As for the news reporters who make up the propaganda machine, critics such as Chomsky or Katrina vanden Heuvel are not trying to shut them up but, rather, to open their eyes to sources of news that they refuse to look at.

Quite contrarily, the right-wing critique of both entertainment and information television constitutes an attempt to stigmatize, marginalize, and hold its targets up to obloquy and to narrow, rather than widen, the sources of representation and inquiry. We can understand the difference if we think of the difference between calling a well-known actor brazenly heterosexual and another brazenly homosexual or calling one script rife with pseudoreligious sentiment and another rife with blasphemous disdain for the sensitivities of believers or complaining that one newscaster has missed the truth about East Timor and another has unpatriotically lied about the alleged (but nonexistent) iniquity of American policy toward the Third World. That is why occasional denials by the flak throwers that they are calling for "censorship" are completely beside the point; they are doing worse. When Ronald Reagan's Secretary of the Interior, James Watt, remarked at the beginning of his tenure that he used to think Americans were either Democrats or Republicans, but now he thought they were "either Americans or liberals," he spoke for the entire conservative critique of culture.

Moreover, although they strenuously object to what they consider to be the stereotyping of minorities, liberals (whoever they are) are otherwise perfectly happy if characters in films and TV series are shown occasionally questioning the morality of abortion or teenage sex; and they are perfectly happy that children be shown growing up in two-parent families and that men and women be shown most of the time engaging in heterosexual exchange: all too happy, some of us might think. By contrast, in a television world inundated with nuclear families, Dan Quayle couldn't bear the thought that even one single mother was being presented as an attractive figure. Worse, Murphy Brown was surely the kind of role model that upholders of social stability should want to see more of. Instead of having an abortion, she had a child; instead of fostering it out, she coped; instead of becoming dependent on welfare, she earned the family's living. What was wrong with this picture? Only that it offended the religious authoritarianism that would restrict women's sexuality to the bonds of marriage. The Right desires not representation of the unrepresented but special recognition for sectarian moral tyranny and political conformity. Liberalism, contrarily, does not always, or even usually, validate otherness, as theorists of difference call for; only on occasion does it make principled efforts to ensure that the other, whoever that may be, has an equal voice. But in principle it insists on the toleration of otherness, on nondiscrimination against otherness, at a minimum. Liberal ideology is pluralistic by conviction, therefore, in the same way that Hollywood's ideology is pluralistic by commercial necessity. Contemporary authoritarian populism, however, denies the ethos upon which dominant visual culture in a pluralistic democratic society is erected and, then, evinces puzzlement or a sense of conspiracy when it cannot find its way into that culture as an equal partner. Its adherents may form a substantial minority of the American populace, but, unlike blacks or gays or feminist women, they are an unassimilable minority; their exclusion from visual culture is a self-inflicted wound.

The Right is not asking for equal time; it already has that and more. There are more religious channels than there are major networks, for whomever might care to watch them. Put simply, the Right wants to replace "dominant television"—a metaphor from the field of cultural studies—with its own domination, literally and not metaphorically. It does not want television to be more open and democratically accessible but, rather, more closed and antidemocratic. It does not want higher quality programs but more ideologically acceptable programs; it calls not for a liberation but for a purge. As only someone tone deaf to visual culture could fail to notice Hollywood's ceaseless endorsement of the status quo, it is clear that the Right's real agenda demands not only, nor even mostly, acceptance of the way things are. On the contrary, what the Right wants is that its own *Kulturkampf* should take over Hollywood.

Contrarily, the fundamental matter of taste behind all the arguments of this essay is that all media criticism ought to have the purpose of bringing not more sanitation to media but more life. A society that is both diverse *and* democratic ought to be diverse in the stories that get told publicly, who gets to tell them, and who gets to appear in them. For example, what was wrong with bringing "Doctor" Laura to TV was not that she's disrespectful of others but that she was granted a monopoly to be disrespectful of others; that is, the offense is that she uses a resource that belongs to all of us for purposes of airing her contempt, a resource that is denied to would-be communicators who would promote instead the respectful treatment of others. Much more effective than preventing her appearance on the broadband would have been to compel the chairman of CBS to appear at the beginning and end of each of her shows, to explain, initially, why she out of so many thousands of possibilities was allocated this precious resource and, finally, what her sponsors and employers thought the public might have gained from listening to her for the past hour. *That* would signal a mass media revolution: not to add more censorship to that which the controllers of media already exercise, but to force them to be intellectually accountable for their uses of our intellectual property; not to restrict diversity to what is inoffensive, but to bring about real diversity in the power to offend. Nothing like this can happen so long as the market for producing and distributing mass images is dominated and controlled by economic giants whose only interest is profit. As for the millions of persons who are quite reasonably dissatisfied with the system and would rather watch programming with more, say, "Christian" content as opposed to censoring what's already there, the fact that it is difficult for them to put that desire into practice on a large scale—to opt out of the commercial system—says nothing about creative elites and everything about the domination of the cultural field by corporate giants whose oligopoly works to exclude any cultural products that might be troubling. The commercial system is toxic, not because its programming is perverse, but simply because of its existence, dominating public space and leaving no room for anything else to be said by anyone else. How that domination might be overthrown is the central question to which we now should turn.

NOTES

1. John Stuart Mill, *On Liberty*, ed. David Spitz, Norton Critical Editions (New York: Norton, 1975), 78.
2. See John Dinwiddy, *Bentham* (Oxford: Oxford University Press, 1989), 114. The context of the phrase I have italicized is that Bentham was arguing against public subsidies to the arts, first, on the grounds that the many should not be taxed for the pleasures of the few and, second, the point I am implicitly making here, that public regulation should not be in the business of making aesthetic judgments. The legislature

may fund an agency that has the professional business of making such judgments (e.g., the National Endowment for the Arts), but should not do so itself. Another way to put this is that aesthetic taste and democracy have nothing to do with each other.

3. See Pierre Bourdieu, *The Rules of Art: Genesis and Structure of a Literary Field*, trans. Susan Emanuel (Palo Alto, Calif.: Stanford University Press, 1996). Bourdieu is more cynical about the legitimate authoritativeness of "the rules of art" than I have allowed myself to be here because I do not wish to rule out *a priori* the possibility that some rules of aesthetic judgment, at least within the framework of a civilization and a broad historical movement, correspond to an apprehensible reality.

4. In Freud's terms, these are respectively the ego and the super-ego. In as much as HBO programs are not subject to the formal and informal censorship of commercial television, the id—untrammeled sexual desire—is also much more honestly represented on *The Sopranos* than on even the most sexualized of commercial TV's programs.

5. Most recently, in the spring of 2002, this happened on an episode of *Philly*. After a juror had to be excused from a jury that was one vote from conviction on a murder charge, the defendant changed her plea to guilty and was sentenced to ten years probation, with no jail time.

6. Eco, "Does the Audience Have a Bad Effect on Television?" *Apocalypse Postponed* (London: British Film Institute, 1994).

7. See *On Liberty*, 46.

8. Michael Medved, *Hollywood vs. America* (New York: HarperCollins, 1992), 327.

9. The quoted phrases are all from chapter headings in *Hollywood vs. America*; the quote about greed is on page 286. Medved's insistence that ideology trumps commerce has its origins in the works of Stanley Rothman cited in chapter 4, note 19. (Though one of the works cited in that note was published after Medved's, it had circulated in draft before then, and Medved might well have seen it in that form). Medved's reasoning about "motivations for madness" goes as follows: "PG," audience-friendly movies earn more at the box-office than "R"-rated, unpleasant movies; thus the insistence of certain moviemakers on making their R-rated losers can only be ascribed to a desire to stuff the minds of audiences with their own anti-American ideology; the same is true of television producers who insist on making audience-losing shows. Unintentionally producing hilarity, he bolsters his argument by constantly quoting producers who say very earnestly that they're not doing it for the money; they're doing it for the art; I would love to have him write my biography. The argument is anyhow disingenuous, in that producers of cultural commodities (actually, of many types of commodities), whatever their real motives, are always behind the curve, which itself is always taking on new shapes. (On television, it should be reiterated, the initial sponsorship of a show based on its audience share is only part of its returns, perhaps even less than syndication, overseas sales, and now DVD distribution.) For

a less tendentious historical explanation of why "the world of entertainment" is as it is today, see chapters 4 and 5 above.

10. As one observer of the "victim" phenomenon puts it, "Critics of victim politics become its practitioners by devising and promoting new groups of worthy victims . . . fighting against the proliferation of victimism can be a way for anti-victimists to establish their own status as victims." From an unpublished manuscript by Alyson Cole, "The Cult of True Victimhood." The epitome of the kind of "anti-victim" polemic that turns directly into its own version of victimhood is Charles Sykes, *A Nation of Victims: The Decay of the American Character* (New York: St. Martin's, 1992). The concept of "worthy victims" traces back to Edward Herman and Noam Chomsky, *Manufacturing Consent: The Political Economy of the Mass Media* (New York: Pantheon, 1988).

7

CONCLUSION:
ABOLISHING THE SYSTEM

In short, this system of public communications for private profit does not provide public goods and services (i.e., goods and services determined by democratically legitimate authority to be "in the public interest"); and for the most part it does not provide (as do the sellers of other cultural commodities) commercial goods or services for user fees or consumer payments. Instead, it delivers consumers to advertisers who, in turn, foot the crucial part of the television bill and, thus, largely determine its content.

Substantively, the purposes of the men who pay the piper and call this tune are not to provide any particular kind of viewing experience but, rather, to cause viewing in general to become habit forming; to bring about a condition in which the television set is never turned off during any audience segment's available time; and, as much as possible, to replace all other ways of looking at the world with their own concomitant ideology of complacency, distraction, and the belief that a lack of intellectual substance, appreciation of moral complexity, or strongly held dissenting views about the social order is a good thing. Conversely, as far as we can tell, whatever their other limitations, this is not the intention of those persons who produce programming that does not serve the goals of advertisers (e.g., films, subscription television) and, thus, is not dependent on absolute audience share for its existence. In this important respect, therefore, commercial television is unique among all contemporary media of communication. Whether its goal is actually achieved we do not know, but it is certainly the case that more time is spent watching commercial television than is spent on any other discretely definable activity (though the internet, which poses entirely different problems, is now challenging this). For this reason, above all, the standards of commercial television have come to replace all other competing standards, most especially distinctive standards of political discourse, moral discourse, and educational and informational discourses. This includes what might be, but is not, the distinctive discourse of news and information television.

This summary provides, I believe, the most appropriate ground for a democratic theory of what ought to be the relationship between mass media of entertainment and democracy. That must be a theory, first, of the virtue of openness and pluralism and, second, of the necessity of withdrawing television's imperial power over both expenditures of time and standards of discourse. These goals require the abolition of commercial television as we know it: the end of the free lunch.

As to the first requirement, the mass media of entertainment ought to constitute a level playing field on which audiences have a chance to make judgments among available consumer products in the ordinary way, that is, by deciding how to spend their money. That option presently does not exist, in that products on which consumers (audiences) do *not* have to spend their money compete with, and drive out, those on which they do. For example, it is impossible to see examples of most art forms anywhere except very occasionally on PBS, and even films can only be seen in a corrupted form on "free" or nonpremium cable TV. This is a particularly powerful instance of Gresham's Law (that bad money drives out good). The marketplace is rigged; it ought to be opened up to all comers on an equal basis, bounded only (ours being a capitalist society) by their ability or inability to find an audience that will pay the break-even price for their product.

The aspect of the existing system that makes monopoly possible—rather, that institutionalizes monopoly—is the use of public licenses to establish private monopolies over *time*. The practice that makes network television possible, and thus puts the control of creative activity and information distribution in the hands of a very small number of persons, is the granting of *sole rights* to a particular television channel (i.e., a portion of the bandwidth) to a private enterprise. That is, at every moment of time, day and night, Channel 2 in New York City is available only to the Columbia Broadcasting System, its owners, and their employees. This particular monopoly is independent of the agglomeration of channels into a *cable television* monopoly—for example, Time Warner, Continental Cablevision. A cable television provider is actually just a packager offering the people who control the actual channels a convenient way of getting access to larger audiences with better reception of programs. Unless it is owned by the same people who own one or more networks, a cable television company is little more than a middleman, making its profit from the service it provides to those owners. We can see this more clearly by comparing Channel 2 in New York with Channel 32 (or channels 201 and 210 for digital television (DTV) customers) and Channel 301 (available only to DTV customers). The owners of Channel 2—CBS—make *their* profit by selling advertising time (together with syndication, overseas rights, and, in some cases, eventual DVD rights) to sponsors. Such advertising time is incredibly valuable and, thus, profitable for the network because the sponsors are *guaranteed* a nationwide audience by virtue of the fact that *no one else* can use CBS's licensed channels anywhere in the United States at any time. Moreover, there is virtually no market in which it, along with ABC, NBC, and Fox, does not have a channel (i.e., own a television broadcast station). Channel 301, in contrast, is one of many pay-per-view channels available to customers of Time Warner Cable in New York City. Those who wish to view, say, a recently released movie pay a fee to Time Warner, which has bought the rights for this particular revenue stream—pay TV—in negotiation with the producing studio (or, more likely, for a package of films). In turn, Time Warner sells viewings of that film to whomever will pay for them (usually, $3.95 per viewing at the time of this writing), but this is merely one distribution stream for those films: they could also have been seen in cinemas, or as videos on VCRs, or on DVDs. In fact, not just any movie is available on the pay-per-view channels; for the most part, only movies that have a notable star or have achieved some kind of general notoriety—a category that includes several channels' worth of soft-core porn films—are available. Furthermore, because many viewers are willing to pay to see these films at home, where they are cheaper than in cinemas, they can be shown as they were made, without interruptions for advertising.

There are also many films not available on pay-per-view that are available from the Independent Film Channel, or Sundance. These will generally be "independent" films (i.e., not financed by a major studio) that can be expected to draw a smaller, but faithful, audience. These films could be shown with advertising interruptions, as are movies shown on Channel 2, but they are not, both because their producers do not see them as commodities in quite the same way as the major studios see their films and because the audience for independent films is a more serious audience that will (it is believed) not put up with commercial interruptions. However, because their audience is relatively small at best, some cable systems will not carry them and others will charge an additional premium for receiving them.

Home Box Office, in contrast to pay-per-view, does not typically sell its offerings per viewing (though it has been offering a pay-per-view archive) but, instead, sells access to its total inventory (over time) to subscribers, who pay a monthly fee to the cable carrier (which has its own separate deal with HBO) in order to be able to view whatever HBO is showing on its various channels that month. These offerings too are shown without commercial interruption, as subscribers support HBO's costs of purchasing rights to show films in this particular revenue stream—subscriber TV—and costs of its own productions such as *The Sopranos*. HBO (and its competitor Showtime as well, though the latter has not achieved quite as much popular or critical success) can in effect do whatever it wants with its film inventory and its own productions, as it needs no support from the cable giants, though in fact it is owned by one of them, Time Warner. And because it is selling its products directly to subscribers, the cable network only being an intermediary, it is free of all the constraints and censorship of both the commercial channels and the cable channels (e.g., Comedy Central, The Golf Channel, etc.), which must satisfy both advertisers and the FCC. Thus HBO, like the pay-per-view channels and unlike IFC and Sundance, can show nudity, broadcast profanity, and so forth, just as though it were a store into which a customer might walk to buy a hard-core magazine. That is why series such as *The Sopranos* or *Six Feet Under* or *Sex and the City* or *Oz* can attain a feeling of liberated creativity that can never be attained on the commercial channels, although the immense popularity of *The Simpsons* and *South Park,* as well as the distancing of content achieved by the cartoon format, have enabled Matt Gruening and his successors to attain a kind of intermediate status for their work.

Obviously, it is not the case that every episode of every television program, not to mention every movie, ought to be rife with the kinds of displays that horrify the would-be censors but, rather, that ideally every cultural production is a transaction between artist and audience, and nothing more. That distinction suggests another important difference, then, between a network channel such as Channel 2, with its monopoly over time, and the pay or subscription channels I've been discussing. With the triumph of capitalism in the nineteenth century, every field of artistic creation has been swept up in the capitalist marketplace. Ultimately, the man (or woman) who pays the piper calls the tune, in negotiation with the musician who offers to play it; this was as true for Bach as it is for Hans Zimmer and as true for Rembrandt as for the clients of Mary Boone. What the capitalist marketplace gradually introduced is the middleman: the publisher, dealer, agent, packager, distributor, who inserts himself (or herself) between artist and audience and comes to determine the conditions of their economic intercourse. (That is why Dickens founded his own magazines in which to serialize his own novels and why Stephen King has attempted to publish his own novels on the Internet.) The producers of an independent movie can hardly hawk their wares directly to Time Warner; they have to find a packager/distributor such as IFC or Sundance. Similarly, the creators of a television series for BBC have to find a producer within the system who will take their proposal to the BBC's board or other vetting entity. But, in both these instances, no third party intervenes with external criteria beyond the ordinary criteria of the marketplace. In these examples, the applicable marketplace criteria would be the track record of the producers (at BBC) or companies (IFC, Sundance) who offer the cultural commodity for broadcast, as indicated by the marketplace ratings they have achieved in the past or by their success in some other market (e.g., a film in cinemas). In other words, the middleman, like any agent, has in some important degree the same interests as the creator (though minus the creator's secret belief that he or she has created the greatest work of art ever seen in its genre, even if absolutely no one else ever sees it). And the middleman's monopoly of certain channels, such as IFC's package of films for distribution to Channel 81 in New York City, or HBO's inventory of films and in-house productions for Channel 32, or Time Warner's pay-per-view schedule, leaves open the determination of content for those channels.

On commercial television, however, neither artist nor producer nor audience is the most important party to the determination of content. Network programmers and advertisers, rather, are in control of content, and their criteria of success are different in that they seek not primarily an audience for programs but programs to carry ads to potential consumers. Thus the people who use public licensing to monopolize time on commercial television are in total control, subject to the dictates of the FCC, of the programming that fills that time; it is this condition that makes them true monopolists in the sense of dominant economic actors whose span of control is incompatible with the freedom of the marketplace.[1] Among themselves, in concert with their sponsors, the networks produce—that is, have final say over the content and placement of—more than 90 percent of episodic, narrative fiction for home viewing. By contrast, even HBO functions like an ordinary producer when soliciting or considering programming, and, in any event, the great bulk of its programming consists of movies produced by other people and purchased by it for selling to home viewers; as for Time

Warner pay-per-view, it produces virtually nothing at all. Thus, on network television, there is no middleman or packager putting together other people's work, as on subscriber channels to which every artist or producer has in principle, to begin with, equal access. On the contrary, no one has any access at all to commercial network television without auditioning their proposals to network representatives. It is as though no song could be sung without being approved by a representative from the Music Corporation of America; no CD played without the approval of Sony. That is what we mean by "monopoly"; it is what is happening to local radio now, as Clear Channel Corporation buys up one station after another, on which it then promotes its own centralized agenda of conventional music (as long as its purveyors do not offend politically, like the Dixie Chicks) and conservative ideas. As well, by virtue of their guaranteed national access, the networks effectively set the costs of a visually interesting production, and the rates for nationwide advertising, well above the level that any independent producers can hope to pay. Neither common carriers nor middlemen of the creative arts, the networks are essentially private profit-making machines with enormous incomes generated by whatever it is they choose to do and guaranteed by public license to monopolize the channels they possess to the exclusion of all others. What they actually produce is a visual culture of almost total alienation.

However we might try to define it, consumer democracy is not really democracy, in any meaningful sense of the word, in any sphere of production and consumption. Given that truth, the alienation of culture's consumers could only be truly abolished in utopia. Where, realistically, only some people are creative artists, and only some people are both knowledgeable followers *and communicators* of the infinite world of public events, the rest of us can never hope, strictly speaking, to imbue the public sphere with our own representations of ourselves and our beliefs about the world. But there are degrees of alienation, even in the realm of mass communication. Cinema, for example, as manipulative and fetishistic as it can be, does not present itself as the very background of life and does not relegate other kinds of understanding and (re)presentation to the sidelines. It presents itself only as one among many varieties of public communication, more ubiquitous than most because it is a mass art but hardly hegemonic. As full of stereotypes as it is, it has comparatively little imperial power over the level and content of public discussion; and, as a medium, it is much more pluralistic in that there is hardly any such thing as "independent film" (or anything), let alone foreign film or "art film" or genuine documentary, on commercial television. That is the level of power, at a minimum, to which we should want to reduce television. In the spheres of both entertainment and information, if implemented, the slogan of "a marketplace of ideas," as tired and misleading as it is, would constitute a tremendous improvement over the existing conditions of monopoly. What is required is not an escape to some utopian condition of total nonalienation but a comparatively simple transformation of television's products to the normal status of commodities in a capitalist society.

We have ceded to the television system, unlike any other producer of commodities, preeminence over *other realms of activity*—politics, sports, the education of children, information about our major institutions, and so on. In actuality, the system doesn't communicate about, or report on, or tell stories about those realms: it reconfigures them in its own image. What we are alienated from most importantly, then, is not ourselves, as in the language of psychoanalysis, or our productive capacities, as in the language of Marx (though both of these accounts are in some part true). We are alienated from the public sphere in its totality because we participate neither in the making and remaking of it nor in discussions about it; all that is done for us. Outside a few major cultural centers, no other way of spending one's time in the evening hours can compete with the pressure to spend it as inexpensively as possible in the privacy of one's own living room. The only way then to combat this structure of alienation is to restore that sphere to itself as much as may be possible, by stripping the system of its power over ourselves, our time, and what ought to be *our* public sphere.

Instead of attempting to imitate the mindless flailings of the conservative moralizers, then, democratic critics of the mass media system should give up any attempts to evaluate its products (beyond the occasional expression of our personal opinions about them), let alone to affect its output, and, instead, consider an entirely different question: how could *the system* be made appropriate for a democratic polity? Obviously, any answer to that question begins with the notion of government regulation, for that is the alternative that exists here and now. The FCC is already so deeply involved in the delivery of television's outputs that it is virtually a full partner in their creation. Language, images, and sometimes even ideological viewpoints must pass muster with the FCC, which, by virtue of controlling the issuance and maintenance of those licenses, has even more power than a pure censor would have. The campaign of harassment and intimidation that the FCC has undertaken against the networks during the second Bush Administration, and especially since the Janet Jackson "nipple" incident, is more evidence than we need of the power inherent in governmental regulation of communications.

On the other hand, stripping this power from the FCC would hardly by itself constitute a viable alternative; nonregulation is not an option in any social order of any kind. That is because regulation does not develop in opposition to some originally pure "free market" but is, rather, a natural outgrowth of any attempts to extend the market's sway. Thus, markets and regulation have a symbiotic relationship. Only the barrage of propaganda from the market's propagandists (i.e., the corporate order) and the theoretical aridity of the academic discipline of economics can conceal this relationship, though never for long. It is simply not conceivable that human beings, with all their diverse needs, injuries, and hopes, will allow any nontrivial social behavior to develop its sway over them without attempting to bring it under some kind of control. The passage from Macpherson quoted in chapter 1 clarifies this. Although individual market transactions (you sell me a pound of hamburger meat) may have only trivial overall consequences (mad cow disease in one person), once transactions come to be enacted collectively and systematically (the cattle *industry* sells its products to millions of customers), their potential consequences (mad cow disease for millions) are no longer trivial. An argument that the sway of mass media over all of us is trivial would be imbecilic. We have to remember only that the same conservatives who support the notion that "free markets" are better than "government bureaucracies" are precisely the same people who are always demanding a say in programming. Nor can it be argued with a straight face that the nongovernmental bureaucracies of the mass media system are somehow less intrusive, less controlling than, say, the FCC. One might as well argue that the distribution of addictive substances should be left in the hands of private enterprise, without any oversight by the bureaucracies of "law and order." To be sure, there are some libertarians who will argue just that, but arguments for anarchy in a complex social order are like arguments for pacifism during a war. They might make some kind of ultimate, abstract sense, but they have nothing to do with what is actually going on. The question of regulation, therefore, is not a question of whether but rather of how, of what, and by whom?

The problem with contemporary governmental regulation of the monopolized media, however, is that it addresses only the truly subjective issues of quality, offensiveness, and so forth, while leaving intact the oligopoly that creates and maintains an undemocratically monopolized public space in the first place. A real, and really implemented, antitrust policy is still the most effective, as well as the least intrusive and safest, form of government regulation in a capitalist society. (It's indicative of this historical truth that the New Dealer Thurman Arnold, who as a theoretical legal realist had written a devastating critique of antitrust policy as being merely "symbolic," when appointed to enforce it, became the most effective trust-buster the Attorney General's office had ever known.) And this is truer for the visual media of communication and their interlocking overlaps with the traditional print media than for any other sector of the economy, for the stakes are even higher than they are in the more traditional arena of means of production.

What would antitrust mean in this realm? In a way, to answer this question requires us to imagine an entirely different system for the delivery of mass cultural commodities. To begin with, I would propose the bedrock requirement that no private person or corporation should be able to "own" more than one television station—more precisely, the access to one television channel—anywhere. This means, effectively, that the primary conduit of mass access to in-home entertainment should be, as it has become, the cable or satellite feed provider, making available consumption packages (or individual sources of programming) at their market price and exercising no power other than the standard market power of being able to make a profit. Given the prohibition against networking, private commercial television could and should only be largely local, having no more access to products intended for the mass market than local entrepreneurs, with their inability to guarantee a producer national or regional delivery, can afford. That being said, however, it is also crucial to assert that ownership by itself is not the real issue. It's not the control of *channels* that creates monopoly power but the control of *time*. Thus, no privately owned television enterprise should be able to use its license to grant long-lasting monopolies for the use of publicly licensed time and space to anyone, filling up time with reruns, infomercials, syndicated talk shows, celebrity hunts, and the like for the sole purpose of attracting advertising. Expensive, habituating programming of the kind that has come to dominate the public sphere can exist only because its purveyors know that they are guaranteed 13, 26, 52, or 260 time slots, and the advertising that those will attract, plus the syndication and overseas sales that will follow from their repetitive nationwide distribution. However, the only justification for the private ownership of public space is its provision of an access to private persons, and this the existing system does not provide. What real access would mean, effectively, is that anyone in the area reached by a licensed station who has something to say, something to show, something to express, should sooner or later (but not too much later) have access to that station to say, show, or express it—and not to be told that the time has been purchased by NordicTrack or reserved for a rerun of *Law and Order*. The real elitism of American television is the systematic denial of that possibility. John Stuart Mill's much quoted sentence is considerably more relevant to the institutions of mass communication than it is to any conceivable legislature: "If all mankind minus one were of one opinion, and only one person were of the contrary opinion, mankind would be no more justified in silencing that one person, than he, if he had the power, would be justified in silencing mankind."[2]

As to the role of "public television" in a democratic society, and given antitrust limitations on private ownership, that ought to be clear by now. Public television stations (or channels) should be owned and operated by truly public entities—state universities, community colleges, city governments. Indeed, as Robert McChesney points out in his history of broadcast regulation, it took a fierce battle in Congress before the would-be privatizers of radio—RCA, NBC, and the like—won out over the higher education sector in the struggle for its control. Basically, meaningful change depends on reversing the outcome of that struggle.[3] Moreover, more truly than it is now, the production and distribution of public television should be divided between a national corporate entity on the model of the BBC and regional or local stations that can function as outlets both for national programming and for their own (or their neighbors') productions. Of course, it's a truism to say that the national sector should be the conduit for all communications events that are truly national and that cannot be generated at the local or regional level and that local or regional public television should be the conduit for programming of local or regional interest. However, such communications events will always be defined in operation and through conflict, as "the public" and its interests must always be defined. Again, I have no interest in imposing my own or anyone else's taste by fiat, as by insisting, say, that coverage of congressional debate is serious and coverage of the O. J. Simpson trial is frivolous (anyone who thinks that is self-evident has never watched a congressional debate on C-Span). To take a more obvious example, should the theater and dance that are found at what is generally considered to be their peak in New York City be recorded and packaged for DVD like any other version of entertainment, or should they occasionally be broadcast to the nation as though their creators are bearers of a public interest? There's no way to answer that question as a matter of principle; making such determinations is what governing boards are for.

As for truly "mass" communications, that is, nationwide information or entertainment, the implications of such a program would obviously be profound, though different in the two cases. As to the latter, there is a strong argument to be made for the idea of easy access to undemanding entertainment. If it did not answer some fairly powerful need, why would there be so many billions of people watching so much of it? I have tried in these pages not to say, "This is wrong" or "This must be done away with." Instead, I have tried to spell out the consequences of the way we provide that access and to suggest the kind of system that might avoid some if not all of those consequences. Whether the destruction of media monopolies, an increase in the democratic uses of public space, and greater pluralism in the sources of artistic production and the kinds of art made available to us would be a fair return for the loss of some ease of access is a judgment I cannot make and have no right to make. I can only point to the possibilities, as I hope I have done. However, it is still necessary to confront the strongest argument for maintaining the existing system. This argument is that TV offers the only "free" and therefore equally available consumer good in a market society— a society in which, because of vast inequalities in income and wealth, all other goods are distributed with gross inequality. There is a free lunch after all, and television is it.

There are several things to be said about this argument for continuing the free lunch. To begin with, it is obviously the case that, the more television a person watches, the more programs that person would be deprived of by having to pay for it. Free (or inexpensive) television, that is, subsidizes heavy watchers. It's not clear that there can be any principled justification for this arrangement, but no justification is needed. The argument really is that, rightly or wrongly, a great many people, especially poor people or people with working-class incomes, or home-bound housewives, will simply not put up with being deprived of their "free lunch." That may well be true, and, in that sense, any proposal for weaning us all from the habituating system may be utopian; we might as well start on alcohol or pornography, with just as much luck. On the other hand, the actual economic facts are not that simple.

In reality, fewer and fewer people get their television for free any more. The basic cable service, providing only a small number of major networks and a few other channels, typically costs about twenty dollars per month, but full cable service averages forty dollars or over and continues to go up— even without access to pay-per-view or any subscription services. Because a changeover to subscription or pay television would render the cable giants irrelevant except as mere packagers, as well as reduce their running costs, much of that consumer expenditure would be freed up to purchase individual programs or even programs amalgamated into a particular package, as say a Soap Opera Channel. Everyone might be in the position of being able to afford only one or two favorite channels or weekly programs without having to pay more than they have to under the present system; this outcome would favor the better off, but to what extent we cannot say. Moreover, we have no idea what television production would cost if deprived of its relationship with advertisers, and, especially, we have no idea what people would actually want to watch *at home* if they had to pay for it. The great popularity of, for example, MTV's "real-life" soap opera, *The Osbornes*, suggests that the intrinsic attractiveness of high-cost programming with expensive production values and major stars might be greatly overrated.

Still, millions of people would certainly view the absence of a full schedule of prime-time television, with which to fill their afternoons or evenings, as a deprivation. Here, however, we have to consider the future of technology as well as the future of popular desire, for the two together actually express an inherent contradiction. At the present moment, most video recorders are being manufactured with a capability of fast-forwarding or otherwise deleting commercials or whole commercial breaks. But, well beyond that, digital video recording technology, as pioneered by TIVO and now available in many guises, stores hours of recordings on its hard drive and eliminates the need for videotape; it is on the threshold of superseding conventional videotape recording. In one way or another, more and more, it will be possible for individuals and families to watch all their episodic television, made-for-TV movies, etc., without commercials, by using the "commercial fast-forward" feature of whatever recording technology they adopt. People will then be able to schedule their own viewing regardless of network scheduling: taping Wednesday night while watching Tuesday night, and so on through the week.[4] Right now the networks are fighting an angry and, in the short run, occasionally successful battle against the makers of these technologies, putting pressure on them to eliminate such possibilities or make them more difficult to access. But, in the long run, they have no hope of success; the technologies that accompany mass entertainment (think of music downloading from the Internet) are propelled by the same dynamic of change and innovation (see chapter 4) that generates mass entertainment itself—and they cannot be forever denied. Ultimately, the law of digital technology is that its components get smaller and faster in a standard progression that takes on an aura of inevitability. TIVO, after all, is nothing but "a few lines of software around a hard drive"; the idea that that kind of technological accomplishment can be short-circuited is totally chimerical.[5]

In this sense, the free-market system is, as always, working against itself. If everyone were to acquire and use the commercial advance capability, the raison d'être of commercial television would collapse and there would be no more free lunch; how could advertisers justify spending billions of dollars on commercials if no one were watching them? Here the system is confronted with the familiar free-rider problem. It is perhaps in the interests of the free riders as a collectivity to go on benefiting from commercial television, but the audience is not in fact a collectivity in any way, shape, or form. It is just a collection of strangers separately engaged in the same activity, with no ideological commitment to what they are doing. It is true that some commercials have been made into mininarratives with massive budgets, and audiences do watch them; moreover, commercials can be made an inextricable part of content. But both fiscally and aesthetically, this effort to maintain a declining form has its limits. It's possible to make a Land Rover, say, the central narrative component of a chase movie; but stopping the action to point out that the batteries enabling you to find the missing briefcase full of plutonium are Evereadys would turn adventure into comedy. No one, as far as we know, really enjoys watching commercials in and of themselves; and, certainly, no one would feel deprived of any important aesthetic pleasure by not watching them. Once the appropriate technology becomes potentially available to everyone, it will therefore be in everyone's interest, operating as individuals, to delete all but embedded commercials from their viewing and, thus, ultimately destroy the system. If we try to imagine, some years down the road, a gigantic advertising campaign in which the networks and corporate giants spend billions of dollars to persuade us that watching commercials is good for us, and that we must do so in order to save their financial power, we can see the limits of electronic manipulation. It does not take some fanciful theory of consumer power or the independence of consciousness to recognize that, in a free, even if manipulative, society, people cannot easily be persuaded of what is manifestly not true, as long as (unlike the "tie" between Saddam Hussein and 9/11 or the rhetorical falsehoods of electoral campaigns) they have any experience of it *or* unless the telling of the story gives them a serious aesthetic pleasure to which they have become habituated. On the whole, this kind of pleasure is not available from advertising in any form, except very occasionally. Otherwise, unless we accept not just that watching television is a pleasure but that this pleasure is such a fundamental human good that more of it is always better, there is no ground on which opposition to a simple development in technology can clearly stand.

Exactly how such a countersystem might develop is a kind of speculative reasoning that I have no desire to engage in. There are many possible futures; here I will briefly describe one in order to free our minds from the trap of the existent. One logical outcome of this historical development in the means of communication is that episodic programming on a mass scale should ultimately be replaced by its availability either as pay-per-view or as store-shelved DVD: a development that again is already underway, as programs such as *The Sopranos* or *24* or *Xena* become available for rental just as though they were movies. The limitation on this substitution, obviously, is that, in the absence of a guaranteed mass market, development of what we now think of as the standard television series becomes a much riskier enterprise. Even with embedded commercials, how could a producer justify spending two and a half million dollars on an episode of the third spin-off of *Law and Order* if there were neither advertisers nor syndication possibilities guaranteed to pay their share of the cost? One possibility is that TV series would then have to be financed like movies, of which there are far fewer, especially in that cost range. Of course, there's no reason that DVDs can't also be sponsored—"brought to you by" the sponsor, even with commercials preceding the actual program. Moreover, privately owned local stations could buy one or more series and provide their own local advertising. Still, it is self-evident that there would be many fewer of these products overall and watching one would not necessarily lead to watching more of the same; and that is exactly the point.

That is what it means to abolish the free lunch. Less choice among expensive products that monopolize time and space equals more choice among a variety of possibilities, including the possibility of spending time doing something else. Above all, what is required in democracies is to break the stranglehold of television on leisure-time activity so that it merely competes with reading, walking, movie going, Internet surfing, and playing together, not to mention political participation and genuine political campaigning.[6] In any such system that we can imagine, cable companies would necessarily become what they ought to be: common carriers providing access to local stations, various versions of pay-per-view (for those who, for example, want to see serials by the week or professional sports), and specialized channels that are cheap enough to produce for a widespread audience that their costs can easily be absorbed by a cable provider (e.g., The Golf Channel). As to who or what might appear on local stations, the answer should always be let the chips fall where they may just as with any product in a capitalist society. The regulation of television stations, no matter how or by whom owned, will always be fought out as it is now, with, however, the single exception that *the one absolute requirement for a democracy is that no public licensee of any kind should be allowed to sell time for political advertising* (except, obviously, to charge a fee for the mere cost of the time itself). Nationwide elections, including the speeches and debates of candidates, should be covered nationally by public television: what is more appropriate programming than the ultimate public event? State and local elections should follow the same principle. As for the promotion of particular political views, that should have no relationship to the money available to be spent on them. Those individuals who want to make speeches to their fellow citizens should line up at the studio door, along with any other persons who want to deliver their personal opinions in public space—be they the local professor of Mideast Studies or the kind of obsessive who wants everyone within range to hear his profound analysis of the Red Sox lineup for 2005. The now-burgeoning institution of the weblog satisfies this urge much more broadly, of course, but it is not as certain of reaching one's "friends and neighbors."

Another obvious complaint about this sort of prescription is that, in an economically stratified society, the going market rate for anything, however low it may be, always has an unequal impact, as poor or, in some cases, even middle-class speakers will not be able to afford the going rate for anything, whatever it is. There are two important points that this familiar kind of critique misses. First, it would not be possible to freeze out more people than are already frozen out of public space except as powerless consumers; any movement away from the total monopolization of almost every segment of time by a handful of oligopolists can only be an improvement. Second, take away the need to support the multibillion-dollar profit levels of public space's present owners, and we would probably have more persons clamoring to be heard than even the digital band could easily accommodate. One can imagine, for example, that some version of George Soros' Open Society Institute would spring into being precisely to help the unheard get a hearing, to pay their way. As with all versions of "participatory democracy," in a truly open system, even within the framework of a capitalist economy, the real problem would finally be not so much providing access as having to ration it.

The main points of difference in the case of a democratic system are fourfold. First, publicly owned space should not have to compete for attention with privately owned space as a weak relation. Depriving private channels of the benefits of nationwide networking accomplishes that end almost automatically; and, of course, the existing, discriminatory, and protectionist statutory prohibition against public television's offering any programming of any kind that would compete with commercial programming would become meaningless.

Second, without any doubt, the key element in any system of public broadcasting, whatever else it provides, must be the dissemination of news, information, and informed discussion for general attention. The overriding interest of any public broadcasting system is in the free exchange and distribution of ideas—and nothing else. In this respect, and in contrast with the imperative not to substitute one's own judgment of what is entertaining for that of the mass audience's, it is neither necessary nor possible for any critic to be agnostic about the extent to which disseminated information is true to the facts. To elaborate the argument of chapter 2 above, in the American television system, all electronically disseminated news coverage is delusive to an unacceptable extent in that, compared with broadsheet daily newspapers (themselves often far from the best source of genuine knowledge), neither the time nor space provided is adequate for making minimal contact with the real world of people and events; and occasional newsmagazine programs merely substitute anecdote for coverage. Moreover, and even more decisively, *visual* news coverage makes reportage more seductively illusory rather than making it more faithful to reality. The coming triumph of digitalization will complete the process, already well advanced, of detaching photography from its original promise of trustworthy materiality. Furthermore, the nature of televised news coverage is dictated by a confluence of the technical demands of a commercial medium, the self-interested demands of the owners of media outlets, and the professional and ideological biases of news and opinion givers. Each of these influences operates to remove news coverage further away from any possibility of striving for "the view from nowhere." However, although it is true that these news and opinion givers, no matter who they are or what their intentions, cannot be representative of the people whom they purport to inform, because of necessity they form a technically trained and educated elite, it is equally true that at least they could be considerably more representative than they are of the plurality of informed elites in general. At the present time, opinion-mongering on television is monopolized by political insiders and ideological elites practiced in sound-bite demagoguery. "The news" mostly consists of a slanted collection of selective images rather than reports; and the control of dissemination of these images is in the hands of interlocking monopolies. Even the overall bias of the system's image-commanding class, whatever that may be, is not as consequential for democracy as is the very condition of monopoly itself. This statement is more than merely a matter of my opinion; *it is a matter of opinion that ought to recommend itself to anyone concerned with the creation and preservation of a democratic social order. Monopolies of information and debate are, over time, the mortal enemy of democracy.*

The state of the print media is bad enough; in the twenty-first century, it is barely possible to start an independent newspaper. Still, it is quite possible to start a magazine, and, in any event, there are many existing, independent magazines that compete with daily newspapers as news and information sources; there are also on-line publications and "news" enterprises that in some instances are becoming more and more accessible, and accessed. But, in the visual delivery of news, no one can compete with the television news monopolists, whose corporate or personal designs set the agendas and often the contents of all coverage. At present, even so-called public television lacks the financial or material capability for offering original coverage of events and can only offer talk about them. This is the condition that has to be reversed; but how can this be accomplished without recreating conditions of the monopolization of opinion?

The answer to this question lies in the third requirement for implementing a system of genuinely public communications. The financing and operations of a public television system ought to be relatively insulated from the ordinary processes of legislation and appropriation; it should be a major event requiring special effort for legislators (as opposed to regulators appointed for that purpose) to assert line-item control over any public broadcasting system. Attainment of this goal would seem to require that public broadcasting be self-financing to the greatest extent possible. The British system of financing the BBC by licensing the ownership of TV sets is impossible in the United States (and is falling short even in Great Britain), but it is not beyond the realm of the hypothetical to imagine the creation of a public broadcasting endowment that would obviate the necessity of such yearly appropriations battles and political obeisances as now afflict, for example, the National Endowment for the Arts.

At the same time, however, and finally, the quid pro quo for what in effect seems to create precisely the kind of monopoly I have been decrying throughout these pages is that public broadcasting itself not be allowed to behave like a monopoly. *The primary purpose of any regulation in this arena ought to be not to constrain public speech but to make sure that it's kept open to all comers.* It doesn't matter how much one respects Peter Jennings, or Wolf Blitzer, or any of their highly paid cohorts. Every report of theirs, no matter how expertly accomplished, comes to us through various institutional filters and is subjected to one among a myriad of possible interpretations; every informed opinion or discussion contains argumentation, if not propaganda, on someone's behalf, no matter how much I may agree with it. There are thousands of their like, persons capable of interpreting current events (at least!), available in a nation of 200 million adults, and left, center, or right, as many as possible of them—of us— ought to have their chance at choosing the filters and interpreting the output. The same is true of the arts, or sports (how much coverage of the Olympics would be enough, and who would pay for it?), or audience-oriented entertainment (the BBC nowadays chiefly features reruns of American commercial television).

Thus, in the end, it is not possible to say beforehand what would be the appropriate mix of programs, the appropriate level of coverage, or the appropriate bounds of taste. Any institution we treat as "public" will be subject to all the push and pull of politics as we know it. In the case of television, there will always be a tug of war between pressures for centralization or localism, for more regulation or less, for more freedom in programming or more accountability of programmers, for less "bias" or more free speech, and for insulated sources of financing or demands to subject that financing to the ordinary tests of budgeting in the political marketplace. If all this were done in the open, in a truly public system, the output might be messy, but the result would be an infinitely more open, pluralist, and democratic system than presently exists.

NOTES

1. As for the FCC, it is not charged with limiting monopoly and has, in fact, encouraged the spread of cross-ownership of media outlets. Rather, it rides herd on the monopolists to be certain that they do not offend whatever pressure groups have the FCC's official ear. Monopoly itself remains unregulated and untouched.

2.. John Stuart Mill, *On Liberty*, ed. David Spitz, Norton Critical Editions (New York: Norton, 1975), 18.

3. See his "Educators and the Battle for Control of U.S. Broadcasting, 1928–1935," in *Rich Media, Poor Democracy: Communication Politics in Dubious Times* (Champagne: University of Illinois Press, 1999).

4. A front-page article by Amy Harmon, "Skip-the-Ads TV Has Madison Avenue Upset," *New York Times*, May 23, 2002, recounts the development of this technology and the anxiety it has been arousing among network executives.

5. From a private communication by Robert O. Green. An article in the Arts and Leisure Section of the *New York Times* of January 30, 2005, by Lorne Manley and John Markoff, reports that do-it-yourself inventors are creating "customized cable boxes" that can record shows and delete commercials as well as search the internet

for illegal copies of television shows that can be downloaded to personal computers. In the words of the reporters, "The industry is terrified."

6. For a more extended description of how the British television system in its heyday achieved this status, see my article "American Television and Consumer Democracy" in *Dissent*, (Spring 1998).

INDEX

ABOUT THE AUTHOR

Philip Green is the Emeritus Sophia Smith Professor of Government at Smith College, Visiting Professor of Political Science at the New School University Graduate Faculty, author most recently of *Cracks in the Pedestal: Ideology and Gender in Hollywood* and *Equality and Democracy*; member of the editorial board of *The Nation*; and recipient of the Charles A. McCoy Career Achievement Award from the Caucus for a New Political Science of the American Political Science Association.